D0408009

ONE-PARTY CLASSROOM

One-Party Classroom

How Radical Professors at America's Top Colleges Indoctrinate Students and Undermine Our Democracy

DAVID HOROWITZ

and

JACOB LAKSIN

Published in the United States by Crown Forum,
an imprint of the Crown Publishing Group, a division of Random House, Inc.,
New York.
www.crownpublishing.com

CROWN FORUM with colophon is a registered trademark of Random House, Inc.

Library of Congress Cataloging-in-Publication Data

Horowitz, David.
One-party classroom / David Horowitz and Jacob Laksin.—1st ed.
p. cm.
Includes bibliographical references and index.
ISBN 978-0-307-45255-9
1. Education, Higher—Political aspects—United States. 2. Universities and colleges—Ratings and—rankings—United States. I. Laksin, Jacob. II. Title.

LC89.H67 2009
378.73—dc22

Printed in the United States of America

Design by Level C

10 9 8 7 6 5 4 3 2 1

First Edition

Contents

ONE-PARTY CLASSROOM

Introduction

An Academic Tragedy*

To appreciate the radical changes that have taken place in America's universities over the past few decades, one could do worse than start with the University of California, Santa Cruz.

Academic courses at Santa Cruz and other California campuses are ostensibly governed by the "Standing Orders" of the university Regents. These state that each school must "remain aloof from politics and never function as an instrument for the advance of partisan interests," and that professors must never allow the classroom "to be used for political indoctrination." In the words of the Regents, such indoctrination "constitutes misuse of the University as an institution."[1]

Unfortunately, this rule and rules like it at academic institutions across the country are increasingly ignored by university professors, and almost never enforced by university administrations. The UC Santa Cruz catalog is itself littered with course descriptions that *promise* indoctrination, almost invariably in radical politics. The clear goal of such courses is not to educate students in the methods of critical thinking but to instill ideologies that are hostile to American society and its values. Contrary to the Standing Orders of the university Regents, these courses teach students *what* to think, not *how* to think.

The Santa Cruz catalog, for example, describes a seminar offered by its "Community Studies Department" as follows: "The goal of this seminar is to learn how to organize a revolution. We will learn what

*The introduction was written by David Horowitz.

communities past and present have done and are doing to resist, challenge, and overcome systems of power including (but not limited to) global capitalism, state oppression, and racism."[2]

This is the outline of a political agenda, not the description of a scholarly inquiry. Moreover, the sectarian character of this course reflects far more than the misguided pedagogy of an aberrant instructor. University faculty are credentialed, hired, and promoted by committees composed of faculty peers.

To create an academic course requires the approval of the tenured leaders of an academic department who have been hired and then promoted by other senior faculty. For a department to survive and flourish, its curriculum must be recognized and approved by professional associations that are national in scope. Consequently, the fact that a course in how to organize a revolution is offered at one of the nation's distinguished academic institutions speaks volumes about the contemporary university and what it has come to regard as an appropriate academic course of study.

The Community Studies Department at UC Santa Cruz is by no means alone in its departures from scholarly principle. The school also boasts a "Department of the History of Consciousness," which was created in the 1960s as a platform for political radicals. Communist Party stalwart Angela Davis—a onetime federal fugitive featured on the FBI's Ten Most Wanted list—has been a faculty icon for decades.[3] Black Panther felon Huey Newton received a Ph.D. from the department by submitting a dissertation that was little more than a political tract justifying his organization's criminal activities. Another prominent radical credentialed in the program and then hired to its faculty is Bettina Aptheker, creator of UCSC's Department of Feminist Studies.

The daughter of a famous leader of the Communist Party, Professor Aptheker was herself on the party's central committee for many years. Aptheker finally left the party in 1981 after her superiors rejected a political tract she had submitted for publication to the party publishing house. Her manuscript was considered unacceptable because it argued that women were oppressed due to their gender and not merely their class position.[4] In a recent memoir, Aptheker explained that she agreed to pursue an academic career only after another professor and long-time Communist Party member told her, "It's your revolutionary duty."[5]

In pursuit of her revolutionary goals, Aptheker devoted herself to revamping the curriculum of the newly created "Introduction to Women's Studies" course, "making it more overtly political" and turning it into a training program in radical feminism and an adjunct of the women's movement.[6] "Teaching became a form of political activism for me, replacing the years of dogged meetings and intrepid organizing with the immediacy of a liberatory practice."[7]

Aptheker was appointed the first professor of Women's Studies at Santa Cruz and went on to build an entire academic department based on her political agendas, shaping its course offerings for a quarter of a century. At her instigation, the department was eventually renamed the Department of *Feminist* Studies, which finally captured her achievement: the embedding of a political program in an academic curriculum, despite the explicit warning by the UC Regents that this "constitutes a misuse of the university."

Bettina Aptheker's academic career is a metaphor for the political trends that have reshaped America's liberal arts classrooms over the past generation. A lifelong political activist, Aptheker regarded the university first and foremost as a fulcrum for revolutionary change. In furthering her political goals, she received extensive support from crucial elements of the university system. This support included, first of all, the academic department that awarded her a Ph.D. for non-scholarly work. Like Newton's, her doctoral thesis was not a scholarly dissertation but the political tract she had previously submitted to the Communist Party publishing house. Once credentialed by the History of Consciousness program as a "scholar," she was hired to the faculty and then promoted by committees dominated by other faculty radicals. These committees then approved the creation of a politically designed Women's Studies program through which she could spread her doctrines. The central university administration then agreed to the expansion of the program into a full-fledged academic department and to its transformation into the Department of Feminist Studies.

Throughout the entire process, Aptheker's ideological curriculum received the imprimatur of the National Women's Studies Association (NWSA), which sets standards of discourse, research, and hiring in the field. Its support was entirely predictable, since the NWSA is itself a political organization whose formal constitution lays out its agendas in blunt fashion:

> Women's Studies owes its existence to the movement for the liberation of women; the feminist movement exists because women are oppressed. Women's Studies, diverse as its components are, has at its best a shared a vision of a world free not only from sexism but also from racism, class-bias, ageism, heterosexual bias—from all the ideologies and institutions that have consciously or unconsciously oppressed and exploited some for the advantage of others. . . . Women's Studies, then, is equipping women not only to enter the society as whole, as productive human beings, but to transform the world to one that will be free of all oppression.[8]

In sum, Professor Aptheker's academic career and her politicized Department of Feminist Studies are made possible by a national movement of academics who share her broad ideological agendas. Over the course of several decades, this movement has instituted massive changes in the structure of higher education, creating new courses, new departments, and new fields that violate the professional standards of the modern research university and undermine its foundations.

These disturbing developments are the subject matter of *One-Party Classroom.* Recent decades have witnessed widespread complaints about the political abuse of university classrooms. But never before has anyone undertaken a comprehensive investigation of what America's college instructors actually say they are teaching their students.

One-Party Classroom fills in those blanks. It documents the results of an in-depth, multiyear study of twelve representative schools—public and private, and ranging from large state universities to elite

Ivy League institutions. Our investigation has systematically scrutinized course catalogs, syllabi, reading lists, professors' biographies, scholarly records, and testimonies.

The outcome of our research leaves no doubt that the failure to enforce academic standards is a problem that is endemic to institutions of higher learning. An alarming number of university courses violate existing academic regulations that have been designed to ensure that students receive professional instruction. Curricula are designed not to educate students in critical thinking* but to instill doctrines that are "politically correct." This is not a claim that professors are "biased." Bias is another term for "point of view," which every professor naturally possesses and has a right to express. For the purposes of this study, professors whose courses follow traditional academic standards do not pose a problem regardless of their individual point of view. What concerns us is whether their courses adhere to the academic standards of the modern research university and the principles of a professional education.[9] And the fact is that a growing number of activist instructors routinely present their students with only one side of controversial issues in an effort to convert them to a sectarian perspective.

Once the widespread nature of the abuses is appreciated, it becomes impossible to argue that the problem is limited to a few aberrant instructors, or to offhand professorial comments, or to an occasional assignment of materials designed to sway students' judgments on controversial matters.

The more than 150 college courses documented in these pages do not exhaust the political offerings at the twelve institutions studied; they are merely the most obvious cases at these schools. The ideologies presented in these courses often reflect prominent and even dominant schools of thought in their respective academic fields. More importantly, these ideological doctrines often shape the core

---

*The term "critical thinking" is widely used by academic radicals as a code for Marxism and its derivative schools. It is used here to mean thinking that is openminded, skeptical of received truths, and guided by the scientific method.

curriculum most undergraduates are required to take to earn their degrees in liberal arts.

If we were to extrapolate from the materials examined here, taking into account the total number of institutions offering advanced degrees, the result would be as many as *10,000* college classes nationwide whose primary purpose is not to educate students but to train them in left-wing ideologies and political agendas. The students who pass through these courses annually are numbered in the millions. In other words, *One-Party Classroom* demonstrates beyond a reasonable doubt that the attempt to indoctrinate American college students is more pervasive and extreme than even the harshest critics of academia have previously suggested.

"No Tipping of the Scales"

Although the courses examined in this text reflect, without exception, a left-wing view of the world, the problems exposed would be just as serious if instructors were instilling conservative or right-wing doctrines. The reason for the absence of such courses in this study was our inability to locate them at the schools examined. This is not surprising. As recent surveys have shown, conservatives are an extraordinarily rare presence in contemporary liberal arts faculties. At several of the schools examined, we could not locate a single conservative professor on the social science faculty. A 2007 investigation by two liberal academics, Neil Gross and Solon Simmons, reported that liberal professors generally outnumber conservatives in the social sciences and humanities by a factor of 9 to 1.[10] In fields such as anthropology and sociology, the ratio approaches 30 to 1. Consequently, in the mainstream university system, which is the focus of our inquiry, conservative professors lack the institutional means to create ideological departments or to design courses for the purpose of training students in right-wing doctrines.[11]

The roots of the present situation lie in the political history of the 1960s and its aftermath. The cultural upheavals of that era saw the accession to academic tenure of a generation of activists who regarded the university as a platform from which to advance their political mission. Drawing on the works of European Marxists such as Antonio Gramsci and Herbert Marcuse, and the educational theorist Paulo Freire, the radicals viewed universities as "means of cultural production" analogous to the "means of production" in Marx's revolutionary *schema.* To these professorial activists, the academic classroom offered a potential fulcrum for revolutionary change. Because the university trained journalists and editors, lawyers and judges, future political candidates and operatives, it provided a path to cultural "hegemony" and an opportunity to promote a radical transformation of the society at large.

The efforts of this radical generation soon led to a dramatic shift in educational attitudes. When the modern research university was created a century ago, it signaled an end to the dominance of religious institutions in the field of higher education. Under the new dispensation, teachers were expected to refrain from imposing their religious or ideological prejudices on students in their charge, to teach according to the precepts of scientific method and not according to what the philosopher Charles Peirce referred to as the "method of authority."

The most important and influential statement associated with this emergence of the modern research university was the "Declaration on the Principles of Academic Freedom and Academic Tenure," a document issued by the American Association of University Professors (AAUP). The Declaration stipulated that a university instructor should "set forth justly, without suppression or innuendo, the divergent opinions of other investigators . . . and he should, above all, remember that his business is not to provide his students with ready-made conclusions, but to train them to think for themselves, and to provide them access to those materials which they need if they are to think intelligently."[12] This statement, issued in 1915, has provided the template for the academic freedom policies of most American universities ever since.

Equally explicit on these matters was a 1934 statement by Robert Gordon Sproul, the president of the University of California and the architect of its rise to academic prominence as an exemplar of the values to which a research university should aspire. In the 1934 statement, Sproul defined the mission of the university as incompatible with the agendas of sectarian political movements: "The function of the university is to seek and to transmit knowledge and to train students in the processes whereby truth is to be made known. To convert, or to make converts, is alien and hostile to this dispassionate duty. Where it becomes necessary in performing this function of a university, to consider political, social, or sectarian movements, they are dissected and examined, not taught, and the conclusion left, with no tipping of the scales, to the logic of the facts."[13]

The Sproul statement was integral to the academic freedom policies of the University of California until 2003, when academic radicals succeeded in suppressing it. In that year, the academic senate voted to *remove* the Sproul statement from its academic freedom template by a majority of 43–3. This removal was engineered by Professor Robert Post, who is currently the principal authority on academic freedom for the AAUP.[14]

The activist mentality behind these moves was aggressively promoted in an article titled "Impassioned Teaching," which was featured in the Summer 2007 issue of the AAUP's official journal, *Academe.* It was timed to coincide with a new statement on academic freedom and was written by Pamela Caughie, a regional president of the AAUP and also a professor of English at Loyola University, Chicago, and its director of Women's Studies.

"Don't be afraid of classroom advocacy; it's not the same as indoctrination," Caughie advised other academics. But her text demonstrated that this was a distinction without a difference: "Feminism is a mode of analysis, a set of values, and a political movement. In teaching students its history, its forms, and its impact, I am teaching them to think and write as feminists. I want to convince my students of the value of feminist analysis and the importance of feminist praxis." In other words, Caughie understands her educational mission as one of persuading students to adopt her point of view, not teaching them how to conduct an intellectual examination of feminism and think for themselves. Caughie is even ready to concede the point in a backhanded way: "In twenty years of teaching I have never gone into the classroom hoping to make converts that day. Still, I feel I am doing my job well when students become practitioners of feminist analysis and committed to feminist politics."[15]

Caughie's defense of the "praxis" of indoctrination in the official journal of the AAUP underscores the predicament in which American liberal arts programs find themselves. The radical cohort to which Caughie and Aptheker belong is now a large and influential presence and in some cases an imposing majority on liberal arts faculties and the governing bodies of national academic organizations. As a result, it has been able to transform significant parts of the academy into agencies of political and social change.

These include traditional professional groups such as the American Historical Association (AHA), which now routinely pass formal resolutions on public controversies that have nothing to do with scholarship, and which take positions on issues that only a handful of their thousands of members would be professionally qualified to judge. In 2007, for example, a tiny but determined minority of AHA members passed a resolution condemning the Iraq war. In doing so they exploited the scholarly prestige of AHA members gained in historical fields far removed from the Middle East in order to promulgate a fashionable left-wing position on current events.

The political subordination of scholarship to political agendas is most evident in fields such as Women's Studies. Almost universally, Women's Studies programs base their courses of study on the ideological (and unproven) claim that gender is "socially constructed"—that behavioral differences between men and women are socially, rather than biologically, determined. According to these Women's Studies programs, gender differences between men and women are artificially created by an entrenched patriarchy for the express purpose of oppressing women. This perspective is presented by Women's Studies faculties as a settled doctrine even though it is a controversial opinion. Recent advances in modern neuroscience, for example, have identified significant differences in the biological makeup of men and women that affect their relative abilities and behaviors.[16] Yet for Women's Studies faculties the issue is settled in favor of social determinants.

Ideological developments in the university have also led to the prevalent phenomenon of professors academically trained in one discipline teaching courses and posing as experts in others. Since radical ideologies require their adherents to make global pronouncements, it is not uncommon to find instructors with degrees in English or Comparative Literature teaching courses that focus on the historical development of economic empires or the complexities of gender and race. This is analogous to a situation where botanists and microbiologists would teach big bang physics or macroeconomics. It is a serious problem for academic professions, which are defined by their specialized knowledge. Entry into these professions is barred to individuals not credentialed as experts in their disciplines, while students pay tens of thousands of dollars for the privilege of being taught by specialists in their fields. Why go through the arduous and expensive process of credentialing experts if anyone is qualified to teach anything?

What we are witnessing in the liberal arts programs of American universities is the collapse of standards on an alarming scale. To describe this problem as one of "liberal bias" or a "lack of balance" is to misrepresent and trivialize it. All faculty, whatever their point of view, have intellectual biases and a right to express them. But the same right comes with an important and long recognized caveat: Professors have an obligation to be professional in their instruction. They are expected to refrain from imposing their personal views on students through the authority they exercise in the classroom, or through the design of the course, or through their power over student grades; they should not represent mere opinion as scientific fact.

The problem posed by the incorporation of ideological agendas into the academic curriculum is not the opinions of a particular instructor or a particular idea introduced in the course of instruction. The problem arises when the course of instruction is not guided by scientific method; when it is not constructed as a scholarly inquiry within a scholarly discipline; when the instructor fails to present students with divergent views on controversial matters or with access to materials that will enable them to think intelligently and for themselves. The problem facing the university today is that many academic courses are designed to train students in sectarian ideologies and recruit them to sectarian causes.

Even as the abuses of university classrooms documented in this study have reached epidemic proportions, faculty unions and professional associations have become increasingly averse to any accountability for the design of academic instruction. Roger Bowen, who until recently served as general secretary of the AAUP, has said in so many words that academics should not have to answer to anyone but themselves: "It should be evident that the sufficient condition for securing the academic freedom of our profession is the profession itself."[17]

But the pages that follow show that left to their own devices, faculty and administrators have consistently failed to defend academic freedom or maintain reasonable academic standards. Routine abuses of the university are also made possible by the passivity of other actors—instructors in the hard sciences who observe traditional professional standards in their own work but choose to remain silent when these standards are traduced by others, non-ideological scholars in the liberal arts who do likewise, education-oriented trustees and alumni, and students abused by the practices described. These academic bystanders constitute a majority of any university community and a majority of faculty as well. But their refusal to speak up has allowed their less scrupulous colleagues to engineer a decline of professional standards, and a consequent debasement of the academic product.

If this passivity continues and the university community does not respond to the assault on academic standards, the credibility and authority of the university will continue to decline and the future of liberal arts education in America will then become bleak indeed.

1

White Devils

DUKE UNIVERSITY
TUITION: $45,121

Duke University, in Durham, North Carolina, is one of the nation's premier educational institutions. In recent years, surveys have repeatedly placed the school among the top ten in the country on the strength of its academics, with its law school and engineering programs emerging at the forefront of their respective fields.

Established in 1924 through an endowment by James B. Duke, the millionaire son of tobacco tycoon Washington Duke, the school owes its existence to the crop that helped launch the economy of the New South and that is now as taboo as the "N-word." Racial tensions in North Carolina were never as bitter as in other Southern states, and the black community thrived there as in few other areas in the region, so much so that by 1949, Durham's business district boasted nearly 300 black-owned firms. The school, too, has sought to bridge race and class distinctions, and today its student body of nearly 13,000 includes 40 percent minority undergraduates.

But in the late winter of 2006, Duke came to national attention because of a scandal that supposedly revealed endemic racism on the campus. On March 13, a black stripper named Crystal Mangum filed assault charges against three white members of the university's lacrosse team, claiming that the students used racial epithets as they raped and sexually abused her.

Of course, as is now well known, the case against the lacrosse players collapsed as it emerged that the accuser had repeatedly changed her story about the evening's events, and that the district attorney, Mike Nifong, had withheld exculpatory DNA evidence. Finally, a full year year after the charges were originally filed, the students were cleared on all counts.[1]

While the Duke lacrosse scandal exposed recklessness on many fronts (Nifong, for instance, would eventually be disbarred for his actions), more than anything else it cast a squalid light on the problems of political radicalism on the Duke faculty, including the outright indoctrination that passes for education at this academically elite institution.

It was bad enough that within weeks of the charges, and before any evidence of the students' guilt had been produced, Duke president Richard Brodhead canceled the lacrosse team's season and forced its coach, Mike Pressler, a former Atlantic Coast Conference coach of the year, to resign, and that the school suspended two of the accused students, Collin Finnerty and Reade Seligmann (a third, David Evans, had already graduated).[2] But the university's response was a model of judiciousness compared with the treatment the three students suffered at the hands of Duke faculty.

Unconstrained by any presumption of innocence or concern for the welfare of their students, a group of 88 faculty members signed a full-page ad in the Duke newspaper titled "What Does a Social Disaster Sound Like?"[3] Composed mainly of anonymous statements alleging widespread racism and sexism on the Duke campus, and expressing support for Crystal Mangum, while referring critically to the lacrosse team, the advertisement was a faculty verdict on the students' guilt—rendered within a month of the original charges, before any indictments had been issued.

"This is not a different experience for us here at Duke," one statement in the ad read; "we go to class with racist classmates, we go to the gym with people who are racists."[4] Other quotes alluded to the "terror" of living on a supposedly racist campus and called for expulsions of the lacrosse players. Perhaps most striking, the advertisement suggested that even if the accused students were innocent, the school was guilty of fostering a climate of racism, sexism, and sexual violence. "The disaster didn't begin on March 13th and won't end with what the police say or the court decides," the ad declared. The statement was signed by the 88 Duke professors and endorsed by 13 academic departments in the liberal arts. "The impact of the ad was devastating," Steven Baldwin, a Duke chemistry professor, later recalled. "This was a large segment of faculty, some highly respected, and it really swung the pendulum against the lacrosse players."[5]

It is a mark of the ideological mania prevalent among many members of the Duke faculty that this was not the most extreme response. Writing in the *Duke Chronicle* in March, Duke history professor William Chafe, one of the 88 signatories, depicted the lacrosse players as the modern-day heirs of white slave masters. As Chafe explained it, "At some point in the past, or present, white males have 'had their way' with black women. White slave masters were the initial perpetrators of sexual assault on black women, subsequent generations continued the pattern." There was little doubt about which "subsequent generations" the professor had in mind. As if the context in which he wanted the rape case to be seen were insufficiently clear, Chafe added that the brutal 1955 murder of black teenager Emmett Till "helps to put into context what occurred in Durham."[6]

In other words, the Duke students (rather than the professors who were attempting to convict and punish them in the court of public opinion) should be viewed in the context of the Southern lynchings of the past. In what would become a pattern among the faculty vigilantes, Chafe concluded by suggesting that whatever the facts in the rape case, the students were guilty of a heinous and racist offense: "Whether or not a rape took place, there is no question that . . . white students hired a black woman from an escort service to perform an erotic dance."[7] Of course, as many were quick to note, engaging the services of an escort service was no crime, and there was a big difference between an erotic dance and a rape. Either the Duke students were guilty or they were not.

Houston Baker, a professor of English and African and African-American Studies at Duke, also wrote a public letter denouncing the Duke administration for what he called the "abhorrent sexual assault, verbal racial violence, and drunken white male privilege loosed amongst us."[8] He then assailed the lacrosse team's (unproven) "racist assaults" and "violent racism," calling its members "violent and irresponsible." As for those who counseled restraint so that the legal process could proceed fairly, Baker sneered at their "timorous piety and sentimental legalism." As Baker saw it, the students were symbols of "white, male, athletic privilege," and therefore guilty. He demanded the "immediate dismissals" of the players, the coaches, and all those "agents" who refused volubly to proclaim their guilt. The Blue Devils had become the white devils.[9]

Echoing Baker's sentiments, English professor Karla Holloway published an article in an academic journal called *The Scholar and Feminist Online,* in which she insisted—without evidence—that the lacrosse players had victimized blacks and women. "At Duke University this past spring, the bodies left to the trauma of a campus brought to its knees by members of Duke University's Lacrosse team were African American and women," Holloway wrote.[10] Like Baker, Holloway dismissed the notion that justice should be allowed to take its course. Justice, she explained, "has an attendant social construction"—a bias toward white male privilege—that cannot be settled in a court of law. Consequently, "judgments about the issues of race and gender that the lacrosse team's sleazy conduct exposed cannot be left to the courtroom."[11] In short, the facts of the case were immaterial; the students were guilty.

That same summer, the university appointed Holloway to lead a group discussion on "race" as part of the Duke Campus Culture Initiative, a university-appointed committee to investigate race relations on campus in the aftermath of the lacrosse scandal. During the school year, Holloway teaches a course at Duke called "Language of Constitutional Law."

Another polemic, suggestively titled "White Male Privilege, Black Respectability, and Black Women's Bodies," was contributed by Mark Anthony Neal, an associate professor in the Department of African and African-American Studies. Neal asserted that "regardless of what happened" on the night in question, "the young men were hoping to consume something that they felt that a black woman uniquely possessed. If these young men did in fact rape, sodomize, rob, and beat this young woman, it wasn't simply because she was a woman: but because she was a black woman."[12] In other words, racism was an attribute of being white.

Unscrupulous and irrational though it was, the faculty campaign to demonize the lacrosse players as racists and rapists who hid behind the shield of white "privilege" shaped the public debate. The Duke faculty's defamatory accusations were repeated in the Raleigh-Durham *News and Observer,* which urged deference to the supposed wisdom of the professoriate. Spurred on by faculty claims of racism and District Attorney Nifong's reckless assurance that the students were "hooligans," militant groups like the New Black Panther Party threatened to march on the Duke campus to distribute brochures asking, "Had enough of disrespect and racism from Duke University?" Protests sprang up on and off campus. Eventually, the climate became so hostile that the lacrosse players had to be moved for their own safety.[13]

Even as the vilification of the students grew louder and shriller, the case against them was revealed to be empty, while the exotic dancer was exposed as a drug-addicted criminal and liar. But the 88 professors expressed little remorse for having pilloried the innocent students and done everything possible to ruin their careers. Karla Holloway responded with outrage when school administrators allowed Reade Seligmann and Collin Finnerty to return to Duke in January 2007—even though the rape charges had been dropped by then. Allowing the exonerated players to return was a breach of "ethical citizenship" by the school, declared Holloway, who resigned from the Duke Campus Culture Initiative.

Of the many other professors who had condemned the students, several now mendaciously insisted that their words did not mean what they did. History professor William Chafe, who a year earlier had put the students in the context of slave masters and the lynchers of Emmett Till, now claimed that his statement "didn't have any reference toward the guilt or innocence of anyone."[14]

The signatories of the infamous advertisement posted a new letter. But far from apologizing for their role in stirring racial hatred on campus, the Duke professors lashed out at their critics, whom they charged with creating the "misperception that the authors of the ad had prejudged the rape case."[15] Houston Baker, who had been verbose in raging against the evils of "white, male, athletic privilege," suddenly developed a case of publicity-shyness. Declining all interviews about the case, he decamped from Duke for a new appointment at Vanderbilt University.

The acquittal of the lacrosse players settled the issue of their innocence, but it left many other questions unanswered. How was it possible that professors at a leading academic institution should be so determined to judge three students guilty on no more evidence than the color of their skin, their gender, and their class status? Why were faculty, themselves privileged, so ready to condemn their own liberal university—whose largest liberal arts center is named for its most celebrated faculty member, African-American historian John Hope Franklin—as a racist institution?

A look into the backgrounds of the academic leaders of the faculty lynch party provides revealing clues. Consider Karla Holloway, one of the most ferocious critics of the lacrosse players. In 1996, then an obscure professor of English and self-identified "black feminist," she was named the acting director of Duke's African and African-American Studies program. Her first book, *New Dimensions of Spirituality,* was a "biracial and bicultural reading of the novels of Toni Morrison." Another, *Codes of Conduct: Race, Ethics, and the Color of Our Character,* was published the year before Holloway's appointment as department head. Written in forbidding academese, it bristled with racial and political agitation. The book anticipated the divisive racial narrative in which she would cast the lacrosse scandal. It was organized around Holloway's conviction that "racism" had shaped and "enforced" the politics of the United States, and that blacks, particularly black women, were its recurring victims. In a rant against what she termed the "tyranny of a white majority," Holloway claimed, "Public policies are racialized; responses to those policies are ethnically inscribed. Social systems are race-coded; reactions to these systems are determined through a filter of ethnicity. Political strategies are race-baited."[16] If there was some facet of American politics untainted by racism, Holloway failed to note it.

As "proof" that black women are routinely abused and victimized in America, Holloway highlighted the 1987 case of Tawana Brawley, the teenager whose proven lies about being assaulted and disfigured destroyed the reputations of six men she accused of raping her. Describing Brawley as "the fifteen-year-old black girl who was found nearly naked, streaked with feces, burned, and otherwise brutally abused," Holloway writes that she "has never spoken out about her trauma. The price of her silence has been a conspiracy of criminal discreditation of the facts of her appearance." One would never know from Holloway's book that in 1988—years before *Codes of Conduct* was published—a grand jury, after conducting an extensive review of the available evidence, found that Brawley had never been abducted, assaulted, or raped, and that her story was in fact a hoax. Holloway's concealment of this record in order to shore up an indictment of white America is quite revealing about her own racial attitudes and regard for the facts. It hardly seems coincidental that Holloway would so vocally condemn the accused when her own school became the stage for a racially charged swindle eerily parallel to the Brawley case.

Holloway's ideological zeal and unscholarly demeanor apparently recommended her to Duke administrators searching for an appropriate figure to head the African and African-American Studies program. Before she agreed to accept the appointment, Holloway insisted that the program's focus would be diversity and multiculturalism, which she interpreted to mean racial hiring and racial politics. She asked for "a commitment from the university" that it would focus on these agendas. "I wanted to be absolutely clear that this is what Duke was going to support. [African and African-American Studies] is not a program that is finished with itself."[17]

In fact, under Holloway, it was just getting started. In keeping with her commitment to "diversity and multiculturalism," Holloway set about hiring professors whose main qualification seemed to be that they were black. Building on Duke's "Black Faculty Strategic Initiative," an earlier effort to increase the number of black professors at the school, Holloway pledged to hire mostly black and female professors. She announced that her first three hires would all be female. Between 1993 and 2003, the number of black faculty at Duke grew from 44 to 88, with the biggest increase coming under Holloway's directorship.[18]

In October 2006, Duke trustees granted the African and African-American Studies program the status of a full department. The reason given for the change was that the trustees wanted to signal their "commitment" to Duke students. Although Holloway, who has since become a professor of English and Law, no longer serves as director of the program, it is clear that her emphasis on race and gender over merit—on politics over academics—has survived her tenure. And the consequences for Duke have been singularly disastrous.

One prominent professor who applauded the direction of the African and African-American Studies program under Holloway was Houston Baker, then at the University of Pennsylvania (and one of the highest-paid humanities professors in the country). An academic trained in Victorian literature, Baker came under the sway of black nationalist politics in the 1970s, finding his new scholarly muse in the guise of militant groups such as the Black Panthers.[19] From that point forward, Baker lost interest in nonideological literary scholarship; as he revealed in his book *The Journey Back,* he shifted his focus not simply to ideology, but to ideology that was "distinctively black."[20]

Baker soon became the archetype of the postmodern academic, who insists that there are no objective criteria for judging artistic value. Baker's brand of intellectual nihilism was best exemplified in his 1988 comment to the *New York Times* that choosing between authors like Virginia Woolf and Pearl Buck was "no different from choosing between a hoagy and a pizza."[21] This attitude, however, didn't prompt Baker to recuse himself when he was elected president of the Modern Language Association in the early 1990s, a position in which he would be responsible for defending standards in language and literature. For such standards Baker showed only contempt. "I am one whose career is dedicated to the day when we have a disappearance of those standards," he explained at the time.[22]

Equally subversive was Professor Baker's philosophy for teaching Black Studies. In a 1995 essay titled "Black Studies, Rap, and the Academy," he issued a racial challenge to his colleagues: How, he asked, could "anyone who is academically well placed doubt that only Black Studies . . . can begin to construct an adequate framework for today's complex black American situation"?[23]

Baker's own "framework" for improving the lives of black Americans was not at all complex. According to Baker, whose own salary is in the six-figure range, "Rich, cynical white citizens and their henchmen are everywhere pounding the hell out of 'the rest of us' average Americans." In a similar racist (and sexist) vein, he condemned "white male profit-making during the 80s," which he claimed "has brought the United States to the precipice of human disaster."[24] Black Studies, as Baker conceived it, was part of the "mandatory academic work of rewriting, reversing, and forestalling" this disaster. In sum, Black Studies was not simply a field of inquiry, it was an ideological weapon to fight the social order.

Professor Baker's contempt for intellectual standards and professional obligations only boosted his academic stock. In 1999 Duke hired him at a premium price and gave him an endowed professorship in English and African and African-American studies; the university brought along his wife, Charlotte Pierce-Baker, as an associate research professor in Women's Studies. Baker wasted no time in burnishing his reputation as a racial provocateur. In a 2001 interview with the *New York Times,* he took pains to distinguish himself from his white colleagues at Duke. "It's not that white academics don't work extraordinarily hard," he explained. "But what they have that I lack is a sense of leisure, an absence of endangerment, a look of being unconcerned that at any moment they could die."[25] Death in the faculty lounge? The multiculturally correct *Times,* of course, withheld comment.

The *Times* interview had been prompted by Baker's new book, *Turning South Again: Rethinking Modernism/Rereading Booker T.* One of the book's absurd claims was that there is a "continuity of American protocols of black imprisonment" that extends from slavery to "today's United States private prison industrial complex."[26] For Baker, there was no meaningful difference between the enslavement of individuals and the punishment of criminals in a society governed by the equal protection of the laws.

If we consider his belief that American society is racist and unjust, there is a perverse logic in the fact that Professor Baker became one of the first faculty members to convict the lacrosse players of the rape they did not commit. It is hardly surprising, given his view that American society favors whites at the expense of blacks, that Baker would claim the lacrosse players enjoyed the "silent protectionism" of the Duke administration for the "racist incident" they had supposedly perpetrated.

Such was Baker's ideological obsession with white racism and black oppression that he could not allow himself to accept the innocence of the white victims in the lacrosse case long after it had been established. In December 2006, when all the exonerating evidence had come to light, Baker received an e-mail from Patricia Dowd, the mother of lacrosse player Kyle Dowd, one of the original suspects. Never charged in the sexual assault case, Dowd claimed he had received a failing grade from his feminist professor for missing class time to meet with his lawyers. In an e-mail to the group of 88 professors who had condemned the lacrosse players, Patricia Dowd made an appeal for civility for her son. Dowd forgave the professors for their earlier rush to judgment, and asked only that they now step forward to concede that the facts exonerated the students. "Our paths may have been different, but I am sure all of us seek the truth and justice," Dowd wrote.

On December 31 Baker wrote back:

> LIES! You are just a provacateur [*sic*] on a happy New Years [*sic*] Eve trying to get credit for a scummy bunch of white males!

> You know you are in search of sympaathy [*sic*] for young white guys who beat up a gay man in Georgetown, get drunk in Durham, and lived like "a bunch of farm animals" near campus . . . umhappy [*sic*] new year to you . . . and forgive me if your [*sic*] really are, quite sadly, mother of a "farm animal."

Another member of the 88—in fact, the leader—was associate professor of literature Wahneema Lubiano. Recruited by Holloway, Lubiano clearly shares her obsession with racial politics, while having even slimmer claims to an academic *oeuvre.* Since earning a Ph.D. in literature from Stanford University in 1987, Lubiano has not produced a single scholarly monograph, unheard of for a tenured faculty member in a traditional academic field. Looking over Lubiano's *curriculum vitae,* one finds only three books listed. Of these, one is not a book of scholarship at all but a collection of political essays that Lubiano helped to edit. The other two books do not exist. *Like Being Mugged by a Metaphor* and *Messing with the Machine: Politics, Form, and African-American Fiction* are listed as "forthcoming." In fact, both books have been "forthcoming" since Lubiano arrived at Duke in 1997.[27]

If Lubiano has not been producing scholarly work, what *has* she been doing in her decade on the Duke faculty? The answer is that this self-identified Marxist—who has written that "corporate capitalism is using racism to manipulate" working-class whites[28]—is a political activist and a leader of the faculty Left. Whether it is an antiwar rally, at which she denounced America's response to the 9/11 attacks as "U.S. war-mongering as terror," or a teach-in about the aftermath of Hurricane Katrina, where she said that "racism is so much a part of our culture that it is always available as a simple tool of convenience," Professor Lubiano can be counted on to promote her racial politics.[29] At the latter event Lubiano suggested that Vice President Dick Cheney, as a member of an alleged "lawless over-class that is looting the state and a state that is looting itself for its friend," should be shot instead of the looters in New Orleans.

In a 1996 essay, Lubiano claimed that she was "at the mercy of racist, sexist, heterosexist, and global capitalist constructions of the meaning of skin color on a daily basis."[30] Fixated on the idea that she is surrounded by white racists, she unsurprisingly emerged as a leader of the faculty lynch mob during the lacrosse scandal. By all reports, she played the lead role in drafting the advertisement that condemned the innocent lacrosse players. When the initial indictments were handed down she said, "I understand the impulse of those outraged and who see the alleged offenders as the exemplars of the upper end of the class hierarchy, the politically dominant race and ethnicity, the dominant gender, the dominant sexuality, and the dominant social group on campus. Further, this group has been responsible for extended social violence against the neighborhood in which they reside."[31] Of this supposed social violence Lubiano offered no evidence. She concluded instead by writing that "regardless of the 'truth' established in whatever period of time about the incident," sexism and racism "continues to occur in everyday and nonspectacular life in this place [i.e., Duke]."[32]

Like many other radical professors, Lubiano considers her politics as integral to her teaching. "Whether I'm thinking, teaching, or engaging in politics (including strategizing) I think that it is part of my privilege, my work, and my pleasure to insist that those three activities are not clearly demarcated."[33] In fact, it is not her privilege, since the academic freedom provisions of the American Association of University Professors explicitly require such a demarcation between teaching and politics.[34] Nevertheless, Lubiano has written that her objective as an educator (one who is "part of the historically marginalized") is "to reconstitute not simply particular curricula, but the academy itself."[35] Because, according to Lubiano, universities are "engines of dominance," it follows that "sabotage has to be the order of the day."[36] In short, Lubiano's academic mission is an assault on the very idea of universities as places of scholarship and learning, with the goal of turning them into platforms for her political agendas.

Lubiano is by no means alone. Mark Anthony Neal, associate professor of Black Popular Culture in the African and African-American Studies program, shares both her political views and her approach to education. A self-styled "black male feminist," Professor Neal has referred to himself as a "ThugNiggaIntellectual." Neal has written that "the 'Thug Nigga' is a dangerous nigger." Of himself, he has said: "I'm the nigga that gonna intellectually choke the living sh*t out of you."[37]

Like Professor Lubiano, Neal teaches that the United States is a racist country. References to the "general demonization of Black men in American society" appear frequently in his writings. When the lacrosse players were arraigned, in April 2006, Neal told ESPN.com that whites regarded black women as promiscuous, which would explain why white students would have raped a black stripper. "There is an historical discourse in this country that suggests black women can't be raped," he claimed. In the same interview, he said, "For me, this is not simply a case of sexual violence or just a case of racism. It's a case of racialized sexual violence, meaning if it had been a white woman in that room, it would not have gone down the same way."[38]

Although no evidence linking the students to the crime had yet emerged—or would ever emerge—Neal had no reservations about describing them as violent and racist. If his attitude is not the embodiment of racist stereotyping, what would be?

When DNA evidence exonerating the lacrosse players was made public, it did not alter Neal's view of the case. Instead, he wrote that he was "less interested in trafficking through declarations of guilt and innocence in the case, but rather interested in illuminating the various perceptions that have been and will continue to be projected onto the body of the black woman who is the focal point of this case."[39] For Neal, as for Lubiano and other Duke professors, the actual facts of the case—the "traffic" in guilt and innocence—were insignificant compared with their greater "truth" about the racism of the Duke campus and of American society in general. This "truth" is wholly unaffected by the revelation that the entire accusation and all the prosecutorial malfeasance were based on a lie.

Not surprisingly, Neal urged Duke administrators to politicize the broader Duke curriculum as an appropriate response to the incident. What was needed, according to Neal, were changes "that will allow our students to engage one another in a progressive manner."[40]

Neal maintains that he is a strong believer in "disciplined study and trenchant scholarship," but there is little evidence of this commitment in the three books he has written since he earned his doctorate. *Songs in the Key of Black Life* is about music that is relevant to his radical politics. In a representative passage of near gibberish, Neal praises *Cookie: The Anthropological Mixtape,* an album by pop singer Meshell Ndegeocello, for being "the first pop-recording that speaks to the era of 'newblackness,'" which Neal inscrutably defines as a "blackness" of "radical fluidity that allows existential 'conversations' within 'blackness' across gender, sexualities, ethnicities, generations, socioeconomic positions, and socially constructed performances of 'black' identities."[41] In his second book, *Soul Babies: Black Popular Culture and the Post-Soul Aesthetic,* he embraced a political project of rescuing black culture from alleged oppression. Outlining his purpose in tortured language typical of his work, Neal writes in the book of "a radical reimagining of the contemporary African American experience, attempting to liberate contemporary interpretations of that experience from sensibilities that were formalized and institutionalized during earlier social paradigms."[42] Neal's most recent production, *New Black Man: Redefining Black Masculinity,* calls for "black masculinity" to embrace "feminism."[43]

A faculty with views such as this can be expected to produce a curriculum to serve them. More than a few courses at Duke bear out that expectation.

"Duke as a Plantation": The Department of African and African-American Studies

Duke's Department of African and African-American Studies—profoundly shaped by Karla Holloway during her time as director—announces the political nature of its curriculum in its official mission statement: "African American Studies programs were born in a context of broader social change. Thus, it ought not be surprising that many of the courses in the African and African American Studies (AAAS) Program reflect a concern with issues of social justice nor that our intellectual stance is often one of critique."[44]

"Social justice" is a term of art for the political Left. It is the rubric under which the familiar agendas of socialism—redistribution of income, political allocation of resources—are subsumed. Consequently, the one-sidedness of the department's intellectual "critique," which is relentlessly shaped by the prejudices of the Left, should surprise no one.

Duke/Durham: *Plantations* *AAAS 49S-01*[45]

INSTRUCTOR: Thavolia Glymph, Professor of African and African-American Studies and History

Those seeking the source of the poisoned relations between Duke University and the surrounding Durham community might consider this course. In an undisguised reference to the cotton and tobacco plantations that were once a feature of the slave economy, the course description asks students to reflect on such politically charged and off-the-wall questions as "What is a plantation and why do some citizens of Durham view Duke as a plantation?"

According to the class synopsis, the "organizers of this course hope to broaden ongoing discussions by locating the question of Duke's relationship to Durham in the global as well as local historical processes on which it ultimately rests." The course covers everything from "indentured Irish workers" to "the forced migration of enslaved African laborers" to the United States. It is difficult to regard this curriculum as anything other than an attempt to stoke racial tension between the university and the mostly black neighborhoods of Durham.

Unfortunately, "Plantations" is not untypical of courses in the African and African-American Studies curriculum.

Marxists and "Queer Black Trouble Makers": The Department of English

Literature Program: Marxism and Society

Duke's Marxism and Society program describes its curriculum as "devoted to the study of Marxist theories of society." Why, then, is it housed under the *English* Department rather than the departments of Economics, Sociology, or History, where study of a theory of history and social organization would be appropriate? This odd placement reflects the unscholarly nature of the program. So does the fact that its director is a professor of literature, Jane Gaines, whose entire academic output consists of writings about the movies. Courses in this interdisciplinary program are also taught by professors from the Art, Cultural Anthropology, and East Asian Studies Departments.

To earn a "certificate" in Marxism, Duke students need to take six courses, chosen from among such offerings as "Soviet Literature," "Third World Culture," and "The Chinese Revolution." Unsurprisingly, none of the courses includes a critique of Marxism, which has been discredited in the world outside the academy by the collapse of the socialist societies it created.

The core course in the program, "Marxism and Society," provides a good illustration of the program's unprofessional character and one-sided advocacy of Marxist clichés. The course is appropriately offered by the Department of Sociology, but the instructor, Michael Hardt, is a professor of comparative literature. Hardt is coauthor of *Empire,* a global theory of society that other ideological Marxists have referred to as a "Communist Manifesto for the Twenty-First Century."[46] Hardt's professional qualifications for constructing such a theory are nil, as he has no academic credentials in subjects relevant to Marxism or society. (His coauthor, Antonio Negri, is a professor of philosophy and a convicted Italian terrorist.)

The description for Hardt's class states:

> This course offers a critical appraisal of Marxism as a scholarly method for understanding human societies. The course considers

> the basic concepts of historical materialism, as they have developed in historical contexts. Topics include sexual and social inequality, alienation, class formation, imperialism, and revolution.[47]

While there is no scarcity of critiques of Marxism or accounts of the historical catastrophes that can be attributed to its flawed theories, there is no indication that students taking this "critical appraisal" are made aware of them or required to read them.

To Be a Problem *English 26S-01*[48]

INSTRUCTOR: Alexis Pauline Gumbs, graduate student in Gender in the African Diaspora in the English Department at Duke University

The synopsis explains, "This class will explore trouble-making, radical performative critique and the transgressive and embattled act of (visual, textual, sonic and multi-media) publishing as possible responses to systemic and individual exclusions." According to the instructor, a graduate student who calls herself a "queer black trouble maker," since "publishing is an act of stolen power for outcasted communities, this class will be a publication of what it can mean to be problematic in a society inflected by race, class, sexuality and gender norms. Our aim is not to solve the problems of classism, sexism, homophobia and transphobia as inflected by race, but rather is to create a space where it is possible to act, speak, write and think otherwise, anyway." In short, the classroom is intended to be a forum for the radical views of instructor Gumbs.

Throughout the course, students are asked to consider American blacks as an "outcast community," a point underscored by questions that they are expected to consider. ("Is outcast status the mark of being 'truly' black, or is it grounds to be kicked out of the 'black community'?") The same themes emerge in the books assigned for the course, which exclusively reflect the instructor's idiosyncratic views. *The White Boy Shuffle,* a novel by Paul Beatty, features as its protagonist a black poet named Gunnar Kaufman, who casts himself as the prophet of "a divided, downtrodden, and alienated people" and voices sentiments such as this: "In the quest for equality black folks have tried everything. We've begged, revolted, entertained, intermarried, and are still treated like shit."[49]

Other assigned texts take an even more strident line on race. Thus, *Sister Outsider,* a book of essays and speeches by the lesbian activist Audre Lorde, describes American society as a "racist patriarchy" that intentionally seeks the "destruction" of its black citizens. The introduction to *Home Girls: A Black Feminist Anthology* claims that the "black feminist agenda" has failed to gain a popular following because of the "virulent racism" of American society. Essays featured in the book decry the "racism of white women in the women's movement," the "prevailing popular culture of racism," and the "racism that is perpetuated by the white male dominant society." No other views need apply.

Attacking "White Supremacy" and Global Capitalism: The Department of Sociology

CompRace/Ethnic Studies *SOCIOL 116-01*[50]

INSTRUCTOR: Eduardo Bonilla-Silva, Professor of Sociology and Center for Latin American and Caribbean Studies

According to the course synopsis, this class concentrates on "race relations in the history of the USA." But it has no intention of examining race relations in a scholarly way. Instead, the course is organized around the radical assertion that racism, particularly white racism, is the distinguishing feature of American society—that "racial dilemmas [are] plaguing the United States." In the words of the course description, "Central to this discussion is understanding that 'racism' is not 'prejudice,' 'ignorance,' or a 'set of beliefs' but a comprehensive historical system of racial domination organized by the logic of white supremacy."

To support such a conclusion, the professor relies on a thoroughly misleading calculus: Because there is no equality of outcomes among racial and ethnic groups in the United States, American society and its institutions must necessarily favor whites over racial minorities. As Professor Bonilla-Silva put it in his book *White Supremacy and Racism in the Post-Civil Rights Era,* "racism is rooted in the fact that races in racialized societies receive substantially different rewards. This material reality is at the core of a phenomenon called racism."

How does this theory account for the fact Asians have higher median incomes than American whites, as well as higher percentage of home ownership and college graduation rates? There is no indication that the course even considers such a question. Or does the theory explain why black immigrants to the United States and their offspring enjoy higher rates of success in American society than native-born blacks? Harvard professor Henry Louis Gates Jr. (who is African-American) has pointed out, for example, that of the black students at Harvard, a clear majority—as many as two-thirds—were West Indian and African immigrants or children of these immigrants.[51] Such statistical realities hardly support the course's contention that discrimination against nonwhites is endemic.

From the dubious assertion that American society is racist because of the mere existence of inequalities between races, Professor Bonilla-Silva proceeds to draw a number of equally dubious conclusions. For example, he claims that whites who do not share his radical critique of American society as racist are themselves racists because "the ideas endorsed by most whites . . . signify postmodern support for the racial status quo." (It should come as no surprise that Bonilla-Silva was a signatory to the original "Group of 88" advertisement, and took an active role in condemning the innocent—but white—lacrosse students.)

Of course, the professor is well within his rights to write a book expounding circular and ill-supported condemnations of American society. But it is an abuse of his position as a Duke faculty member to make such tendentious, and apparently obsessively personal, claims the foundations of a university course.

Poverty, Inequality, and Health SOCIOL 299S[52]

INSTRUCTOR: Sherman A. James, Professor of Public Policy Studies and Professor of Center for Health Policy

Presented as a course in public policy, the class is in fact a political attack on globalization—the spread of free-market economies and liberalized trade—and on America's largely private health-care policies. The sole required text is *Health and Social Justice: Politics, Ideology, and Inequity in the Distribution of Disease,* which, as one sympathetic reviewer noted, "is unapologetic in bringing together readings that share a similar ideological construct."[53] The book—and therefore the course itself—presents free trade as increasing class inequalities globally and denying health care to the poor. For example, the volume claims that free-market economies, especially in the United States, produce inferior health-care outcomes for the poorest members of society. Nor does the book attempt to engage contrary arguments. As the same reviewer notes, "no attempt is made to convince the skeptical reader."[54]

The recommended (as opposed to required) books for the course share a similar political agenda. Among these books is *Profit Over People: Neoliberalism and the Global Order*, by MIT linguist (and prominent far-left activist) Noam Chomsky. In this book, Chomsky, who is neither an economist nor a public-policy expert, tendentiously defines neoliberalism—the spread of free markets—as "policies and processes whereby a relative handful of private interests are permitted to control as much as possible of social life in order to maximize their personal profit."[55]

Only one book on the recommended reading list, *The Lexus and the Olive Tree,* by *New York Times* columnist Thomas Friedman, makes a case for global capitalism. That this book has been recommended for students is encouraging, but it is the exception rather than the rule. The other recommended books, such as *Dying for Growth: Global Inequality and the Health of the Poor* and *When Work Disappears: The World of the New Urban Poor,* reinforce the view that capitalism is the enemy of prosperity and health.

Course assignments also betray the one-sided perspective. One asks students to "choose a US or Non-US population and describe how globalization might have contributed to a major health inequity currently experienced by that population." Thus, instead of examining *whether* globalization is a cause of "health inequity"—a legitimate question for objective inquiry—students are expected to assume it is a matter of fact. It is just one example of how the course confuses political indoctrination with pedagogy.

Ignoring Modern Science: The Department of Cultural Anthropology

Gender and Culture CULANTH 113[56]

INSTRUCTOR: Irene Silverblatt, Associate Professor of Cultural Anthropology

This course takes as its starting point the ideological view that gender is a "cultural construction" rather than the product of innate biological differences between the sexes. Although this claim contradicts the finding of modern neuroscience, evolutionary psychology, and biology, it is advanced as a central tenet of cultural anthropology: "Anthropology's most important insights point to the cultural construction of gender as well as to the complexities of gender constructions. This course will develop a critical stance toward the study of gender by taking anthropology's insights into the cultural construction of gender as its point of departure."

In other words, a controversial claim is to be treated as a given—an unexamined assumption on which the entire course is premised.

Sadly, these courses represent only a small portion of the radical indoctrination that goes on at Duke. But just from these samples it becomes clear how such a large group of professors, supposedly committed to rational thought and the pursuit of the truth, could have so quickly and furiously condemned the accused lacrosse players before they had even been formally charged with any crime, let alone convicted.

The courses documented here reflect how even America's most prestigious universities honor and provide platforms for professors who treat their teaching as an opportunity for radical propagandizing and left-wing indoctrination.

This epidemic has spread to large state-run institutions as well, as the case of the University of Colorado, in the next chapter, demonstrates.

2

Ward Churchill U

UNIVERSITY OF COLORADO
TUITION: $5,643 IN STATE
$24,797 OUT OF STATE

Situated just beneath the red sandstone cliffs of Colorado's stately Flatiron Mountains, the University of Colorado at Boulder is the flagship school in the state's higher education system. Its colleges of engineering and applied sciences are among the best in the country; it has become a center for advanced research in environmental law and physical chemistry; and the school boasts a significant number of alumni who have gone on to work for the NASA space program (including an impressive sixteen astronauts). As a result, the University of Colorado, which is now home to more than 28,000 students, enjoys a reputation as a so-called "Public Ivy," a state-supported institution that delivers an elite education.

But in 2005, the University of Colorado made headlines not because of its academic programs or the triumphs of its athletic teams, but because of an Ethnic Studies professor named Ward Churchill who described the victims of the World Trade Center attacks as "little Eichmanns" and likened the United States to Nazi Germany, as a "genocidal" nation.

Churchill's questionable scholarly credentials had been a subject of discussion in academic circles for years. But it was only the scandal generated by his statements, and the accompanying calls from public officials (including the governor) that he be fired, that finally persuaded the university administration to take action. In 2006, the school convened a panel of Churchill's academic peers to investigate his work and the charges from scholars that had dogged his career.

After holding hearings and interviewing Professor Churchill, the panel issued a devastating 125-page report. Among its findings were that Churchill had plagiarized other scholars' works, falsified historical evidence, and even invented historical events in the service of his political agenda. Focusing solely on Churchill's academic work, and resolutely ignoring his extreme anti-American views, the panel found "repeated instances of his practice of fabricating details or ostensible written evidence to buttress his broader ideological arguments," and noted that Churchill lacked any formal academic training in his areas of "expertise." He had written about legal issues, for instance, without any academic training or background in the subject. And although he had been hired as an Ethnic Studies professor (on questionable grounds that he was a Native American) and promoted to full professor rank, his only advanced degree was an M.A. in "communications studies" from an experimental college that offered no grades and was now defunct. In the panel's collective judgment, Churchill was unqualified to teach in his academic field and did not understand the principles of academic inquiry.[1]

Although Churchill's fabrications and weak credentials became national news, less noticed was the panel's equally severe assessment of his employer. The report noted that the university's investigation was long overdue, since a number of the charges against Churchill "had apparently been well known by scholars in the field, although perhaps not by responsible University personnel, for years before the University took any action whatsoever concerning them, and it did so only after the controversy over Professor Churchill's essays became national news." As a result, the report stated that it was "troubled by the origins of, and skeptical concerning the motives for, the current investigation."

Amazingly, even after another academic panel recommended that he be fired for his "repeated and deliberate" violation of the standards of scholarship, Churchill managed to evade disciplinary action. In

June 2006, CU's interim chancellor, Phil DiStefano, issued a notice of intent to dismiss Churchill from his post. But it was not until July 2007—two years after the original scandal—that the university Regents voted 8–1 to fire Churchill (who had remained on the faculty, though prohibited from teaching). The only thing surprising about the Regents' action was the statement of its chairman, Patricia Hayes, who told reporters that firing an incompetent, dishonest, and unqualified professor "was not an easy decision for the board."[2] Perhaps no other statement could so sum up the plight of the American university as it had devolved in the past several decades.

It would be easy to dismiss Ward Churchill as an aberration, but in fact the scandal highlighted the entrenchment of political ideologues on university faculties such as Colorado's. Throughout the controversy, Churchill received support from hundreds of university professors across the country.

More specifically, the case signaled the radicalism infecting the university in Boulder. It is telling, for instance, that Churchill's entire department had voted to promote him to tenure rank and to make him its chairman despite "well-known" allegations about his misrepresentations. Not surprisingly, despite Boulder's strong engineering and science programs, the university's liberal arts faculty offers a disturbing number of courses that are neither academic nor scholarly, but blatantly ideological.

The Trinity of Class, Gender, and Race: The Department of Sociology

Modern Marxist Theory *Sociology 5055*[3]

INSTRUCTOR: Martha E. Gimenez, Professor of Sociology[4]

Like Duke University's "Marxism and Society" course, Martha Gimenez's "Modern Marxist Theory" does not ask whether Marx's theoretical insights are valid, or whether his ideas have any application to current topics of theoretical or political importance, as an academic inquiry normally would. Instead, it assumes that Marxism has the character and validity of Newtonian physics, its propositions verified by centuries of empirical data.

The course description actually defines its agenda as instructing students in how to "apply Marx's theoretical and methodological insights to the study of current topics of theoretical and political importance." Specifically, the class shows students "the relevance of Marxist theory" to such topics as "class, gender, and race/ethnic inequality; population growth/limits to growth; the changing nature and significance of work; information technology and inequality, and democracy, markets and the underdevelopment of development."[5]

An academic course on a sectarian doctrine like Marxism would presumably teach about its origins, history, and texts, and examine the arguments of critics. An academic course on "modern Marxist theory" might also be expected to confront the question of how a doctrine that appears to have been discredited by the collapse of so many societies based on its theories could continue to find adherents. But as is evident from its own course description, "Modern Marxist Theory" is not intended as an academic course about Marxism and does not propose to follow a scholarly approach to its subject or the questions it provokes. This is, rather, a course *in* Marxism, taught by a proponent of Marxist theory: it seeks to indoctrinate students in a Marxist view of the world and to amplify Marx's original paradigm by incorporating views of gender and race that fit its intellectual framework. Its reading list, needless to say, does not list a single text that is critical of Marxism—nothing by Leszek Kolakowski, Ludwig von Mises, Thomas Sowell, Martin Malia, Richard Pipes, or any other prominent critic of Marxist theory or practice.

Such a course would be appropriate to a political academy; it is not appropriate to a modern research university.

Since professors do not have the authority to invent courses and insert them into the curriculum without departmental approval, the adoption of this course indicates that the lack of standards begins with the department itself. This is borne out by other Sociology Department course offerings that are similarly ideological in their approach.

Feminist Theory *Sociology 5006*[6]

INSTRUCTOR: Martha E. Gimenez, Professor of Sociology

Professor Gimenez brings her Marxist perspective to this course as well. Gimenez is described by one biographical website as using "Marx's methodology and theoretical framework for understanding the oppression of women in the capitalist mode of production."[7] The same website notes that Gimenez has sought to "demonstrate the continuing relevance of Marx and Marxist theory for feminist theorizing and feminist politics." According to the course description, her "Feminist Theory" seminar is "designed to examine the materialist feminist challenge to postmodern feminist theorizing, tracing the development of materialist and marxist feminist theory" and examining "the connections between class, gender and race and the contradictory implications of identity politics in the context of the global economy."[8]

This is clearly not an academic course that examines "the materialist feminist challenge" using the critical methods of an academic discipline, which are the methods of science rather than what the philosopher Charles Peirce once referred to as the "method of authority." Instead, the controlling authority of this course is radical feminism, as is evidenced by the required readings for the course. These essays and book chapters, all written by feminist theorists and polemicists, advance feminist and Marxist critiques of capitalism and other subjects.

Two of the required essays were written by the professor herself: one is a "Marxist-feminist analysis" of the effects of "reproductive technologies," while another is a feminist review of "gender struggles under capitalism." To study the role of capitalism the students are required to consult not the work of an economist but rather an essay by Teresa Ebert, a Marxist "queer theorist" and an advocate of what she calls "red feminism." In her essay, Ebert surveys "late capitalism" through the ideological lens of what she labels "ludic feminism." On the subject of U.S. foreign policy, the course assigns feminist philosopher Judith Butler rather than a political scientist or an academic trained in international relations; Butler's essay claims that the 1991 Gulf War to repel Iraq's invasion of Kuwait was actually an imperialist and racist attack on the Arab "other."[9]

Only through such ideological fulminations do students in this course examine complex subjects such as war and peace.

Feminist Theory *Sociology 5036*[10]

INSTRUCTOR: AnnJanette Rosga, Assistant Professor of Sociology

This Feminist Theory course does not make Marxist theory its focus, but its aims are no less radical than those of Professor Gimenez's class. The course description makes clear that the objective is to teach students feminist doctrine, not to instruct them on how to think about feminist doctrine. The synopsis readily acknowledges that the course does not make "any pretense to comprehensiveness" and endeavors "to ensure that students acquire sufficient vocabulary and familiarity with key texts *to understand and work with these {feminist} theories.*"[11] In the now-familiar babbling of academic discourse, the description states that "the course will prioritize a reckoning with the epistemological ramifications of poststructuralist feminist theory."

Having first been indoctrinated in the theory, the students are then asked to apply it to the social universe:

> During the second half of the term, we'll set out to explore specific applications of feminist poststructuralist theory. The course will focus particularly on the ramifications of these theories—theories that arise out of, and analyze, the experience of living in and through the mediations of "marked" categories (woman, queer, [post]colonial)—for the study of lives lived in/through/via "unmarked" experiences and institutions. Put another way, the course will ask: of what use are poststructuralist feminist, queer, and/or postcolonial theories for the analysis of topics that are not primarily identified in terms of their connection to "oppressed" groups? To this end, we will examine feminist theories of masculinity, heteronormativity, "white"-ness, the state, nation and empire.[12]

The instructor, Professor Rosga, attempts to string together these radical clichés into a unified field theory that allows gender to explain virtually every aspect of experience. The scope of this task is breathtaking, encompassing the theory not only of gender, but of the state, the nation, and empire as well—an especially difficult challenge for someone with Rosga's professional qualifications. She has a Ph.D. in the "History of Consciousness" (itself an impossibly vague concept) from the University of California, Santa Cruz.[13] Her "areas of specialty" as listed on her website are "hate crimes in the U.S., and feminist and critical jurisprudence," although she has no law degree. She has no professional expertise in the theory of the modern nation-state or political and economic empires. Instead, she is practiced in the manipulation of ideological concepts like "heteronormativity." And that is what this course is about—how to manipulate ideological concepts that are presumed to be true and therefore left unexamined.

Graduate Feminist Methods *Sociology 5026-001*[14]

INSTRUCTOR: Joanne Belknap, Professor of Sociology

This is self-evidently a course for feminists, not a course for scholars interested in assessing whether feminist methods are useful or not. The synopsis features the bold headline "Course Ideology," under which runs this description: "This graduate seminar is an overview on feminist research methods, focusing on the discipline of sociology, but also addressing some other disciplines in far more limited means." Professor Belknap also frankly announces her intentions to train students in the methods of a sectarian ideology under the headline "Teaching Ideology," by writing, "My goal is to have students leave the course with a strong knowledge base in feminist research methods."[15]

Sex and Gender in Society *Sociology 1016*

Colorado's "Sex and Gender in Society" is premised on the same controversial assumption that forms the basis of "Gender and Culture" at Duke—that is, gender is merely a cultural construct. One instructor for this class—Jadi Morrow, a graduate student in the Department of Sociology—begins her course description by stating, "Many sociologists agree that gender is mainly constructed during socialization as a child through the various socializing institutions (family, school, religion, the media)."[16] Many (feminist) sociologists may agree with this claim, but of course most neuroscientists, biologists, evolutionary psychologists—and psychologists generally—would not.

Nevertheless, Morrow indoctrinates students in her extreme and unproven theory of gender and society, failing to assign any texts that challenge the view she favors.

"Sex and Gender in Society" is a required course for Boulder's sociology majors, which makes its tendentious foundations both disturbing and instructive. This course reflects not just the idiosyncrasies of the instructor, but rather the ideology of the department, which is precisely what an academic department should not have.

Boulder offers multiple sections of this required course, but rather than considering multiple points of view, as a survey of "Sex and Gender in Society" would legitimately do, other instructors champion the same troubling perspective that Morrow does. One instructor, Alison Hatch, informs students that she too will teach "Sex and Gender in Society" exclusively from an ideological perspective—declaring in the course catalogue that "gender roles are learned behaviors (not biological) that are socially-constructed by culture (not innate) and contextually specific and malleable (not universal or fixed)."[17]

A third section is taught by Elaine Enarson, who also frankly explains in the catalogue description that her course is taught from a sectarian point of view: "I teach from a feminist perspective, by which I mean . . . that knowledge of how gender relations are constructed, maintained and challenged can be empowering."[18]

What is the fate of students in these courses who raise challenges to the view that gender is not "constructed" but is a fact of nature? What latitude do they have to disagree if the agenda of the course is to teach them the opposite?

A fourth section of "Sex and Gender in Society" is taught by

Adam Morenberg, whose course overview predictably states, "Our work will focus on the social construction of gender, privilege and difference." He goes on to say:

> We will identify patterns of gender oppression and privilege, and we will discuss possible responses to social inequality. . . . With a "feminist consciousness," we take our gender consciousness and look for ways that gender differences grant or deny power. . . . With a gender consciousness, we note differences; with a feminist consciousness we see what difference those differences make. The point of this class is not to convince you to be a feminist. Rather, I want you to understand sociological feminist thought; it is your decision whether you adopt a feminist consciousness as your own.[19]

The caveat at the end of this statement seems disingenuous in light of the views announced quite candidly above. Morenberg has already informed his students that the point of the course is to teach them to look at the world with a "feminist consciousness." It is not an academic examination of feminist consciousness but a training *in* feminist consciousness. Any decision a student made to accept or reject feminism must take place outside the curriculum, since no provision is made for a critical analysis of the subject. Similar courses could be taught in how to think as a Republican or a Democrat, or as an Islamic jihadist for that matter.

Social Conflict and Social Values *Sociology 1005*[20]

INSTRUCTOR: Brett Johnson, Graduate Student in the Department of Sociology

The first goal of this class, according to instructor Brett Johnson's course description, is "to better understand the discipline of sociology." But the goals subsequently listed reveal this objective to be mere boilerplate; sociology is an academic discipline that requires skepticism, disinterested inquiry, and an empirical approach to complex social issues, while Johnson's synopsis shows that he is teaching left-wing politics. The other goals read as follows:

- To think critically and question authority (e.g. politicians, corporations, teachers).
- To understand how power and privilege are unequally distributed across economic classes, races, genders, sexual orientations, and countries.
- To understand that social institutions (e.g. media, education, economy, government, health care) often reflect the interests of the more powerful (e.g. whites, men, wealthy, heterosexual, U.S.)
- To appreciate the struggles that underprivileged groups have fought and are still fighting for economic, social, and cultural justice.
- To consider concrete actions you can take to make your life more meaningful and will contribute to the creation of a better world.[21]

Johnson may want students to "question authority," but evidently that does not extend to feminists or Marxists, since the other goals assume a feminist/Marxist view of these issues. That perspective is not surprising considering that Johnson is the author, along with other University of Colorado instructors, of *The Better World Handbook,* a guide to "progressive" political action. Sure enough, that book is a required text for the course.

In describing the "purpose" of the course, Johnson highlights his interest in not merely studying radical movements but actually *creating* such a movement. His stated purposes are:

- To understand the influence that society has upon us and to realize our power to shape society with our every action.

- To embrace the world with passion and determination and have an intense desire to make a contribution to the world.
- To become citizens that promote the creation of a just and ecologically sustainable world.[22]

Such political activism is entirely unsuitable to a publicly supported classroom.

Whiteness Studies *Sociology 3171-001*[23]

INSTRUCTORS: Eleanor A. Hubbard, Senior Instructor Emerita in the Department of Sociology, and M. Duncan Rinehart, Research and Educational Program Assistant in the Division of Student Affairs

Sociology 3171 is a course in "Whiteness Studies," which applies the concept of "social construction"—a staple of University of Colorado gender courses—to race. The readings assigned exclusively reflect the views of radicals that America is a racist society and that whites dominate all other groups. Readings by academic critics of these views—Thomas Sowell, Walter Williams, Shelby Steele, John McWhorter, Stephan and Abigail Thernstrom—are entirely absent from the course's reading list.

In the only perspective legitimized by the course, the concept of "whiteness" is allegedly imposed on society (or by society) to oppress other groups. The course includes class sessions devoted to such topics as "Remedial Education for White Folks," "White American Culture," "History of Whiteness," "Is the Social Structure White?," and "Whiteness: The Power of Privilege." Thus, while Black Studies is designed to make African-American students proud and empowered, Whiteness Studies is designed to make white students feel guilty and illicitly privileged. In fact, it is not really a program of "studies" at all; it lays out a racially motivated agenda.

For example, class sessions single out white students: "Whiteness Assignment #1 for White Students (due 10/6): Write an essay interrogating your whiteness identity. The issues you should address in this essay are: your understanding of race, the role of whiteness in your community and country and how that has impacted you, your socialization into being white in a white dominated culture." Notice the loaded premise—the culture is not "majority white" but "white dominated," as though in twenty-first-century America there is a determined and largely successful effort to keep the Oprah Winfreys and Toni Morrisons and Barack Obamas and Michael Jacksons and P. Diddys and Denzel Washingtons and Hank Aarons and Shaquille O'Neals from having their day.

The course description further notes that nonwhite students have a separate assignment, to describe "how whiteness as an identity has impacted you." In this way has segregation returned to American schools fifty years after *Brown v. Board of Education.*

U.S. Values, Social Problems, and Change

Sociology 2031[24]

INSTRUCTOR: Sara Steen, Assistant Professor of Sociology

Despite the course description's promise of "using a sociological perspective" to examine its subject, none of the assigned texts for this course is by a sociologist. Instead, students are required to read Jonathan Kozol, a radical left-wing education writer and an admirer of Cuban dictator Fidel Castro, whose book *Amazing Grace* is a polemic about racism and poverty in the inner-city Bronx; Barbara Ehrenreich, a socialist reporter whose book *Nickel and Dimed* is a political tract about minimum-wage jobs[25]; Joseph Hallinan, a reporter whose *Going Up the River* is an attack on privatized prisons; and Barbara Kingsolver, a left-wing novelist and author of a diatribe against American patriotism in the wake of 9/11, whose book *Small Wonder* is a collection of her political and philosophical essays.

More accurate is the objective of the course stated in the synopsis: "The goal of this course is to prepare you to be a more educated and more active citizen. . . . We will use what we learn about social problems to begin to think about possible solutions and to identify specific actions we as individual citizens can take to work toward these solutions."[26] In short, this is a frankly political course designed to recruit students to left-wing activism.

Race and Ethnic Relations in the United States

Sociology 1021[27]

INSTRUCTOR: Liam Downey, Assistant Professor of Sociology

The instructor teaching this course claims that his first goal is to introduce his students to "different explanations of racial and ethnic inequality in [the] United States." But shouldn't an academic course inquire whether or to what extent there is still ethnic and racial inequality in the United States, instead of simply presuming that there is, and inquiring what causes it? In fact, the curriculum for this course reveals no interest in these questions. Every assigned text is written by a well-known leftist whose thesis is that the United States is a racist society.

In one of these texts, *Living with Racism,* author Joe Feagin—a former head of the American Sociological Association—asserts that "in the United States, every part of the life cycle, and most aspects of one's life, are shaped by the racism that is integral to the foundation of the United States," and that "racial discrimination remains at the heart of U.S. society." He also claims, "Almost any encounter with whites [in the United States], in workplaces, schools, neighborhoods, and public places can mean a confrontation with racism."[28] In Feagin's ideological universe, evidently, whites alone are capable of racial bigotry, an absurd statement that is itself an example of racial bigotry.

Racism also figures as a central theme in another text used in this course, Kozol's *Amazing Grace* (clearly a popular work among radical academics). Here Kozol attributes the social pathologies of Mott Haven, a poor black and Hispanic section of the South Bronx, to the indifference and alleged racism of society at large. In a typical passage, Kozol suggests that Mott Haven is like a medical quarantine that is actively sustained and supported and by "all the strategies and agencies and institutions needed to contain, control, and normalize a social plague."[29] At another point, Kozol claims that the "most vulnerable people in our population" are intentionally "consigned" to "educational denial, medical and economic devastation."[30]

A Different Mirror: A History of Multicultural America is another required text, written by Ronald Takaki, a professor of ethnic studies at the University of California at Berkeley, which presents the history of the United States through the prism of racism and discrimination. Blacks, Hispanics, Asian-Americans, Indians, Irish, and Jews—all are, in Takaki's estimation, victims of exploitation by American society and the capitalist economy, instead of beneficiaries of the opportunities they offer.[31] According to Takaki, the founding of the United States was premised on "economic acquisition and expansion" rather than a desire for liberty.[32]

Sociology of Race and Ethnicity *Sociology 3015*[33]

INSTRUCTOR: Jason D. Boardman, Assistant Professor of Sociology

While the course description claims that the primary goal of this class is to "introduce students to research" and that the reading materials "will be structured around . . . empirical pieces," the only assigned academic text is by tenured radical and racial extremist Joe Feagin. Feagin telegraphs his political agendas in the title of the required book: *Racist America.* Here he offers the following measured analysis of domestic race relations: "One can accurately describe the United States as a 'total racist society' in which every major aspect of life is shaped to some degree by the core racist realities. . . . In the United States racism is structured into the rhythms of everyday life. . . . Every part of the life cycle, and most aspects of one's life, are shaped by the racism that is integral to the foundation of the United States."[34]

Contrary to what the course description says, Feagin's book is anything but empirical. According to Feagin, "Historical data on white images of and attitudes toward black Americans suggest that for centuries the overwhelming majority of whites have been openly and unapologetically racist."[35] But he provides no compelling evidence to support this sweeping assertion, for the simple reason that there are no "historical data" to suggest anything of the kind. Such argument is typical of this book, which is the sole analytic text required for the course.

Feagin's racism-obsessed writing is also featured in a second assigned text, *Race and Ethnic Relations in the United States: Readings for the 21st Century*.[36] Not surprisingly, the book's running ideological theme is that minority groups in the United States are victims of pervasive racism and discrimination; it contains only one essay (by Shelby Steele) criticizing such views.[37]

Resist the "Axes of Domination": The Department of Women's Studies

The departmental website for Women's Studies asks, "What knowledge will I gain with an undergraduate degree from the Women and Gender Studies Program?"[38] Among the answers it provides to the question are these:

- the ways in which ideas of masculinity and femininity shape and interact with other axes of domination, such as class, race, ethnicity, sexuality, ability and nation
- the centrality of gender at the local, national and international levels of society, politics and the economy . . .
- how power and privilege function in relation to the intersection of gender, race, class, sexuality and nation . . .
- women's activism and resistance to oppression . . .

None of these degree goals represents academic values or implies academic knowledge. The idea that "class, race, ethnicity, sexuality, ability and nation" represent "axes of domination" is an ideological perspective of the Left. The idea that gender is central in all areas and all levels of society is an ideological claim. The knowledge of "women's activism and resistance to oppression" is the statement of a political agenda, not an academic program. Since students are expected to display such knowledge—or prejudice—in order to earn a Women's Studies degree, this entire department is self-evidently devoted to indoctrination, not education.

Introduction to Feminist Studies

Women's Studies 2000-100[39]

INSTRUCTOR: Jill Williams, Assistant Professor of Sociology

The description for this course declares that students will examine "the social construction of knowledge by considering feminist critiques of scientific knowledge." It adds, "An underlying project of the class will be to address the questions 'How do we know what we know?' and 'How do our particular positions within the race, class, gender and sexuality systems affect our knowledge?'"[40]

Do our particular positions within the race, class, gender, and sexuality "systems" really affect our *scientific knowledge?* Is there a feminist theory of relativity, or working-class theory of gravity? Only for an ideologue. Not surprisingly, the theoretical texts for this course are exclusively written by radical feminists.

Antimilitary Prejudice: The Peace and Conflict Studies Program

Peace and Conflict Studies *PACS 2500-001*[41]

INSTRUCTOR: Patricia Lawrence, Instructor in the Department of Anthropology

The description of this "foundation course in the Peace and Conflict Studies Certificate Program" announces that it is "designed as an introduction to nonviolent methods and approaches to resolution of conflict. The course provides an intellectual exploration and historical understanding of prominent ideas advanced by nonviolence adherents working actively for social change."[42] In other words, it candidly proclaims the ideological nature of both the course and the entire Peace and Conflict Studies Program, which is designed to indoctrinate students in the antimilitary prejudices of its instructors. The rationale for the military in a democracy is the preservation of peace. A commitment to nonviolent methods is a religious conviction, not an academic perspective. The absence of a professor of military science in this department is prima facie evidence of the ideological character of its curriculum.

"Voodoo Methodology": The Black Studies Program

The field of Black Studies was not so much created by universities as forced on them during the turbulent decades of the 1960s and 1970s, through species of political blackmail. The first Black Studies program was created in 1967, during a general strike that shut down San Francisco State College. The academic issue was whether the traditional disciplines—history, sociology, literature—whose intellectual standards had been established over generations, could accommodate the subject, or whether a new field with no such standards was required. To avoid continuing chaos and the obstruction of their academic programs, the university administrators at San Francisco State capitulated to the demands of the radical Black Student Union and sanctioned the creation of a highly politicized program.[43]

Radical sociologist Nathan Hare was hired by San Francisco State administrators to organize the curriculum. Hare envisaged the new field of Black Studies as first and foremost a morale-raising exercise for black students, and proposed that the courses offered through Black Studies departments primarily speak to their black identity. Thus, instead of learning science, students would take "black science," which would stress the contributions of black scientists and otherwise make science relevant to "the environment of black Americans." Instead of taking math, students would take "black math," which would devote special attention to math as it served "the black community's needs." The same principle was applied to any number of other subjects, including history, philosophy, and literature. Whether students learned anything of substance was irrelevant. What mattered was that the courses raise black students' pride and racial consciousness.[44]

Similarly successful political assaults on the curriculum soon followed at other universities. In October 1968, twenty members of the Black Student Union at the University of California at Santa Barbara stormed the campus building housing the computer center, effectively shutting down the entire university. Their intimidation was rewarded by the creation of a Black Studies Department and Center for Black Studies a year later.[45] The following April, more than a hundred black students at Cornell University, brandishing shotguns and wearing bullet-filled bandoliers, occupied the administration building. Their demand for ending the standoff was a Black Studies Program in which only blacks would be allowed to teach. When Cornell faculty resisted, one black leader warned that "Cornell University has three hours to live."[46] The university yielded, prompting several professors to resign in protest over its "abject capitulation." A third politicized program, this time at a private Ivy League institution, had been incorporated into the academic curriculum.[47]

Under pressure from political activists, liberal administrators across the country began introducing agenda-driven Black Studies programs. In the three years between 1968 and 1971 alone, more than three hundred black studies programs were created, all without the academic standards and guidelines that might ensure that their scholarship and teaching would be professional.[48] This movement was driven entirely by radical activists, not scholars or even students. In fact, as Princeton professor Noliwe M. Rooks noted in her sympathetic history of what eventually was relabeled (again for political reasons) "African-American Studies," many of the programs were "begun on campuses where students had not actually expressed an interest."[49]

Florida Atlantic University professor Clevis Headley has defended the political nature of Black Studies, writing that it should not be seen as a field of intellectual study like other academic programs.

Rather, he writes, Black Studies is "an ethical endeavor to the extent it seeks to give voice to the other, in this case the racial other, those not part of the Eurocentric hegemony." Not to be confused with an academic program, Black Studies is fundamentally a training in racial politics.[50]

Black America and the War in Vietnam

Black Studies 4650-30[51]

INSTRUCTOR: William King, Professor of Ethnic Studies

Despite its title, this course is not an academic survey of black Americans' service in the Vietnam War. Professor King concedes as much in his syllabus, when he writes, "My intent in this course is to provide a view of the War in Vietnam from an Afrocentric perspective." What this "perspective" amounts to is the tendentious claim that the defining feature of black service in Vietnam, as for blacks in the United States, was racism. "Racism in the rear [of the Vietnam War] was alive, well and virulent," students are informed in the course description. They are also expected to repeat these views in their assignments. A paper that counts toward 45 percent of the students' final grade asks them to respond to the following statement:

> In 1903, W.E.B. DuBois wrote, "The problem of the twentieth century is the problem of the color-line,—the relation of the darker to the lighter races of men in Asia and Africa, in America and the islands of the sea." In what ways does the black American experience in Vietnam illustrate his comment?

In his syllabus, King explains that grading is "purely and simply the exercise of power through the authority of the teacher. Its end is purposely political: to limit access to smaller and more elite groups as a means of preserving the status quo." Students who do poorly in this course presumably could object that they were victims of political discrimination.

The politicized presentation of racial issues is inevitable given the Afrocentric perspective that underlines the course content. Afrocentrism puts Africans and their descendants at the center of world history regardless of the historical evidence, as classical scholar Mary Lefkowitz meticulously documented in her book *Not Out of Africa: How Afrocentrism Became an Excuse to Teach Myth as History.* Afrocentrism is based on the dubious insight that history is "culturally determined," from which it follows that any group of people can dispense with evidence and write history according to its choosing. For that reason Eugene Halton, a professor of humanities at Notre Dame, has described Afrocentrism as "racially based form of relativism."[52] Harvard professor Henry Louis Gates Jr., perhaps the nation's preeminent black scholar, has called Afrocentrism a "voodoo methodology."[53]

The Civil Rights Movement in America *Black Studies 4650*[54]

INSTRUCTOR: William King, Professor of Ethnic Studies

Professor King is characteristically blunt in his description of this course, writing that "it is my contention that the Black Civil Rights Movement in America is a kind of domestic war created and sustained by white people (or their surrogates), whose origins may be found in the involuntary transportation of Africans to the New World." He adds that black "self-determination" has been "resisted at every turn by those in power who fear a loss of identity whenever black people advance to a place they have not been before."[55]

King's description ignores the role played by non-Africans in establishing racial equality, beginning with the American founders, who provided the legal and philosophical basis for the civil rights movement in the Declaration of Independence. Moreover, presenting the civil rights movement as a "war" between blacks and whites does a grave injustice to what is in fact a far more complex historical development. Countless historians have documented that whites (including many white Southerners) played a critical role in the movement's ultimate triumph.

In this course, however, the complexities of history are flattened in favor of the professor's one-sided view of the United States as a racist society and its black minority as forever under siege. This is the central theme of the assigned readings for the course, including *Black Movements in America,* by Black Studies professor and self-styled "Black Marxist" Cedric Robinson. In this work, Robinson depicts the United States as one of the most racist countries in the world. "The Second World War was followed by decades of race war on a global scale," he writes at one juncture, elaborating that the "most intensive sites of the war" were "the United States and South Africa."[56]

This course should be about one of the greatest and most successful social movements in history. Instead, it is a reflection of its own theme—racial disparagement of blacks and the confirmation of black impotence. The syllabus actually articulates the view that blacks do not have individual agency but are only acted on by superior forces: "Structurally, the course is a helix. One branch addresses black people as objects—'things' acted upon. The other branch addresses black people as limited access actors in a play not always of their own making." The possibility that blacks might assume control of their own destinies is nowhere contemplated. Such low-level racial demagoguery not only aborts a significant educational opportunity but debases the black experience as well.

"Queer Service-Learning Projects": The Lesbian, Gay, Bisexual, Transgender Studies Program

Queer Rhetorics *Program for Writing and Rhetoric 3020-026*[57]

INSTRUCTOR: Geoffrey Bateman, Graduate Student in the Department of English

"This course," the description announces, "presumes that the best way to learn how to write is by writing—by engaging frequently and intensively in the arts of composition. We will do so by immersing ourselves in the exciting ideas of queer theory and LGBTQ studies and in the local Boulder lesbian gay transgender queer community, which will provide the context for our practice to become effective and adept writers. Throughout the semester, we will survey a number of different types of queer writing—including history, theory, coming out stories, journalism, political activism, and academic research—and will use this writing to generate thoughtful discussion and analysis of queer rhetorical contexts and to help us develop our own voices as writers."

The time-tested rule of learning to write is to study *good* writing, not to study writing with the correct political views. Yet the syllabus for this course conflates "effective" writing with advocacy for "queer politics." The first book, by journalist Richard Goldstein, is a strident political *j'accuse* against gay writers who have distanced themselves from what they regard as the excesses of more radical elements in the gay community. In the book, sneeringly titled *Homocons,* Goldstein rages against authors Andrew Sullivan, Camille Paglia, and Bruce Bawer for their failure to endorse the sexual promiscuity favored by many gay activists during the AIDS crisis and for their refusal to support specific items on the agenda of the gay Left. Goldstein acknowledges that not all of the "homocons" he identifies are political conservatives. Nonetheless, the fact that they do not share his radical views effectively makes them traitors to "their own queer kind."[58] No writings by Sullivan, Paglia, or Bawer are included in the course's required readings.

In fact, the only other required text is *The Trouble with Normal,* by Rutgers University English professor and queer activist Michael Warner. Warner is best known for his defense of gay sex clubs and sex with anonymous partners at a time when both were contributing to high rates of HIV infection and AIDS-related deaths in the gay community. Not only does he oppose practical regulations to impose health standards at such clubs, but employing postmodern theory, he also rationalizes the most destructive practices of the gay community. "The phenomenology of a sex club encounter is an experience of world making," Warner writes. "It's an experience of being connected not just to this person but to potentially limitless numbers of people, and that is why it's important that it be with a stranger. Sex with a stranger is like a metonym."[59] Warner insists that there are no sexual norms, and suggests that the role of the "gay and lesbian movement" is to "challenge" any and all restraints on sexual behavior.[60]

To regard Warner's theoretically dense, jargon-laden academese as a model of clear writing is to divest the concept of all meaning. His and Goldstein's books are assigned not to support a course in "queer rhetoric," as the course title and description suggest, but to school students in the politics of an extreme queer sect.

Another course requirement is that students participate in "queer service-learning projects." The course description states, "To help us hone our skills as writers and rhetoricians, we will also spend about one-third of our class doing 'service-learning.' That is, we will explore the LGBTQ communities in Boulder, volunteer time at a few organizations, and develop our own queer service-learning projects. (Please note: you do not have to identify as queer, or as any other such non-normative sexual/gender identity, to take or succeed in this class; you do need to maintain an open mind to the intellectual and critical possibilities of queerness.)"[61]

This is hardly a course in rhetoric, let alone one designed "to generate thoughtful discussion and analysis," as its catalogue description suggests. Imagine if the instructor offered a parallel course in conservative rhetoric that included internships with conservative organizations like the Heritage Foundation and political causes like the Republican National Committee, and stipulated that "you do need to maintain an open mind to the intellectual and critical possibilities of conservatism."

The "service-learning" requirement of this course is clearly designed to immerse students uncritically in a radical worldview and to expose them, again uncritically, to radical organizations and political agendas, all under the guise of providing them rhetorical skills.

This is recruitment, plain and simple.

Introduction to Lesbian, Gay, Bisexual, and Transgender Studies *Women's Studies 2030*[62]

INSTRUCTOR: Jill Williams, Assistant Professor of Sociology

This course clearly states its sectarian viewpoint and agendas in the description, which affirms that "this class takes a decidedly feminist and social construction approach to studying LGBT issues."[63] In other words, the course assumes that homosexuality and other sexual orientations are environmentally determined (socially constructed). This is not an academic course about lesbian, gay, bisexual, and transgendered people; it is an indoctrination in the radical feminist approach to the subject.

The foregoing cases are not, in any sense, an exhaustive list of the radical courses offered at Boulder, but even these examples make clear that many University of Colorado professors consider their classrooms as appropriate arenas for political activism, and confuse scholarship with political advocacy. They violate the fundamental principles of academic freedom to which the university community is pledged.

If there were any doubt that Ward Churchill was not an anomaly at Boulder, consider how another member of the Ethnic Studies Department describes her mission. Professor Elisa (Linda) Facio—a Churchill acolyte—declares in her departmental biography:

> As racial/ethnic women scholars, I feel our works are attempts to explore our realities and identities (since academic institutions omit, erase, distort and falsify them) and to unbuild and rebuild them. Our writings and scholarship, built on earlier waves of feminism, continue to critique and to directly address dominant culture and "white" feminism. However, our works also attest to the fact that we are now concentrating on our own projects, our own agendas, our own theories, in other words on our own world views. This process is recognized by racial/ethnic

> scholars as "decolonization of the voice." For others, it is considered unscholarly, unscientific. . . . Chicana scholarship reveals our struggles as Chicanas in the United States, and expresses in a society which attempts to render us invisible. . . . Rooted in the political climate of the late 1960s and early 1970s, our scholarship, like other currents of dissent, is a Chicana critique of cultural, political, and economic conditions in the United States. It is influenced by the tradition of *advocacy scholarship, which challenges the claims of objectivity and links research to community concerns and social change.* It is driven by a passion to place the Chicana, as speaking subject, at the center of intellectual discourse.[64]

Professor Facio's statement reflects the values and standards not of a scholar but of a political campaigner. It is difficult to imagine how someone with such a low opinion of the academic mission could observe any reasonable academic standards in her classroom or in her scholarship.

Unfortunately, the same could be said for any number of professors at the University of Colorado—and at universities, prestigious and otherwise, throughout the country.

3

Uptown Madrassa

COLUMBIA UNIVERSITY
TUITION: $36,997

Among the first colleges founded in colonial-era America, Columbia has educated American leaders for some 250 years, from diplomats and statesmen such as John Jay and Alexander Hamilton to American presidents such as Theodore Roosevelt and Franklin Delano Roosevelt.[1] Dwight Eisenhower served as the school's president before leading the nation. To give the long list of academic honors claimed by the school throughout its history is an all-but-impossible task. But the fact that several of its constituent schools—including the Columbia Business School, Teachers College, and the prestigious School of Journalism—are ranked among the best not only in the country but in the world is sufficient testimony to Columbia's academic standing.

In recent years, however, the school has been beset by a succession of high-profile scandals, which reflect the disturbing intrusion of political influences on its academic culture. In March 2003, at an antiwar "teach-in" on the Columbia campus, Professor Nicholas DeGenova provoked national outrage when he publicly wished for "a million Mogadishus"—the site where eighteen U.S. Army Rangers were massacred by al Qaeda–trained Somali forces—and he told Columbia students that "U.S. patriotism is inseparable from imperial warfare and white supremacy," and that "[t]he only true heroes are those who find ways that help defeat the U.S. military."

The following year, Columbia's name was again identified with academic extremism when a documentary film titled *Columbia Unbecoming* featured several students and former students in Columbia's Department of Middle East and Asian Languages and Cultures recounting incidents of faculty anti-Semitism, political sermonizing, personal harassment, and general intolerance. According to the students, professors used their courses to spew political venom against Jews, Israel, and "Zionism," treated the Arab-Israeli conflict as a closed subject rather than an opportunity for academic inquiry, and fostered a culture of classroom intimidation.[2]

Disdain for intellectual diversity expressed itself even more thuggishly in October 2006, when a rowdy mob of student political activists shouted down guest speaker Jim Gilchrist, the founder of a public interest group opposing illegal immigration, slandered him as a "racist," threatened him physically, and drove him off the stage. One student protester expressed the group's anti-intellectual, antidemocratic attitude, saying of anyone who shared Gilchrist's view that immigrants should be admitted only through a legal process, "They have no right to be able to speak here." Columbia president Lee Bollinger deplored the incident as a violation of free speech and the University did take disciplinary action against the perpetrators.

The following fall, Bollinger again defended free speech, this time for an anti-Semite and self-declared enemy of the United States, Iranian president Mahmoud Ahmadinejad. While many condemned the school for providing a podium to a man who has called for the destruction of Israel and denied the Holocaust, and whose theocratic regime was waging a proxy war in Iraq against American servicemen, Bollinger personally introduced Ahmadinejad and prefaced his critical introductory remarks with this affirmation: "I want to say . . . as forcefully as I can, that this is the right thing to do and, indeed, it is required by existing norms of free speech, the American university, and Columbia itself."[3] Ahmadinejad had been invited by

Columbia faculty, such as international relations professor Gary Sick, and his attacks on President Bollinger were applauded by a significant number of the students present.

Apologists for Columbia's administration claim that these are isolated incidents. But they did not occur in a vacuum. Nonacademic agendas have been making their way into the heart of Columbia's liberal arts curriculum for a quarter of a century. In many classrooms, controversial left-wing perspectives are no longer analyzed and dissected but are instilled as received doctrine, while other points of view are ignored and, in effect, suppressed. Reading assignments reflect the one-sided nature of lectures delivered by professors who behave like political activists instead of scholars.

In turning their classrooms into political platforms, such faculty activists have had to violate (and administrators have had to ignore) explicit Columbia regulations that obligate professors to observe an academic discipline in the classroom. These standards are codified in Columbia's Statement on Professional Ethics and Faculty Obligations and Guidelines for Review of Professional Misconduct. It states that while faculty members have the freedom to decide what they teach, they have a "correlative obligation of responsible self-discipline." More precisely:

> Every effort must . . . be made to be accurate, to be objective, to demonstrate appropriate restraint, and to show respect for the opinions of others. Faculty members may not enroll or refuse to enroll students on the basis of those students' beliefs, or otherwise discriminate arbitrarily or capriciously among them. Evaluation of students and awards of grade and credit must be based on academic performance professionally judged, not on matters extraneous to that performance.[4]

These obligations find additional support in Columbia's Code of Academic Freedom and Tenure, which stipulates that professors are granted the academic freedom "in the classroom in discussing their subjects," but that concurrently "they should bear in mind the special obligations arising from their position in the academic community."[5]

An inquiry into Columbia's curriculum reveals, however, that many professors—along with many departments and affiliated programs—fail to observe such a discipline and instead promote ideological agendas that have little to do with the educational mission or the professional expertise that Columbia is supposed to provide.

Teaching for "Social Justice": Columbia Teachers College

Generally regarded as the premier graduate school of education in the country, Columbia Teachers College provides an example of the corrosive influence of ideology and political activism on an academic curriculum. The school's "Conceptual Framework," which sets forth "the rationale and organizing principles" behind its curriculum, is premised on the radical idea that education is at bottom a political act. In line with this view, the framework stipulates that teachers are expected to be "participants in a larger struggle for social justice."[6] Indeed, the school's website specifically states that one of its "expectations" is that students demonstrate "dispositions" and "commitments" to "social justice." For the faculty of Teachers College, there appears to be no distinction between teaching and politics. Summing up the reigning philosophy, Margaret Crocco, an associate professor of social studies and education at Columbia, has said, "Social justice is at the heart of our program."[7]

To an outside observer, the term "social justice" can seem vague, but at Teachers College there is no confusion about its meaning: it is a template for socialist political agendas. Thus the school defines the mission of a teacher in this way: "To change the system and make schools and societies more equitable, educators must recognize ways in which taken-for-granted notions regarding the legitimacy of the social order are flawed."[8] It follows from this that students who hope to be teachers are expected to share a radical view of American society and to consider their mission to be not educating the young but attacking the legitimacy of the social order.

The school's website informs prospective teachers that "social inequalities are often produced and perpetuated through systematic discrimination and justified by societal ideology of merit, social mobility, and individual responsibility."[9] In other words, the foundational values of American society—merit-based advancement, upward mobility, and personal responsibility—are suspect. No wonder students who attend the school often come away with a belief that teaching is part of a larger effort to create, as one recent Teachers College graduate has put it, a "progressive democratic community."[10]

One can learn a good deal about the Teachers College's educational philosophy from a series of books titled Teaching for Social Justice, published by Teachers College Press. The fourteen-book series—the brainchild of Maxine Green, a professor emerita of philosophy and education at the college, and her protégé William Ayers, a onetime leader of the terrorist group called the Weather Underground, an unrepentant bomber, and a graduate of the college—focuses on K–12 education and shows the extent to which teaching "social justice" means promoting left-wing activism.[11] One particularly telling example is the book *Teaching Science for Social Justice,* which is forthright about its aim: to replace science education with political activism. "By illustrating how science brings about different kinds of change, we make the claim that all teaching and learning science is political," the authors declare.[12] Rather than viewing science as a body of empirical knowledge, the authors say that it should be seen as a "tool for social change."

Notwithstanding its titular concern with education, the book has the feel of a political tract, something the authors readily concede. "Drawing from feminist theories," they write, "we show how the students in our study find strength—political and ideological—by carefully and critically understanding how society supports separations between individuals and groups of individuals based on race, ethnicity, social class, and gender."[13] Plainly, the authors believe that it is this "political and ideological" purpose that science education should serve.

Kindred themes inform other titles in the Teaching for Social Justice series. In the introduction to *Refusing Racism: White Allies and the Struggle for Civil Rights,* one learns that education in the United States suffers from an "unacknowledged racism that has been present in the U.S. school system."[14] To combat this racism, the book's white author, Cynthia Stokes Brown, writes that American whites must first recognize that they are racists: "Only after we white people work our way through understanding racism, a painful and difficult part of our growth, can we realize how stunted we were before."[15]

Nor is political activism reserved for K–12 schools. On the contrary, a typical course indicates that Teachers College professors practice what they preach inside their own classroom.

Human Rights in Africa: Politics, Policies, and Pedagogies

ITSF 4094-2

INSTRUCTOR: Fran Vavrus, Associate Professor of Education and Associate Director of the Teachers College Center for African Education

Although the description states that this course "examines the historical conditions that have given rise to human rights violations in particular African countries and the efforts to protect human rights through policy and education," the class avoids a scholarly examination of human rights in Africa. Rather, the course makes a political argument: that human rights abuses in Africa, past and present, can be attributed to Western colonialism. Indigenous sources of human rights abuses are off the table from the start.

For example, the course's section on the 1994 tribal genocide in Rwanda, when Hutu militias massacred the country's Tutsi minority, is grounded in a single text, *When Victims Become Killers: Colonialism, Nativism, and the Genocide in Rwanda.* which argues that "the Rwandan genocide needs to be thought through within the logic of colonialism."[16] According to author Mahmood Mamdani, the "historical legacy of colonialism and postcolonial politics" created a "dynamic leading to the genocide."[17] In other words: blame the white guys—the tribal nature of the conflict notwithstanding.

Apart from Mamdani's tendentious text, there are only two other required readings: Mark Mathabane's *Kaffir Boy: The True Story of a Black Youth's Coming of Age in Apartheid South Africa*, which is a memoir of the author's childhood in a South African ghetto, and Adam Hochschild's *King Leopold's Ghost: A Story of Greed, Terror, and Heroism in Colonial Africa,* which is not an academic text but a left-wing journalist's indictment of Belgian colonialism in the Congo under King Leopold II.[18] None of these books explores the history of slavery in Africa predating colonialism, or the ongoing tribal conflicts, or the corruption and genocide that have plagued the continent since the dissolution of the colonial empires half a century ago.

School for Agitators: The Teachers College Peace Education Center

Political rather than academic criteria frame the curriculum for the Teachers College Peace Education Center, an adjunct of Columbia's Teachers College. The center's purpose is to train students to look upon teaching as a way to promote various political agendas, from environmentalism to antiwar activism. The center's mission statement makes this intention plain, declaring that its goal is "to further the development of the field of peace education, particularly in recognition of the unprecedented need to address issues of security, war and peace, human rights and social justice, sustainable development and ecological balance." The underlying principles of peace education are enumerated as "non-violence, human rights, social, economic, political and ecological justice."

Elsewhere, the center reveals that its teaching methods are rooted in "a philosophy of education grounded in the role of education in social change." Citing the influence of Maxine Green, who argues that political activism is a proper role for an educator, the center states that "[o]ne of its primary purposes" is "to capacitate learners to take action in the larger society." In plain English, the center is more concerned with turning out committed political agitators than with producing able teachers.

Human and Social Dimensions of Peace *ITSF 4603*

INSTRUCTOR: Peter Lucas, professor in the Department of International and Transcultural Studies

This course is designed to teach "peace education" and to strive for "substantive social change." Students are required to review the website of the People's Decade of Human Rights Education, a left-wing group whose mission is to "advance pedagogies for human rights education relevant to people's daily lives in the context of their struggles for social and economic justice and democracy." No attempt to supplement this with an alternative point of view is made.

A section of the course titled "Mass Imprisonment in America" requires students to read left-wing journalist Eric Schlosser's article "The Prison-Industrial Complex," which is a slogan of the movement launched by Communist and black activist Angela Davis to free all minority criminals under the presumption that they are "political prisoners." Rather than analyzing other views of the criminal justice system, students must scrutinize the websites of activist groups like Books Not Bars, a radical campaign that seeks to close down California's juvenile detention centers.

Another section of the course, called "The Politics and Material Practices of Occupation," is a political attack on the state of Israel. The course endorses the view that Israel's "occupation" of Palestinian land is the principal cause of the continuing conflict between Israel and the Arabs. Students are required to read a book called *A Civilian Occupation: The Politics of Israeli Architecture,* which argues that Israeli architecture is actually a form of "territorial control" and that Israeli settlements are "devices for the surveillance and the exercise of power." Students also must visit the website of Peace Now, a left-wing group that is routinely critical of Israel's defense policies, as well as the anti-

Israel website of the PLO Negotiations Affairs Department. The clear impression left by the course is that the social dimensions of peace are synonymous with opposition to Israeli and American policy.

Fundamental Concepts of Peace Education *ITSF 4613*

INSTRUCTOR: Peter Lucas, Professor in the Department of International and Transcultural Studies

According to the course description: "We will . . . note how peace education works both within the formal educational system and through non-formal channels such as community-based associations and NGOs. In the schools, education for peace includes programs such as diversity education, peace and justice education, conflict resolution, civic and democratic education, and violence-prevention education."

This is the menu of a political movement, not an academic course of study, as the class assignments further illustrate. Students are asked "to reflect on a certain concrete situation using a peace education lens. For example, a previous student wrote about her school where she works as a teacher, critically reflecting on the institution from a peace education perspective and drawing from the peace education theories used in the class." Thus the course urges students to view education as essentially a political vocation.

For inspiration, students are assigned solely those books that regard "peace education" as synonymous with left-wing political activism. A representative text is *Peace Education,* by Ian Harris and Mary Lee Morrison. Declaring that their motivation is to change "human consciousness," the authors write that peace education is based on the "philosophy [of] nonviolence" and dogmatically assert that war is not a "legitimate" way of solving problems. "Peace education," they state, "tries to inoculate students against the evil effects of violence by teaching them the skills to manage conflicts nonviolently and by motivating them to choose peace when faced with conflict." The authors do not address the fact that some conflicts do not lend themselves to peaceful solutions, and that the goal of education is not to promote their own distinctive political ideologies. They concentrate instead on isolating the root causes of violence, which they identify as "structurally violent societies that deny [poor people] economic and social security" and "state systems that invest in police forces and armed forces rather than quality education and social justice." Clearly, the authors are talking about America, one of whose evils is that it is not a socialist state. In the course of lamenting the rise of "corporate capitalism and its impact upon human communities," the authors reveal that their goal is to "see that resources are controlled equitably."

Polemical, heedless of contrary perspectives, and inspired by the radical theory that education equals political activism, the book crystallizes the nonacademic mission of the Peace Education Center.

Fundamentals of Activist Reporting: The Columbia School of Journalism

Columbia's School of Journalism has long been regarded as the leading institution for training in the field. But some of the courses offered are concerned less with acquainting students with the fundamentals of the journalistic craft than with encouraging them to embrace the political convictions of their (left-wing) professors. Here is an example, approved—as are all courses—by the school authorities.

Human Rights Reporting *JOUR J6002*[19]

INSTRUCTOR: Peter James Spielmann, Adjunct Faculty Member in the School of Journalism

The official description of this course reads more like a newspaper editorial than an academic instruction in the fundamentals of objective reporting:

> America's new anti-terror war has spawned an array of setbacks for human rights. In the United States these range from

> the roundup and detention of Middle Eastern men after 9/11 to the erosion of civil liberties and privacy rights. Overseas, the example of the U.S. crackdown has been eagerly adopted by Russia, China and Israel in their battles against local uprisings; Washington will have little moral leverage if it wants to criticize their human rights practices. In the name of enforcing order worldwide, the United States also now claims exemption from the jurisdiction of the new International Criminal Court. . . .

After this prologue, Professor Spielmann gets down to business:

> Students will examine and report on international rights abuses, and problems in the New York City region. These may include subjects such as immigrants seeking refugee status, migrants held indefinitely without trial on "secret evidence," police tactics, racial profiling, prison overcrowding, the death penalty, sweatshop labor, the moral responsibility of multinational business for human rights, recovery from atrocities through therapy, and the difficulty that artists and writers grapple with in representing human tragedies.[20]

The aim of this course is not to teach students how to report on issues of human rights but rather to tell them what to think about such issues. It is based, quite explicitly, on the partisan judgments of the professor—an approach that would be inappropriate even in a course on opinion journalism, let alone one purportedly devoted to objective reporting.

It is not clear whether Professor Spielmann regards himself as an academic, a journalist, or a political partisan, or whether his intention is to train journalists or activists. According to Spielmann, "[the] course is designed for students who will work as reporters and editors, and those who may join advocacy organizations or international institutions."[21]

DeGenova's Playground: The Department of Anthropology

Latino History and Culture *LATS W1600*[22]

INSTRUCTOR: Nicholas DeGenova, Assistant Professor of Anthropology

As anthropology professor, Nicholas DeGenova is entitled to believe that all patriotism amounts to "imperial warfare and white supremacy" and that the United States must be defeated in the War on Terror. But as a professional educator, he is obligated to conduct objective and scholarly classes that do not promote his extreme political convictions to a captive audience.

The design of this course shows, however, that Professor DeGenova has no respect for legitimate academic inquiry or the "intellectual pluralism"—in other words, a range of perspectives—that the American Council on Education has called one of the "central principles of an American higher education." Instead his course adopts the rigidly dogmatic view that Latino history and culture have been shaped by the twin forces of American imperialism and racism.

This theme runs through every book assigned for the course, without exception. In *Harvest of Empire: A History of Latinos in America,* author Juan Gonzalez sets out to "trace the seamless bond between Anglo dominance of Latin America . . . and the modern flood of the region's people to the United States." Gonzalez is neither a scholar of Latin America nor a historian of immigration. He is a political columnist and activist who cofounded the Young Lords, a radical Puerto Rican group in the late 1960s.

With a similar poverty of nuance, Ramón A. Gutiérrez's *When Jesus Came, the Corn Mothers Went Away*—a book referenced repeatedly in the course—assails the "flag-waving apostles of American democracy" for conquering New Mexico in the mid-nineteenth century and condemns the "rising American empire" of the "Anglos" for initiating an "intense cycle of cultural conflict" that is "very much alive in New Mexico to this day." Likewise, Ronald Takaki's assigned book, *Iron Cages: Race and Culture in 19th-Century America,* tendentiously identifies imperialism, capitalist repression, and "racism" against nonwhite minorities as the distinguishing features of the United States in the nineteenth century. Reginald Horsman's *Race and Manifest Destiny: The Origins of American Racial Anglo-Saxonism* describes America's self-conception as flowing from the racist certitude that "a superior American race was destined to shape the destiny of much of the world." Students are also required to read a chapter from Howard Zinn's Marxist indictment of the American experiment, *A People's History of the United States,* which reduces the impulses underpinning American foreign policy to an "ideology of expansion," "racism," "paternalism," and "capitalism." In addition, DeGenova forces the class to read ideological polemics such as the speeches of Fidel Castro's notorious executioner, Ernesto "Che" Guevara, and "El Plan Espiritual de Aztlán," a manifesto of the radical Chicano separatist group MEChA.

DeGenova's course provides no contrary historical interpretations, such as those of Humberto Fontova, Maurice Halperin, Hugh Thomas, Marc Falcoff, or Thomas Sowell. Nor, in fact, does it assign any dispassionate academic inquiries, which would afford students the opportunity to arrive at their own conclusions about these controversial subjects. The course is a comprehensive introduction to nothing more than the radical politics of Professor DeGenova and the bitter tirades of America's radical critics.

Labor and Exchange, Measurement and Value

ANTH G6129[23]

INSTRUCTOR: Paul Kockelman, Assistant Professor of Anthropology

This is a course in Marxism as seen through the lens of Marx's magnum opus, *Das Kapital,* one of only two texts assigned for the course. Apart from the dubious propriety of uncritically teaching Marxist economics in any course—let alone an anthropology course—it is unclear what academic credentials qualify its instructor to do so. As a linguistic and psychological anthropologist, Professor Kockelman can claim no academic expertise in economics. The fact that he is nonetheless free to engage in scarcely camouflaged political advocacy is another indication of the extent of the intellectual corruption in this particular department.

Revolutionaries in the "Ebony Tower": African-American Studies

Introduction to African-American Studies *AFAS C1001*[24]

INSTRUCTOR: Professor Manning Marable, Professor of History and Political Science

This is the introductory course required of all African-American Studies majors. Its catalogue description equates its subject with radical political protest, with an emphasis on promoting "social change." The instructor, Professor Marable, engages in such political activism, as a member of the "central committee" of a Communist splinter group associated with Angela Davis called the Committees on Correspondence, which emerged from the wreckage of the Communist Party USA after the fall of the Berlin Wall.

Rather than offering a scholarly inquiry into the history, status, and condition of African-Americans, the course portrays the history of black Americans as a struggle against racist oppression from slavery to the present. Its themes include "ways for the black community to survive discrimination and oppression" and how "black people have managed to sustain themselves in the face of almost constant adversity."[25]

The course assigns only texts that reinforce this ideological message. For example, *Let Nobody Turn Us Around: Voices of Resistance, Reform, and Renewal: An African-American Anthology* is a volume of political tracts edited by Professor Marable himself. The work includes essays by "black Bolshevists" such as Communist poet Claude McKay, who pays tribute to the "freedom" and the support for "the Negro" in Soviet Russia, as well as by Communist writers Langston Hughes, Paul Robeson, and Angela Davis. Also represented are Nation of Islam spokesman and anti-Semite Stokely Carmichael, Black Panther felon Huey Newton, and convicted cop killer Mumia Abu-

Jamal, who is described simply as "America's most celebrated and controversial prisoner on death row."[26]

Students are encouraged to watch films and visit the websites of antiprison activists associated with the movement headed by Marable's party comrade Angela Davis. These include films such as *Critical Resistance to the Prison Industrial Complex,* made by the Video Activist Network, and websites such www.thetalkingdrum.com, which campaigns against the "prison industrial complex" and lobbies to set all minority felons free.

Beyond inundating students with its relentlessly pessimistic view of "oppressed" black Americans, the course includes a "service-learning" component. Students are required to volunteer with four preapproved organizations that work with the black community in order to better understand the "theory you are exposed to in the classroom and throughout the assigned texts." By doing so, the students are informed, they will be "empowering those who have no voice." This work will also teach students to "understand your *social responsibility.*" (Emphasis in the original.) In other words, it is the students' social responsibility not to become educated citizens, but to become left-wing activists.

Because the assumption of the course is that black communities are "oppressed," students are informed that by volunteering they will be "empowering those who have no voice." Since black Americans have their own television network (BET); until recently ran the biggest media corporation in the world (Time Warner); are secretaries of state, presidential candidates, and chairs of powerful congressional committees; and are prominent figures in television and film, it is not apparent how empowering the voiceless should be a central concern of an African-American Studies course, except to feed the political prejudices of the instructor.[27]

Once the volunteer project is completed, students must write a "reflection paper" relating the political themes promoted in the course to their community activism. To ensure that they will arrive at predetermined political conclusions, students are asked to consider a series of leading questions, such as:

> How have your experiences in the community helped you learn about structural racism today?
>
> In what way did you encounter structural racism at your organizations or with the people you worked?
>
> What change is needed for the groups of people you worked with?
>
> How can this change be accomplished: with individual action or collective action—within the system or challenging the system?
>
> What privilege did others bring? What systems are the sources of such privilege? How are you or others disempowered by your/their lack of such privilege?

A proper academic course would pursue the question of *whether* there exists "structural racism" in a society whose laws and Constitution prohibit discrimination on the basis of race, but Marable's class takes "structural racism" as an unquestioned point of departure. That the course promotes one-sided political views and racist attitudes is objectionable enough; even worse, the students' grades depend on the extent to which they embrace its party line, which is a violation of their academic freedom.

Critical Approaches to African-American Studies

AFAS G4510[28]

INSTRUCTOR: Manning Marable, Professor of History and Political Science

Here is another course in which Professor Marable trains students for political activism in his radical causes. Paraphrasing Marx's famous dictum that philosophers have only interpreted the world and the task of revolutionaries is to change it, the course description asserts:

> Black Studies is "prescriptive," presenting theoretical and programmatic models designed to empower black people in

> the real world. By its very nature, it requires a "praxis"—the unity of critical analysis and social action, the production of new ideas, not merely designed to interpret the world, but change it.[29]

The statement that Black Studies is "prescriptive"—that it has agendas beyond a scholarly examination of its subject—is itself a violation of academic standards and of the instructor's professional obligations as a Columbia faculty member. The Marxist idea that theory must always be connected to a practical agenda is repeated in Professor Marable's introduction to *Dispatches from the Ebony Tower: Intellectuals Confront the African-American Experience,* a book that is required reading for his course. In it, Marable writes there is "a practical connection between scholarship and struggle, between social analysis and social transformation."[30] But scholarship connected to struggle is not scholarship; it is political propaganda. Marable goes on to describe African-American Studies as a "means to dismantle powerful racist intellectual categories and white supremacy itself," and to state that "black studies must . . . be an oppositional critique of the existing power arrangements and relations that are responsible for the systemic exploitation of black people."[31] In other words, in Professor Marable's view African-American Studies involves the racist assumption that twenty-first-century America is built on "white supremacy" and the "systemic exploitation of black people."

As in his introductory course, Professor Marable provides students with a menu of texts that reinforce his ideological prejudices and promote his agendas. Prominent among them is his own polemic *Living Black History: How Reimagining the African-American Past Can Remake America's Racial Future.* In this book, Marable rejects the historical "master narrative" that the United States has extended rights and benefits to its black citizens, declaring instead that American society is "historically organized around structural racism."

Topics in the Black Experience Seminar: Lyrics on Lockdown—Hip Hop and Spoken Word vs. the Prison Industrial Complex *AFAS G4080/004*[32]

INSTRUCTOR: Bryonn Baine, a "spoken-word poet" and activist

To assume that there is a "prison industrial complex" in America is already a political rather than a scholarly statement. And that is only the first of the ideological conclusions students are required to make if they enroll in this course. Students are assigned readings that "will examine the origin and evolution of the prison industrial complex in the U.S., the development of the criminal/juvenile injustice [*sic*] system, the sociological and psychological impact of mass incarceration on families and children, the role of the arts in social justice campaigns and resistance movements, and the use of popular culture as a pedagogical tool for popular education." To fulfill the requirements of the course, students must attend workshops where "hip hop or spoken word poets" discuss "the prison crisis in America." They must also devise their own workshop "related to the criminal (in)justice system."

Relatedly, students are required to study "community-based" organizations recommended by the professor and document their "best practices" (but evidently not their worst practices). The recommended groups unfailingly reflect the course's ideological prejudices; not one treats prisons or incarceration policies in the United States as anything other than a function of omnipresent white racism. For instance, the Ella Baker Center for Social Justice is founded on the belief that criminal justice policies in the United States are "racist," with "communities of color" being the primary victims of "racist policing" and unjust "over-incarceration."[33] Likewise the Malcolm X Grassroots Movement asserts in its mission statement that the "collective institutions of white-supremacy, patriarchy and capitalism have been at the root of our people's oppression."[34] This group calls for the "liberation" of "Afrikan" people in the United States, including unnamed "political prisoners," "by any means necessary."[35]

The extreme views of this course are those of the instructor, Bryonn Bain. A longtime antiprison radical, Bain has made a number of allegations about the criminal justice system in America, few of them supported by fact. He has claimed, for example, that with the passage of the PATRIOT Act, Arab-Americans were "detained by the hundreds of thousands," a statement ridiculous on its face.[36] Bain has also said that the American prison system is proof that "[t]ere is slavery in this country," while American sentencing laws are "racially motivated."[37] Bain's views are straightforward. The only puzzle is why Columbia University would offer such rantings as an academic course.

Soros-Funded Activism: The Africana Criminal Justice Project

The Africana Criminal Justice Project is directed by Professor Marable and funded by the Open Society Institute, the grant-making arm of financier and leftist George Soros.[38] The project represents itself as a research institution at Columbia, when in practice it functions as an indoctrination center for Professor Marable's conspiratorial view that American society is pervasively racist. In Professor Marable's own words, the project's work is part of his "struggle against systemic or structural racism" in the criminal justice system, and more broadly his "struggle to overturn the violence that is being meted out against millions of American citizens . . . particularly for citizens of African descent."

Consistent with this vision, the Africana Criminal Justice Project "supports initiatives seeking to address a response to the contemporary crisis of racialized criminal injustice, especially through the promotion of black civic capacity and leadership in communities impacted by mass criminalization and incarceration." A creditable research project might be expected to grapple with such discomfiting data as crime rates for black men, which are well above the national average of other demographic groups and which may account for their high levels of incarceration. Correspondingly, it might consider the implications of the fact that black citizens are also disproportionately the victims of black crime, and that if the "mass incarceration" were ended, there would be many more black victims. But no such considerations are evident in the syllabus or readings for this course. The Africana Criminal Justice Project ignores the basic data on black crime and incarceration and the complex issues that the data suggest, instead promoting the political view that white racism is the source of the problems the black community faces.

Conferences sponsored by the Africana Criminal Justice Project reflect its political agendas—namely, its desire to overthrow existing criminal justice structures and power relations. In April 2003, the project sponsored a conference entitled "Africana Studies Against Criminal Injustice: Research-Education-Action." An open academic inquiry would not be "for" or "against" anything, and would enlist research and education not in the cause of "action" but in the cause of knowledge. But this is a political program rather than a course of study, as the project's promotional statement clearly signals: "Africana Studies is poised to make valuable contributions to a growing body of work on the collateral consequences of racialized mass incarceration, informing new strategies of critical research, education, and collective action."

In November of that year, the Africana Criminal Justice Project sponsored a similarly political symposium titled "Chanting Down the Walls: Using the Arts to Combat America's Prison Crisis." The project invited former Black Panther Party leader and Black Liberation Army cofounder Dhoruba Bin Wahad to deliver a keynote address. Bin Wahad was introduced simply as a "U.S. political prisoner"—never mind that his Black Liberation Army publicly claimed credit for a 1971 machine-gun assault that left two New York police officers seriously wounded, and that in 1973 he was convicted of two counts of attempted murder for his role in that attack.

Sexist Tyrannies: The Department of Women's Studies

Like African-American Studies, the Department of Women's Studies is a narrowly conceived ideological program, not an academic discipline. Its introductory course is devoted to propagating various schools of radical feminism that view American women as victims of male oppression and America as a social order characterized by rigid hierarchies of power.

Introduction to Women's and Gender Studies

WMST V1001x[39]

INSTRUCTOR: Alice Kessler-Harris, R. Gordon Hoxie Professor of American History

According to its catalogue description, one of the principal themes of this course "pertains to systems of power and discrimination. We explore issues of hierarchy and domination, ask whether and how women have been subordinated and what the consequences of those constraints have been. We also want to know how women have challenged, resisted, and adapted to their devaluation and subordination. In addition we will analyze the practices and institutions women have created that have enabled them to survive and thrive."[40]

Notice the unquestioned assumptions that provide the basis for this course: the course does *not* ask whether and how women have been subordinated, but accepts that subordination as a given. Consequently all that remains is finding out "how women have challenged, resisted, and adapted to their devaluation and subordination." By presenting ideological claims as undisputed facts, this course closes off any such discussion in advance, and closes its students' minds as well.

This required introductory course does not make students aware of the wider spectrum of views on the status and condition of women, such as the arguments of conservative feminists such as Christina Hoff Sommers and dissenting liberal feminists such as Camille Paglia. The first assigned text, *Myths of Gender: Biological Theories About Women and Men,* by Anne Fausto-Sterling, is a polemical attack on the view that gender differences are biological in origin. The author accuses sociobiologists of justifying "the domination and hierarchy" of men over women in society with their "biologically based argumentation," thereby impeding "political efforts to obtain male/female equality."

Even more stridently political is the tone of another assigned text, *Feminist Theory from Margin to Center,* by the radical bell hooks (the lower case is hooks's whimsy). Amplifying the theme of the course, hooks describes the United States as a "political system of imperialist, white supremacist, capitalist patriarchy," and portrays American women as victims of "sexist tyranny," a "patriarchal mass media," and "sexism, racism, classism." Though one would hardly guess it from her prose, hooks is a professor of English Literature.

In an assigned reading titled "Capitalism, Patriarchy, and Job Segregation by Sex," author Heidi Hartman argues that Western men have used capitalism to establish "hierarchical organization and control" over women; that "job discrimination by sex" is the "primary mechanism in capitalist society that maintains the superiority of men over women"; and that "accommodation between patriarchy and capitalism has created a vicious circle for women." An identical theme animates another assigned text, Catharine MacKinnon's *Sexual Harassment of Working Women,* which begins: "Intimate violation of women by men is sufficiently pervasive in American society as to be nearly invisible." As an example of this totalistic but somehow "invisible" violation, MacKinnon cites sexual harassment of women, which she claims is "institutionalized" in the U.S. labor force.

Only one course text departs from these orthodoxies: an article by Andrew Sullivan arguing that men and women differ because men have more testosterone. Because this argument runs contrary to the course's political agendas, students are required to disagree with it by writing a "critical response," using Fausto-Sterling's *Myths of Gender* as their "primary reference" and imitating its "methodological criteria."

Anti-Israel Soapbox: The Department of Middle East and Asian Languages and Cultures

This department has generated sustained controversy as a result of student claims that several of its faculty are political partisans who intimidate those who disagree with them in the classroom.

Joseph Massad, an associate professor who teaches modern Arab politics, is one focus of these student complaints.[41] Students have charged that Professor Massad repeatedly used his course "Palestinian-Israeli Politics and Societies" as a soapbox to attack Israel. According to one student's report, Massad became outraged when asked in class whether Israel provided warnings to civilians before striking residential areas, telling the questioner that if she was going to "deny the atrocities" committed against Palestinians, she should "get out of his class." Another student complained that the professor referred to Zionism as a "male-dominated movement," and erroneously informed his students that the word "zion" means "penis" in Hebrew.

Students have made public their lecture notes to prove that Professor Massad uses the course to express his anti-Israel views. According to these notes, Massad on more than one occasion likened Israel's Zionist character to the racism of apartheid-era South Africa. "We were not presented with any material that argued that Zionism is not racist," one student said. On other occasions, students assert, the professor told jokes intended to present Zionism as a fringe phenomenon with virtually no following among Jews. "What makes a Zionist a Zionist?" the professor is alleged to have asked. The answer: "A Jew who asks a Jew to send a third Jew to Palestine."

Further, while omitting any mention of human rights abuses in other Middle Eastern countries, Professor Massad devotes consistent attention to crimes allegedly committed by Israel, even going so far as to question Israel's right to exist. The point is made more explicitly in the assigned text *Israel, a Colonial Settler State?,* by the French Marxist Maxime Rodinson, which includes a map of 1967 Israel that is labeled "Palestine." This polemical book assails Israel's right to exist and argues that it was created in order to "dominate [Arab peoples] economically and politically."

Professor Massad concedes that he is critical of Jews and Zionists in his classroom, but has said that his anti-Israel perspective is necessary to counterbalance what he alleges is the "Israel-friendly angle" of other department offerings. Massad provides no specific examples of such courses, but even so, this is hardly a methodologically sound way to ground a course on any subject. He also tries to justify his bias by saying that "Palestinian-Israeli Politics and Societies" is an "elective course which no student is forced to take," which does nothing to defend the academic soundness of the course.

Following the controversy generated by student protests, Massad stopped teaching the class, complaining that he did so "under the duress of coercion and intimidation" by critics. Since no disciplinary action was taken against Massad, it is difficult to credit this particular excuse.

Like Professor Massad, George Saliba, a professor of Arabic and Islamic Science, has been criticized by his former students, who allege that he uses his courses "Islam & Western Science" and "Intro to Islamic Civilization" to attack the West and the United States. Students also say that Saliba makes a point of criticizing Israel, and referring to it as "Palestine." When a student asked whether this usage was intended to deny the legitimacy of Israel, Saliba responded with a political sermon: "Oh, so that's the ax that you have to grind? Why Israel is being called Palestine in my class? What about the plight of the Palestinians? Why isn't that what you are talking to me about?"[42]

More notoriously, Saliba once informed a Jewish student of his that Jews like her had "no claim to the land of Israel" because of the color of her eyes. "You have green eyes, you're not a true Semite," Saliba lectured the student. "I have brown eyes, I'm a true Semite."[43]

Saliba does not deny the incendiary substance of the student's charge: that he tells students that the right to live in the land of Israel is crucially dependent on eye color. "I do sometimes use the metaphor that inheriting a religion or converting to one is not the same as inheriting the color of one's eyes from one's parents . . . and most certainly it does not come with a deed to a specific lot of real estate," he has said. The professor evidently sees nothing wrong with subjecting students to his bizarre and racist ideas about genetics and the conflict in the Middle East, or with making his students the targets of his ethnic slurs.

Despite being subjected to political harangues by their professors—Dan Miron, a professor of Hebrew Literature at Columbia, reports that Jewish students visit his office weekly to bemoan anti-Israel bias in their courses—many Columbia students have been reluctant to file complaints with school administrators. Their reluctance can be explained in part by the fact that the head of the Middle East and Asian Languages and Cultures Department is Iranian Studies professor Hamid Dabashi.

Professor Dabashi has his own record of unprofessional conduct and has shown little sympathy for students concerned about anti-Israel bias in the classroom. Dabashi canceled his courses so that he and sympathetic students could attend a pro-Palestinian rally where activists called for the destruction of Israel. The professor unapologetically defended his "attendance at a political rally where both students and faculty could benefit from access to accurate information on the Middle East that is never reported by the newspapers 'of record' nor is it even allowed to be reported by any member of the press as Ariel Sharon's army prohibited access to the press when he was committing his massacres in Jenin and for days, now weeks, after that."

In addition to permitting these professors to vent their grievances against Israel in the classroom, Columbia has devoted academic "conferences" to anti-Israel themes. In January 2005, the university sponsored a panel discussion under the title "One State or Two?: Alternative Proposals for Middle East Peace." The notion of a "one-state" solution remains a fringe political view; it is widely interpreted to mean the effective destruction of Israel. But three of the four professors who participated in the panel discussion—Columbia professors Joseph Massad and Rashid Khalidi[44] and Haifa University professor Ilan Pappe[45]—endorsed the "one-state" solution. During the discussion Massad repeatedly denounced Israel as a "racist apartheid state," while Pappe announced that Israel had committed a "Holocaust against the Palestinians." Despite such radical activism, many parts of the Columbia community sponsored the panel discussion—including Qanun, the organization of Arab students in Columbia University's School of Law; the Human Rights Program of the School of International and Public Affairs at Columbia; the Office of the University Chaplain; Columbia's Student Services; and the Student Senate.

Columbia has consistently proven itself unwilling to hold professors accountable for their behavior. For instance, in response to student complaints about Massad, Saliba, Dabashi, Khalidi, and other professors in the Department of Middle East and Asian Languages and Cultures, Columbia president Lee Bollinger in December 2004 appointed a five-member panel to adjudicate their concerns. But while students raised a number of incidents that in their view illuminated a pattern of academic misconduct, the panel ignored all but three. Among those complaints the committee did not consider was one brought by a Jewish student who accused Professor Massad of declaring, as if it were a matter of fact rather than unfounded speculation, that it was official "Israeli policy" for soldiers to rape Palestinian women in Israeli jails so that they would be killed for adultery upon returning to the Palestinian territories.

Ultimately, the panel dismissed all but one complaint and ruled that it had "found no claims of bias and intimidation in classrooms"—a conclusion that does not square with the statements of the professors themselves, who acknowledge and defend their biased teaching. Even the one instance of intimidation the committee took seriously, in which Professor Massad threatened to expel a student from his class for disagreeing with his political conclusions, was downplayed as merely a "rhetorical response," a momentary and inconsequential lapse in judgment. Similarly, of Professor Saliba's harassment of a Jewish student for the color of her eyes, the committee astonishingly decided that "however regrettable a personal reference might have been, it is a good deal more likely to have been a statement that was integral to an argument about the uses of history and lineage than an act approaching intimidation." Would the committee have taken such a charitable view of the professor's conduct had the complaining student been an African-American reporting a comment about skin color?

Measurably more severe was the committee's verdict on the students. Indeed, the committee's final report suggested that it was the students, rather than the professors, who most imperiled academic freedom. "There is a thin line between participating fully and enthusiastically in a discussion, and intervening in a fashion which significantly disrupts the class," the report chided.

The panel's soft-line ruling regarding the professors does not seem accidental. Two of the committee's members—Farah Griffin, a professor of African-American Studies, and Jean Howard, a professor of English and vice provost for diversity initiatives at Columbia—had previously signed a petition condemning Israel and appealing to Columbia to divest its holdings in companies that conduct business with the Jewish state. Another committee member, Lisa Anderson, at that time the dean of Columbia's School of International and Public Affairs, had served as a dissertation adviser to Joseph Massad and, prior to joining the committee, had defended him from outside criticism, which she called a "campaign of defamation."

There is a certain irony in the department's portrayal of Massad as a victim of defamation, not least because the professor holds views that Columbia University's politically correct faculty might be expected to find unacceptable. Thus, while Iranian president Mahmoud Ahmadinejad drew derisive boos when he declared during his appearance at Columbia that Iran, unlike the United States, does not have homosexuals,[46] Professor Massad was the proponent of strikingly similar antigay bigotry. In a 2002 article titled "Re-Orienting Desire: The Gay International and the Arab World," Massad insisted that there were no homosexuals in the Arab and Muslim world, only "practitioners of same-sex contact," and blamed organizations like the International Lesbian and Gay Association for suggesting otherwise.[47] "It is the very discourse of the Gay International which produces homosexuals, as well as gays and lesbians, where they do not exist," Massad claimed.[48] He also found a way to rationalize the widespread persecution of gays in Islamic countries, writing that Islamic governments were targeting not gays but "the sociopolitical identification of these practices with the Western identity of gayness and the publicness that these gay-identified men seek."[49] In other words, stay in the closet.

In October 2007, Columbia denied Professor Massad's application for tenure, a small but not insignificant consolation for those concerned about the state of the university's academic curriculum. Still, given

Columbia's weak response even when its faculty's radicalism has generated national controversy, the school seems destined to be plagued by professors who recklessly pursue political agendas in the classroom. The university's Ivy League pedigree goes a long way toward disguising the radical indoctrination that substitutes for real education in so many of its courses.

Penn State University, meanwhile, uses another fig leaf: its clearly articulated policies on academic freedom.

4

Breaking the Rules

PENN STATE UNIVERSITY
TUITION: $12,844 IN-STATE
$23,712 OUT-OF-STATE

Chartered in 1855 by the Pennsylvania State Agricultural Society as "The Farmers' High School," Penn State University has grown into one of the ten largest public institutions of higher learning in the country, with twenty-four campuses, 84,000 enrolled students, and a $3 billion-plus operating budget. Where once it drew young laborers eager to learn the crafts of carpentry and metalworking, today Penn State is known for its top-ranked programs in business, economics, and the hard sciences.

The university should also, in theory, be a model of academic freedom. For more than fifty years it has had one of the country's strongest policies on academic freedom. Known as HR 64, the policy bars Penn State professors from indoctrinating students with "ready-made conclusions on controversial subjects."[1] It instructs professors "to train students to think for themselves, and provide them access to those materials which they need if they are to think intelligently." It warns that "in giving instruction on controversial matters the faculty member is expected to be of a fair and judicial mind, and to set forth justly, without supersession or innuendo, the divergent opinions of other investigators"—in other words, to present students with more than one perspective on the subject. Finally, it declares, "No faculty member may claim as a right the privilege of discussing in the classroom controversial topics outside his/her own field of study. The faculty member is normally bound not to take advantage of his/her position by introducing into the classroom provocative discussions of irrelevant subjects not within the field of his/her study."

There is nothing ambiguous in this policy. It clearly and forcefully defines the standards of professionalism that Penn State University professors are expected to observe. But examination of a dozen courses in the Penn State curriculum reveals that these principles are often ignored, and the professional standards the policy sets forth are systematically violated. Too many professors feel free to teach the contentious issues of race, gender, and "social justice" through the framework of sectarian political ideologies, making no attempt to familiarize their students with the broad spectrum of scholarly views as required in Penn State's academic freedom policies. Others presume to teach subjects for which they lack academic credentials, introducing subjects (such as "empire" and the "global economy") into their courses to support political rather than academic agendas. In some instances, the curricula of entire departments, such as Women's Studies, are organized to instill sectarian doctrines, a practice expressly forbidden by Penn State's academic freedom policies.

Oppressor Nation: The American Studies Program

Ostensibly, this program is an academic survey of American history and culture. But its course descriptions reveal a one-sided view of American history and culture that reflects the political prejudices of its instructors.

Introduction to American Studies *American Studies 100*[2]

INSTRUCTOR: M. P. Wilkins, Senior Lecturer in English

According to the Penn State catalogue, "American Studies 100 is a broad-ranging introduction to American culture. While specific topics may vary from class to class, the course examines what 'America' means and what it means to be 'American.' These issues will be examined from a variety of perspectives: literature, history, politics, film, race, gender, and geography."

The course is taught by several instructors, among them M. P. Wilkins, whose syllabus depicts American culture as the manifestation of a history of uninterrupted brutality and oppression, in which minority groups suffer while their white oppressors write a bogus narrative of unfolding freedom. This is fairly representative of the curricula offered in other American Studies 100 sections.

The sole historical text assigned for this course is James Loewen's *Lies My Teacher Told Me.* This book is not a scholarly work, but—as the title suggests—a polemic that rails against "elite white male capitalists who orchestrate how history is written" and obscure the black record of the American past, such as the U.S. government's supposed "participation in state-sponsored terrorism."

A typical chapter in Loewen's book is called "1493: The True Importance of Christopher Columbus." Loewen summarizes the achievement of Columbus in these words: "Christopher Columbus introduced two phenomena that revolutionized race relations and transformed the modern world: the taking of land, wealth, and labor from indigenous peoples, leading to their near extermination, and the transatlantic slave trade, which created a racial underclass."

The statement is demonstrably false. The taking of land, wealth, and labor from indigenous peoples, leading to their near extermination, was a practice going back at least to the Romans, long before Columbus arrived in the Americas. Moreover, the intercontinental slave trade in Africans, conducted by Muslims, long predated Columbus, making his role hardly revolutionary in terms of race relations.

Loewen's dubious and sometimes risible views are not offered as a text to be examined critically and objectively, although a course with any real academic standards would probably not examine it at all. Instead, *Lies My Teacher Told Me* is the only required historical text for Wilkins's introductory course, and its chapters are assigned in lessons throughout the semester to provide historical background to students as they study American culture. Since the class presents no alternative views—that is, since the instructor does not provide students with "access to those materials which they need if they are to think intelligently"—Loewen's book defines the tunnel vision of the course.

While Loewen provides the course's perspective, other assigned texts, literary in nature, underscore the darkest chapters of American history, including the African slave trade and the misconduct of American soldiers during the Vietnam War. While there is nothing inherently wrong with examining cultural reflections on American history, none of the assigned texts, fictional or otherwise, offers a perspective at odds with Loewen's extreme historical viewpoint. This is a course designed to present students with ready-made (and radical) conclusions on controversial issues, in violation of Penn State's academic freedom policy.

Introduction to American Studies (Berks Campus)

American Studies 100[3]

INSTRUCTOR: Ray Mazurek, Associate Professor of English

Another section of Introduction to American Studies is taught by Ray Mazurek and titled "Work in America." This course purports to examine "work in America in the 19th and 20th centuries, with an emphasis on the last 40 years." But the course description and syllabus reveal it to be anything but an objective survey of American labor history. Instead, the course offers students a relentless political attack on free-market capitalism.

Of the assigned books, only one—Frederick Douglass's account of his enslavement and freedom—is an American classic. The others include *Nickel and Dimed,* socialist Barbara Ehrenreich's journalistic assault on American capitalism in which she likens the condition of low- and medium-wage workplaces in the United States to life in a "dictatorship."[4] Another text, *No-Collar: The Hidden Cost of the Humane Workplace,* is by Andrew Ross, a well-known academic leftist, whose political activism focuses on antiglobalization and whose work is featured in ideologically driven venues like *The Nation* and *The Village Voice*.[5] Although Ross is not an academically credentialed economist, his book calls for an "alternative economic arrangement" to replace what he presents as the failures of free-market capitalism. Professor Mazurek also assigns *Working Classics: Poems on Industrial Life,* an anthology of poems that collectively paint a negative portrait of working-class life in capitalist America. The remaining texts are *A Short History of the U.S. Working Class,* by Marxist Paul Le Blanc, and *Working,* by another *Nation* leftist, Studs Terkel. None of these texts are academic; all of them reflect a single-minded radical agenda.

By presenting students one-sided views of "Work in America," this course fails to adhere to the Penn State academic freedom policy, which stipulates that "in giving instruction on controversial matters the faculty member is expected to be of a fair and judicial mind, and to set forth justly, without supersession or innuendo, the divergent opinions of other investigators."

Radical Prejudice: The Women's Studies Department

Much like the Women's Studies Departments at Duke and Colorado, the Penn State program provides little more than for-credit training sessions in radical feminist politics. The departmental template describes the Women's Studies program in these words: "As a field of study, Women's Studies analyzes the unequal distribution of power and resources by gender."[6] Here we see another instance of a familiar but nonetheless deeply troubling pattern in the modern university: taking a highly controversial claim (in this case, the notion that "power and resources" are distributed unequally "by gender") and using it as the unquestioned assumption that justifies the existence of an entire academic department.

Introduction to Women's Studies

Women's Studies 001, Section 8[7]

INSTRUCTOR: Michael Johnson, Associate Professor of Sociology, Women's Studies, and African and African-American Studies (Emeritus)

A catalogue description of the Introduction to Women's Studies course taught by emeritus professor Michael Johnson begins, "Men are privileged relative to women. That's not right. I'm going to do *something* about it, even if it's only in my personal life."[8] Professor Johnson explains that he will "spend most of the course on just a few of the ways that men are privileged relative to women. We'll look at how and why women face more barriers to happiness and fulfillment than do men, and how we might go about helping our world to move in the direction of gender equity." These contentious propositions are raised not as a potential object of disinterested academic inquiry, but as "truths" students are expected to embrace. The professor recommends his course to those students who "want a really full feminist experience." This is an appropriate invitation to join a political party, not an intellectual discussion.

Although Professor Johnson retired in 2005, his courses (there are several, all as ideological as this one) are still listed in the catalogue. No authority in the Women's Studies Department or in the Penn State administration appears to have regarded them as problematic, which is not surprising since, however eccentric they may seem, they are perfectly in accord with the intellectual guidelines of the Women's Studies Department.

Introduction to Women's Studies

Women's Studies 001, Section 4[9]

INSTRUCTOR: Yihuai Cai, Graduate Student in Departments of Curriculum and Instruction and Women's Studies

This section of the Introduction to Women's Studies course, taught by graduate student Yihuai Cai, is quite frankly aimed at recruiting students to radical feminist causes. To this end, students are asked to consider a number of politically spun "questions" clearly designed to impress on them the feminist claim that America's democratic society is hierarchical and oppressive:

> How do various forms of oppression (e.g. sexism, racism, classism, ageism, heterosexism, and ablebodism [*sic*]) operate to divide oppressed peoples from one another and consequently facilitate the continued oppression of each group?
>
> Examining your own previous values and knowledge, have you consciously or unconsciously participated in one or more of those oppressive ideologies and discourses?
>
> What is feminist activism?
>
> How shall we develop strategies that address issues of power differentials in our society?[10]

These questions—especially the last—reflect the mentality of a political operative rather than an inquiring scholar.

Consistent with the stated goal of the Women's Studies Department "to connect theory and scholarship with feminist activism," students in the course are required to volunteer for organizations that are both feminist and activist. One of them is the Penn State Center for Women Students, which is not a student center in the traditional sense but an advocacy group that protests "institutionalized sexism, sex-based discrimination, violence against women and other conditions which impede women students' personal and academic development." Another university-sponsored organization, Peers Helping to Reaffirm, Educate, and Empower, conducts campus programs about "healthy body image." Still another, Men Against Violence, is a "peer education group" that focuses on "gender violence." Two other approved organizations are the Lesbian Gay Bisexual Transgender Support Network and the pro-abortion group Planned Parenthood.

These programs are housed in the Paul Robeson Cultural Center, named after the American singer. Although Robeson was famous as a Communist and fervent supporter of Stalin, an official announcement from the center antiseptically describes him as a "human rights" activist who became "an eloquent, often controversial spokesperson against racism and discrimination."[11] Robeson has no historical connection to Penn State other than his political affinity with those who named the center.

Only two of the organizations approved for the students' volunteer work appear either ambiguous or nonpolitical: the HIV/AIDS Risk Reduction Advisory Council, a student organization that focuses on "health promotion and activism," and the Mid-State Literacy Council, which promotes adult literacy programs. No conservative activist groups with interests in women's issues are included, nor is there indication of any awareness that encouraging political activism in an academic program might be problematic.

At the conclusion of their volunteer project, students are asked to write a paper that "summarizes the project and makes connections to the course readings and your own learning experience." Since *all* the course readings are written by radical feminists or "critical theorists" sympathetic to feminism, it is evident that the sole function of this course is to turn students into feminist activists. This is precisely the sort of classroom environment that is specifically prohibited by the Penn State academic freedom rules under HR 64.

Introduction to Women's Studies

Women's Studies 001, Section 006[12]

INSTRUCTOR: Marla Jaksch, Lecturer in Women's Studies

Yet another section of the Introduction to Women's Studies course, taught by adjunct lecturer Marla Jaksch, is described as "an introductory feminist survey course." This is a course *in* (rather than about) the ideology of radical feminism, as students have no option to take different or dissenting views. Jaksch reveals her political mission when she explains that her motivation is to "examine (and challenge) the nature of power and privilege in our lives and institutions."

One of the principal texts assigned to Jaksch's students is *Femi-*

nism Is for Everybody, by bell hooks, the radical ideologue who is also an assigned authority in Columbia University's Women's Studies Department.[13] Professor hooks explains to readers that her book is an exercise in "revolutionary feminist consciousness-raising." More precisely, it is a manifesto devoted to hooks's extreme views, including the claim that black women are "never going to have equality within the existing white supremacist capitalist patriarchy." This phrase—"white supremacist capitalist patriarchy"—recurs frequently in hooks's "academic" writings to describe (and denigrate) America's democratic system. Credentialed as a Distinguished Professor of English Literature at the City University of New York, hooks has no apparent expertise on the subject of capitalism, race, or patriarchy, but extreme views make her a favorite in ideological courses such as Professor Jaksch's.

Jaksch expects students to practice the radical politics she preaches. To this end, the course is designed to "create possible strategies for change through appreciation and engagement with many creative strategies that women have employed historically and contemporarily." What such strategies entail is explained in her course assignments. One requires students to write a biographical paper on a "feminist" artist, activist, or writer in order to "familiarize you with feminist strategies for telling unique and possibly untold stories." Students are also required to attend events that promote feminist activism. An entire section of the course is given over to the subject of this activism and presented under the title "Social Justice & Global Feminism," which makes no secret of its underlying socialist and anticapitalist political agendas.

In common with other professors in the Women's Studies Program, Professor Jaksch states that she encourages "critical thinking" and that she "critically examines" the issues discussed in the course. But the term "critical thinking" (like "social justice" and other cant phrases) is a common political code among academic radicals, which refers to the Marxist and post-Marxist tradition of providing critiques of capitalism—not of its alternatives. "Critical thinking" in the usage of academic radicals is not a commitment to scientific skepticism and intellectual pluralism such as the Penn State policy requires. It is a commitment to left-wing ideology.

Professor Jaksch's Introduction to Women's Studies section is a course in "ready-made conclusions in regard to controversial subjects," which HR 64 specifically rejects.

Global Feminisms *Women's Studies 502*[14]

INSTRUCTOR: Melissa Wright, Associate Professor of Geography and Women's Studies

"Global Feminisms" is a politically lopsided attack on international capitalism and the free-market system taught by Associate Professor Melissa Wright. Although Wright has a Ph.D. in geography, she makes her commitment to feminist ideology clear. Her Ph.D. thesis, titled "Third World Women and the Geography of Skill," was a study of women in Mexican *maquiladora* factories, while her academic website notes that she "studies the dynamics linking economic and cultural processes. . . . Her recent work has focused on the emergence of an international social movement that protests violence against women along the Mexico-U.S. border."[15]

A required text for Wright's course is *Feminism, Theory, and the Politics of Difference,* by Chris Weedon, which proposes to examine the "political implications" of feminist theory. For Weedon, capitalist societies are "both oppressive and hierarchical"; they are also governed by racist stereotypes applied exclusively to Third World people. These stereotypes are used to demonize victims of American imperialism: "Irrationality and violence are stereotypes regularly applied, for example, to Saddam Hussein's Iraq and Muslim fundamentalist regimes."[16] Racial stereotypes directed at white Americans don't count in Weedon's calculations, since white Americans don't qualify as oppressed people.

A second required text for Professor Wright's course is Chandra Talpade Mohanty's *Feminism Without Borders: Decolonizing Theory, Practicing Solidarity.* A radical feminist and antiglobalization activist, Mohanty is frank about her political (and therefore nonacademic)

goals in writing her polemical book, which she describes as a "transnational feminist anti-capitalist critique." Mohanty describes her target readership as the "progressive, left, feminist, and anti-imperialist scholars, intellectuals, and activists"; these are not the words of an objective intellectual ready to lead the student on a balanced, dispassionate tour of challenging subjects.[17]

Wright's course also requires students to read *The End of Capitalism (As We Knew It): A Feminist Critique of Political Economy*, by J. K. Gibson-Graham—an amalgam byline for "feminist economic geographers" June Graham and Katherine Gibson. Employing a Marxist analysis defaced by postmodern gobbledygook ("For capitalism to exist in difference—a set of concrete specificities, or a category of self-contradiction—it becomes necessary to think the radical emptiness of every capitalist instance"[18]), the authors assail "globalization" and "capitalist hegemony" and "oppression." They assert, for instance, that women are "allocated to subordinate functions of the capitalist system," as though there were no women CEOs of Fortune 500 companies, or as though two of the last three secretaries of state and the current Speaker of the House—third in line for the presidency—were not female. Of the other texts used in this course, all but one, Azar Nafisi's *Reading Lolita in Tehran,* advance a polemical feminist or anti-capitalist agenda.

Professor Wright devotes part of the course to promoting radical activism, specifically supporting the cause of the antiglobalization movement. A section of the syllabus titled "World Forums, Women's Solidarity, and the Human Rights Discourse" amounts to a celebration of the World Social Forum, an international conference of Marxists and anticapitalist radicals such as the Colombian FARC terrorist organization and Venezuelan dictator Hugo Chávez. The World Social Forum's *Manifesto* states, "We are building a large alliance from our struggles and resistance against a system based on sexism, racism and violence, which privileges the interests of capitalism and patriarchy over the needs and aspirations of the people." The *Manifesto* further declares that "an urgent task of our movement is to mobilize solidarity for the Palestinian people and their struggle for self-determination as they face brutal occupation by the Israeli state."[19]

A training course in the politics of the far Left—or any sectarian movement—is not appropriate to an academic institution, let alone to a taxpayer-funded public university.

Feminist Theory *Women's Studies 507*[20]

INSTRUCTOR: Joan B. Landes, Ferree Professor of Early Modern History and Women's Studies

"Feminist Theory," taught by Professor Joan Landes, adopts the language of intellectual pluralism while sharply limiting its scope to the *idées fixes* of the radical feminist Left. According to its catalogue description, the course "aims to introduce students to the range of debate among feminist theorists on questions of patriarchy and male domination; gender, sexuality and desire; identity and subjectivity; experience and performance; maternity and citizenship; universalism and difference."[21]

"Range of debate" is a promising phrase, but in this course the "debate" is held among a narrow range of left-wing "feminist theorists." This is the narcissism of small differences; such disagreements as exist among these "feminist theorists" pale in comparison with their shared beliefs and assumptions.

Professor Landes's assigned readings promote a political agenda that views American society and free-market capitalism as racist and oppressive, and urges radical "resistance" to both. For example, the required essay "Theory as Liberatory Practice," by the omnipresent bell hooks, makes no pretense to being a scholarly work, instead urging readers to engage in "feminist struggle" against the "patriarchal norm" of American society—assuming without analysis that there is such a norm. The feminist writings of conservative and liberal academic thinkers who do not share these views—Professors Christina Hoff Sommers, Daphne Patai, and Camille Paglia come immediately to mind—are simply ignored.[22]

Like hooks's essay, the required text *Feminist Practice and Poststruc-*

turalist Theory, by Chris Weedon, suggests that feminist theory is largely the instrument of a political cause. Specifically, it "must always be answerable to the needs of women in our struggle to transform the patriarchy." A theory that must always be answerable to the needs of the "women's struggle," as defined by a group of sectarian ideologues, cannot by its nature be scholarly, since it lacks the freedom to challenge such assumptions as the idea that the "women's struggle" has definable "needs" that everyone can agree on.

The political agendas that make up the course in Feminist Theory find their most explicit expression in its concluding section. Titled "Transnational Feminism in the New Age of Globalization," this is yet another left-wing critique of capitalism, a subject in which the course instructor has no academic credentials.

Typical of the readings in this section is a chapter from Chandra Talpade Mohanty's *Feminism Without Borders* entitled " 'Under Western Eyes' Revisited: Feminist Solidarity Through Anticapitalist Struggles." Here Mohanty laments her disenchantment with what she calls the "increasing privatization and corporatization of public life" in the United States, calls for the revival of a more radical feminist movement, and boasts that her "site of access and struggle has increasingly come to be the U.S. academy."[23] The purpose of a university is not to provide a freelance radical with a site for struggle; nor is it to provide faculty members a megaphone for their left-wing ideas. Yet this is exactly what has happened to an entire department at Penn State.

Women, the Humanities, and the Arts

Women's Studies 003[24]

INSTRUCTOR: Stephanie Springgay, Assistant Professor of Art Education and Women's Studies

On its face, a course on art might seem to offer a respite from the feminist ideology and political activism promoted throughout the department. But Women's Studies 003 shows that even a subject with no obvious connection to politics can become a canvas for the political agendas of activists posing as academics.

While Assistant Professor Stephanie Springgay claims that her course does not propose a "right answer" for students to accept and encourages them to think "critically," there is little evidence that she conducts the course in accordance with these appropriate academic standards. As the course description makes clear, students in this class will not simply learn about art. They will also be trained to "challenge the nature of power and privilege as it relates to gender, race, class and sexuality and in particular how it shapes the lives and experiences of women."[25] Additionally, they will be expected to "find spaces of resistance within these terms" and to "understand how women have, at times, been silenced by the constructions of gender, race, class, sexuality, and nationality, and how they have also reformulated those constructions through a variety of creative expressions." Once more we see a glaring omission from the curriculum: any hint that vast bodies of scientific research conflict with the idea that gender is "socially constructed" rather than innate.

Not the least of the problems with this course is that it is unclear what expertise the instructor has to lecture about such complex topics as class, race, nationalism, and globalization. Professor Springgay earned her doctorate in *art education.* Meanwhile, the section of her course on globalization is based on three feminist instructional texts—two by bell hooks, whose academic credentials are in English literature.

In a typical reading assignment from this class, author Linda Nochlin asks, "Why have there been no great women artists?" Her answer is that the problem lies with the "social structure and institutions" of the art world—specifically, that they are dominated by white, middle-class males: "As we all know, things as they are and as they have been, in the arts as in a hundred other areas, are stultifying, oppressive, and discouraging to all those, women among them, who did not have the good fortune to be born white, preferably middle class and, above all, male."[26] Ignoring great artists like Georgia O'Keeffe and Mary Cassatt, this argument also fails to explain why there have been so many great women *writers* throughout history, since they experienced the same social restrictions. Sappho, Jane Austen, George Eliot, Emily Dickinson, and the Brontë sisters come to mind, not to mention the greatest writer in a famously patriarchal society, Murasaki Shikibu, the tenth-century author of the *Tale of Genji,* which is regarded as the *Iliad* of Japanese civilization.

The few reading assignments that cannot be classified as feminist are nonetheless overtly political. For instance, in the essay "The Other History of Intercultural Performance," visual artist and activist Coco Fusco describes a performance-art project intended to "dramatize the colonial unconsciousness of American society." According to Fusco, "even though the idea of America as a colonial system is met with resistance—since it contradicts the dominant ideology's presentation of our system as a democracy—the audience reactions indicated that colonialist roles have been internalized quite effectively."[27]

Students learn about the convergence of art and political activism; one section of the course is actually titled "Activism." Here students read essays that encourage them to participate in political—particularly feminist—activism. For instance, in her essay "Bringing Feminism *a la Casa,*" feminist writer Daisy Hernandez asks students to consider this query: "How do you go off to college, learn about feminism in English, and then bring it home to a working-class community where women call their children in from the street at night in every language—except 'standard' English?"[28] Such a question in an academic context puts a leftist spin on the notion of homework.

Professor Springgay, like so many of her feminist colleagues, is not content to have her students simply learn about radical political activism; they must actually engage in it. In fact, a full 15 percent of students' final grade depends on their participation in a "public art project as a form of student activism on the Penn State campus."

Racism Is for Whites Only: The African and African-American Studies Program

Penn State's African and African-American Studies Program propagates the view that American society and its institutions are racist, discriminating against black Americans. Students earning a major in the program are given several related areas of study, known as "options" within the program. One such area is called the Law and Social Justice Option. As noted, "social justice" is not an academic concept but a politically loaded code; there is in fact no societal consensus about how justice is best achieved, and the term itself is historically associated with only one set of beliefs—those of the political Left.

Inequality in America

African and African-American Studies 409[29]

INSTRUCTOR: David McBride, Associate Professor of African and African-American Studies

Professor McBride's course requires only two texts, both of which reflect a one-sided view of the race issue. The dubious premise of Joe Feagin's *White Racism* is that "few whites are aware of how important racism is to their own feelings, beliefs, thinking and actions,"[30] and that all whites harbor unconscious feelings of racism against blacks. But blacks evidently have no such feelings against whites: "From the perspective of this book, black racism does not exist." Feagin also claims the United States is governed by "a centuries-old system intentionally designed to exclude Americans of color from full participation in the economy, polity, and society." This would be news to the richest woman in America, Oprah Winfrey; to billionaire media magnate Robert Johnson; to the former CEO of the largest media company in the world, Time Warner's Richard Parsons; to President Barack Obama; and to the 49 percent of African-Americans who are part of America's middle class.

The second required text, *Race, Ethnicity, Gender, and Class: The Sociology of Group Conflict and Change*, by Joseph F. Healey, argues that the defining feature of America's minority groups is that they are discriminated against by the "dominant" white majority. The book claims that the "four crucial concepts for analyzing dominant-minority relations are prejudice, discrimination, ideological racism, and institutional discrimination." This course, seemingly stuck in the time warp of the 1960s, never bothers to question whether there even is such a dominant group in a society as ethnically diverse as America's, whose civil rights laws make such discrimination a crime.

Status of Blacks in the Twentieth Century: Interdisciplinary Perspectives

African and African-American Studies 100[31]

INSTRUCTOR: Darryl C. Thomas, Associate Professor of African-American Studies

The instructor's description of this course is little more than an extended rant against the United States and free-market capitalism:

> Through an examination of African-American contestation and engaging of Globalization, Democratization and Empire from the contested Presidential election of 1876 to the recent disputed 2000 Presidential election and its' [*sic*] aftermath in 2004, we can analyzed [*sic*] the divergent strategies employed by this non-state actor to changed [*sic*] the set of unequal power relations within the United States and to transformed [*sic*] the power relations that governs [*sic*] human rights practices, racial capitalism, and the global apartheid international regimes supported by the United States during divergent waves of globalization and racial capitalism.[32]

Not even written in coherent English, this course description relies on language—"racial capitalism," "global apartheid international regimes supported by the United States"—that brings to mind radical publications like *The New Masses.* The instructor further demonstrates his ideological prejudices by asking students leading questions obviously intended to influence their answers. For instance, they are asked to write a paper explaining how "racial capitalism" has ill-served "underdeveloped African-Americans in the past" and how it "continues to stifle African-American financial and economic development today." Such "questions" are of the "Are you still beating your wife?" variety.

Students are also asked to ponder whether the ideology of "Afrocentrism" provides "the essential instruments for combating the 'new racism' in the new era of colorblind America." But Afrocentrism is itself a racialist ideology, which is based on tendentious claims that Egyptians were black and that the Greeks "stole" their contributions to civilization from them.[33] In another assignment, students are asked to "develop a case why liberalism has failed African-Americans." No assignment asks them to assess whether radicalism has failed African-Americans.

Minority Health

African and African-American Studies 297C[34]

INSTRUCTOR: David McBride, Associate Professor of African and African-American Studies

According to its course description, "Minority Health" concentrates on "social and cultural factors, poverty, racial and ethnic discrimination, and health care barriers that are causing minority groups to have much higher rates of illness and disease." Once again, a controversial conclusion is presented as a given. A truly legitimate academic examination of health care might be expected to ask, for instance, whether minority groups have higher rates of illness and disease as a result of genetic factors or cultural behaviors. But this course insists on an ideological perspective that renders such crucial medical issues irrelevant.

Its two required texts are *Social Injustice and Public Health* and *Mama Might Be Better Off Dead: The Failure of Health Care in Urban America.* The first is edited by a team headed by well-known political activist Marian Wright Edelman, who famously—and wrongly—claimed that the Clinton administration's welfare reform would cause a million poor children to starve.[35] The second is by Laurie Kaye Abraham, an "investigative journalist" with the *Chicago Reporter,* a local throwaway published by a community activist group.

This course is not interested in educating students in the range of factors that affect minority health, including inadequate care. It is interested in persuading students that racial discrimination and racially determined economic inequalities are to blame for minority health problems.

"Peace" Studies: The Department of Science, Technology, and Society

Peace Seminar and Peace and Conflict Studies Program

Science, Technology, and Society 490[36]

INSTRUCTOR: Wenda Bauchspies, Associate Professor of Science, Technology, and Society and Women's Studies

This course is described as an "advanced study of major contemporary issues of peace and conflict." In fact, the course is primarily intended to promote the belief that violence is under no circumstances a legitimate solution to conflict. Only two books are used in this course. One is *Approaches to Peace: A Reader in Peace Studies,* written by David Barash, an animal psychologist.[37] Barash is a self-described "progressive" and an activist for nonviolence who makes exceptions for "revolutionary violence"—a cliché from the sixties originating in the work of Frantz Fanon—if it is used to good ends as in countries such as Cuba.[38] The other book, coauthored by a professor of peace studies, reveals its slanted perspective in its title: *An Anthology of Historic Alternatives to War.*

Presenting the students with the "ready-made conclusions," the instructor requires students to attend several lectures featuring antiwar radicals. Pennsylvania leftist Barbara Ballenger, for instance, speaks to students about "personal peace activism after 9/11." Another antiwar radical, Peter Shaw, delivers his "reflections on a career of peace activism."

This is only a small sampling of the problematic courses that violate Penn State's academic standards and academic freedom policies. But the violations are so flagrant that we submitted them to the Penn State administration and faculty—specifically to the university president, the provost, the vice provost, the president of the Penn State faculty senate, and the dean of the College of Liberal Arts. Speaking for the administration, the vice provost referred the matter to the faculty senate. Only the dean of the College of Liberal Arts, Susan Welch, responded. The exchange of letters follows:

August 7, 2007

Dean Susan Welch
College of the Liberal Arts
Penn State University
University Park, Pennsylvania

Dear Dean Welch,

The following analysis focuses on several courses, which were listed in your online catalogue this year, that appear to me to be in clear violation of HR 64. If I am mistaken, I would like to know the reasoning under which you regard these as courses that observe Penn State's academic freedom standards. If I am correct in my analysis, I would like to know what steps you plan to take to advise your faculties of the Penn State regulation and their obligation to design their courses in conformity with it.

I thank for your consideration of these serious matters.

Sincerely,
David Horowitz

August 14, 2007

David Horowitz Freedom Center
4404 Wilshire Blvd, 4th Floor
Los Angeles, CA 90010

Dear Mr. Horowitz,

Thank you for your letter of August 7 concerning Penn State's HR-64. I have recently reminded our department heads about this policy, and, more generally, asked that they make sure that the training of our graduate students and part time instructors, in particular, emphasize expectations, not just for grading standards and work expectations, but for subject matter appropriate to the course. (Most of the courses in our college that you have flagged were taught by those categories of instructors.) That said, however, the choice of classes that you are focusing on suggests that you may object to the topics of some classes as much as to the lack of balance. After all, in how many business courses would you find assignments requiring reading of leftist critiques of American business practices? Some, perhaps, but not many, and yet I did not see any of those on your list. Business courses generally promote or assume the values of capitalism and American business just as women's studies courses promote the values of feminism.

HR-64 does remind faculty that it is not appropriate to use the "academic freedom" rhetoric to preach on topics unrelated to the subject matter of the course. Similarly, it infers that students are to be graded not on the outcomes of their arguments but on the quality of evidence and logic used to make those arguments. These are sound principles that are inherent in the original definition of academic freedom, but HR-64 provides a useful reminder.

Thank you for your interest.

Regards,
Susan

August 23, 2007

Dean Susan Welch
College of the Liberal Arts
Penn State University
University Park, Pennsylvania

Dear Dean Welch,

Thank you for your prompt attention to my letter and the thoughtfulness of your reply. I am pleased that you have taken the step of drawing the attention of your department heads to HR 64 and trust that they will pass on your advisory notice to all their faculty and adjuncts. . . . [39]

I want to turn now to the more serious and complex matter you raise concerning Women's Studies. You suggest that what I am really objecting to is the subject matter of Women's Studies rather than the way it is taught, and that I seek to hold the Women's Studies Department to a higher academic standard than, for example, the School of Business.

First, let me say that I have absolutely no objection to the academic study of women. My concern here is that the treatment of women by the Penn State Women's Studies Department is not academic, as defined by current Penn State codes, but is partisan and sectarian.

As the analysis I sent you makes clear, many Penn State Women's Studies courses, including the crucial introductory courses, present students with a one-sided perspective on the condition and status and history of women. Moreover, they do so to the virtual exclusion of other perspectives—including feminist perspectives that are not based on the radical theory of the social construction of gender. Worse, the Department itself defines its curriculum in terms that are appropriate to a sectarian ideology, not to a scholarly inquiry. This is how the curriculum is described on the departmental website: "As a field of study, Women's Studies analyzes the unequal distribution of power and resources by gender."

The idea that power and resources in a democracy are distributed according to gender—rather than, for example, ability or merit—is a controversial claim that flies in the face of most modern economic theory, neuroscience, evolutionary psychology, and biology. It is also counterintuitive, since American society is ruled by laws that make gender discrimination illegal. The view held by the Women's Studies Department (and imposed on its students) might be a legitimate perspective to examine among other perspectives, but it is surely inappropriate as a statement defining *a departmental curriculum in a modern research university (let alone in a state-funded institution).*

What if a student does not subscribe to this claim? How can such a student, who may be just as interested in the study of women as others, receive a good grade if he or she does not accept the very premise of the curriculum as it has been currently defined? Are such students to be denied the ability to study the subject of women at Penn State? Are all students to be denied instruction in perspectives that challenge this view (as a glance at the reading lists for many current Women's Studies courses show they are)?

To make my position as clear as possible: I am not *suggesting that the Women's Studies program be abolished. Nor am I suggesting that its curriculum should overlook injustices that may have been done to women historically or in the present. I am suggesting instead that no academically sound curriculum should be so ideologically rigid or committed to one controversial perspective on women. In short, the Women's Studies curriculum should be reformed to meet generally accepted academic standards. One would not expect the Department of Physics to teach only one side of a physics controversy. Similarly the Department of Women's Studies should not take one side in a controversy over the causes of the distribution of power and resources in a democratic society.*

You argue that there is an analogy to be made with the Business School and that "business courses generally promote or assume the values of capitalism just as women's studies courses promote the values of feminism." I do not think this analogy will hold. The Business School is a professional school whose purpose is to train students in accepted business practices so they can pursue careers in the business world. Students enroll in business courses to learn these practices, not to examine the philosophical or sociological foundations of the business system, which is the appropriate subject matter for sociology, anthropology, economics and philosophy—all subjects offered in the College of Liberal Arts.

The purpose of a professional school is to train graduate students for a career in their chosen profession. An undergraduate liberal arts education is quite different, and was explicitly created to be different. Otherwise, why have a College of Liberal Arts in the first place? Students could just enter professional training programs directly.

The liberal arts curriculum was designed from the outset to create well-rounded citizens who would learn to respect different perspectives, and the pluralism of ideas. The purpose of a liberal arts education is to foster an inquiring intelligence, and to introduce students to the varieties of human experience and the ways in which individuals interpret the world. It was designed to teach students the scientific method, which suspends judgment and subjects hypotheses to the test of divergent opinions, and ultimately to the verdict of empirical evidence. By contrast, the Women's Studies Department insists on one interpretation of matters that are controversial.

To illustrate the point, let me ask you whether you think it would be appropriate to establish an Evangelical Studies Department in the College of Liberal Arts at Penn State, taught exclusively from an Evangelical point of view; or a Department of Conservative Studies taught exclusively by conservatives; or a Department of Communist or Fascist Studies taught exclusively from Communist and Fascist perspectives?

The liberal arts by nature deal with subjects over which there can be no ultimate agreement, no resolution of controversies that have sustained for centuries. Departments that deal with such controversies should not try to resolve them by ideological fiat. Feminism may be a career choice for some students, just as Republican Party activism might be a career choice for others. But training students in a sectarian ideology such as gender feminism is not what a liberal arts education should be about, and HR 64 makes that quite clear. I believe a rethinking of this curriculum is in order.

Thank you again for your consideration of these matters. I look forward to your response.

Sincerely,
David Horowitz

September 25, 2007

Dear Mr. Horowitz,

Thank you for your letter of August 27 in response to my earlier letter. I have reviewed your letter carefully, but do not think further action is warranted.

I'd be pleased to talk with you about this. My assistant was trying to set up a telephone call, but perhaps you would prefer to come by the next time you are on campus.

Sincerely,
Susan Welch

If even a university with an unequivocal academic freedom policy like Penn State can't be bothered to take action to cope with the problems of radicalism and political activism in the curriculum, what hope is there for other colleges and universities across the country? If the University of Texas is any guide, any such hope is slim.

5

Radical Degrees

UNIVERSITY OF TEXAS
TUITION: $7,670 IN-STATE
$24,544 OUT-OF-STATE

The University of Texas at Austin is not only the flagship of the fifteen-school University of Texas system but one of the most distinguished academic institutions in the country. On the strength of its highly rated programs in business, law, and engineering, the school has attracted some 50,000 students to its sixteen constituent colleges. The university urges its students to continue in the tradition of achievement well beyond their academic years, with the school's official song, "The Eyes of Texas (Are Upon You)," reminding them that they will remain in UT's sights long after leaving its classrooms.

But if the people of Texas were really watching what goes on at their flagship university, they would probably be surprised to see a degree-granting curriculum that includes, in effect, a comprehensive training and recruitment program in the theory and practice of radical politics.

The University of Texas's academic freedom policies are contained in the "Rules and Regulations of the Board of Regents," and are derived from the 1940 Statement on Academic Freedom and Tenure of the American Association of University Professors. The policy is listed under "Rights and Responsibilities of Faculty" and bars professors from introducing "controversial matter that has no relation to the subject," an injunction clearly designed to prevent indoctrination in the classroom.[1]

Many courses offered in the University of Texas curriculum violate these standards. They lack an appropriate dispassion and skepticism about sources and doctrines, and do not fall within a scholarly discipline. Instead, these courses are designed to recruit students to particular forms of social activism and to train them in the sectarian ideologies that guide these agendas. Some make only a cursory effort to even represent themselves as appropriate to the academic fields in which they are located, and are often taught by professors without any apparent academic expertise in the subject matter they teach. Frequently, the courses are cross-listed in several cooperating departments.

Consider Dana Cloud, an associate professor of communications. Cloud makes no secret of her radical political agendas; her academic website describes her as "a longtime activist and socialist."[2] She is a member of the International Socialist Organization, a self-styled Bolshevik party that seeks the establishment of a "dictatorship of the proletariat" in the United States. Professor Cloud's academic website lists five courses driven by political agendas. For example, she teaches "Communications and Social Change," the purpose of which, according to her own description, is "to encourage your engagement with the tradition and ongoing practice of movement for social change in the United States." The course requires students "to become involved as an observer and/or as a participant in a local social movement"—specifically, "the movement against the death penalty and the movement of University staff for higher wages and better treatment."[3] The only two required texts are both by political Marxists, Howard Zinn and Robert Jensen (an associate professor at the University of Texas).[4] Insofar as this course is about communications at all, it is a course in conducting propaganda for radical political movements.

How have Professor Cloud's overt political agendas passed unnoticed? How did a course like Communications and Social Change secure departmental approval? Does the Department of Communications

Studies have academic standards that would distinguish between an academic course and a course in political propaganda? Does the Liberal Arts faculty? Does the University of Texas?

Professor Cloud's courses are not alone in disregarding academic standards. Take the course "Manifest Destiny and the Environment: The Fur Trade to Globalization," whose description asserts, "In the past few decades multinational agreements for global 'free' trade have increased environmental degradation and brought social and economic disruption. The United States has been a leader in these developments, whose roots can be traced back to the Fur Trade Era that began in 1822."[5] This course, in short, does not examine the effects of trade on the environment; it declares from the start—and therefore asks students to assume—that commercial malignity is responsible for "environmental degradation." The instructor, Professor Richard Richardson, is a biologist with no professional training in history or economics.[6] Richardson teaches the class with the assistance of Bobby Bridger, a folksinger whose sole book is a little-known biography of the entertainer Buffalo Bill; he appears even less qualified to teach a course on the environmental effects of trade—a formidable undertaking even for a serious economic historian.

As these examples indicate, the radical academic project at the University of Texas is not confined to just one professor or even one academic department. It spreads across multiple departments, tarnishing the academic mission of a prestigious university.

"Prepare to Refute It": The Center for Women's and Gender Studies

As is so often the case in Women's Studies programs, the Center for Women's and Gender Studies at Texas builds its supposedly academic program around an ideological claim: that gender structures society. The UT Center describes its mission as advancing the "knowledge and understanding about women's lives, and the role that gender plays in structuring society."[7] The Women's Studies program at Texas is designed not to study women but to school students in the doctrines of radical feminism.

Introduction to Women's and Gender Studies *WGS 390*[8]

INSTRUCTOR: Katherine Arens, Professor of Germanic Studies

The problems with this course begin with the professor and the curriculum. The course deals with complex historical, sociological, and psychological issues, and yet it is taught by a professor, Katherine Arens, who is trained in Germanic Studies. Also, it is the introductory course for the entire departmental curriculum, and yet the curriculum makes no pretense of approaching the study of women from a scholarly perspective. Instead it is an indoctrination in radical feminist and Marxist theories.

Of the books assigned in this course, only one is critical of radical feminism: *Professing Feminism*, by feminists Daphne Patai and Noretta Koertge, who explain that they left Women's Studies because the field was devoted to political ideology rather than academic scholarship. Professor Arens does not even pretend to present a dispassionate evaluation of the authors' views, however. This is the way her syllabus refers to the book: "Daphne Patai and Noretta Koertge, *Professing Feminism,* passim (note that this represents ANTI–women's studies—prepare to refute it)."

Feminist Theories *WS 391 & RTF 386C*[9]

INSTRUCTOR: Janet Staiger, the William P. Hobby Centennial Professor of Communication

The focus of this course is "the richness and diversity of the feminist and gender theories guiding the work of feminist and gender scholars at the University of Texas at Austin."[10] This is a clear, if somewhat parochial, statement that "Feminist Theories" is not really an academic course analyzing feminist theories but a course that presents feminist theories as the only legitimate explanations of the status of women. All the section headings for the course are devoted to an uncritical presentation of radical feminist theory. Typical are: "Early Feminist Theories," "Second-Wave Feminisms," "Feminisms and Freud," "Feminisms and the Arts," "American Feminism," and "Revisions of Second-Wave Feminisms."

Rhetoric of Feminist Spaces *RHE309K*[11]

INSTRUCTOR: Kristen Hogan, Graduate Student in the Department of English[12]

This course is offered through both the Division of Rhetoric and Writing and the Women's and Gender Studies Program. It is not, however, a course about rhetoric or writing. Rather, its clear purpose is to recruit students to radical feminist causes. Toward this end, students are required to sign up for a "service learning" research project that requires them to work with what the course description refers to as "Feminist-Space Community Organizations." Although the course does not specify which organization students must select, it stipulates that it must be a "feminist space."

A typical organization mentioned in the syllabus is the Third Wave Foundation, which is described as an "organization [that] offers scholarships to students 30 years old or younger (the generation of the Third Wave of feminism) who are involved in social justice work/activism and have financial need." Specifically in reference to the foundation, the course description notes that "[y]our service learning for this class definitely qualifies as social justice work, so take a look at the application." In other words, the course encourages students to join political organizations that advance its (nonacademic) radical feminist agendas.

Theories of Gender and Sexuality *RTF386C*[13]

INSTRUCTOR: Mary Celeste Kearney, Assistant Professor of Radio-Television-Film

This is a related and equally sectarian course. It applies radical feminist theory to television media:

> Although we will begin with second-wave feminist explorations of gender and the cultural representation of women, our particular concern will be contemporary poststructuralist theories which move our understanding of gender and sexuality beyond the normative binaries of male/female, masculine/feminine, and heterosexual/homosexual.

After taking this course, students are expected not only to be familiar with but also to espouse feminist theories. Among the stated objectives of the course is that students "understand and discuss various feminist approaches used in critical and cultural studies of television" and "apply various feminist theories and methodologies to the relationship of women, gender, and feminism to television history, programming, and reception." Such a goal may be appropriate for the training of feminist television critics, but it is indefensible for an academic course.

The required texts include Chris Weedon's *Feminist Practice and Poststructuralist Theory* (also required in Women's Studies courses at Penn State), which presents feminism first and foremost as a type of politics. Weedon argues that feminists "take as our starting point the patriarchal structure of society" and declares that "the task of this book" is "to make a case for recent poststructuralist developments . . . which will serve feminist interests."[14] A second required text, *Screening the Male,* is an anthology of feminist essays addressing "heterosexual masculinity in the mainstream cinema." The all-but-unreadable essays adhere faithfully to feminist boilerplate, and few pass on the opportunity to condemn what they call the "dominant patriarchal organization of US culture."[15]

While the professor's syllabus encourages students to make suggestions about "additional readings and research materials,"[16] they will recommend critiques of feminist politics at their peril. After all, the instructor's refusal to include alternative viewpoints in the required reading list suggests that, in her judgment, there is only one "truth."

Women and Media Culture *RTF 359s & WGS 324*[17]

INSTRUCTOR: Mary Celeste Kearney, Assistant Professor of Radio-Television-Film

Although this course purports to be a "critical analysis of women and media culture," such a critical stance is nowhere in evidence. Likewise, although the description states that the course will consider a "variety of theoretical perspectives," there is no sign that it goes outside the limited spectrum of feminist viewpoints—"feminist and gender theory, critical race theory, lesbian/gay/queer studies." Students are expected to "apply various theories of gender and media in critical analyses of women-oriented media texts, women media consumers, and women's alternative media production."[18]

"Dilemmas" of the Left: The Department of Sociology

American Dilemmas *SOC 336C, URB 354, and AFR 320*[19]

INSTRUCTOR: Penny Green, Lecturer in the Department of Sociology

The "American Dilemmas" examined in this course are a mishmash of left-wing issues: the "economy and political system, social class and income inequality, racial/ethnic inequality, gender inequality and heterosexism, problems in education, and problems of illness and health care." All these issues could theoretically be examined in an academic manner from varying perspectives. But this course, in its very description, provides students with a ready-made answer to these controversial issues, namely that the social problems it identifies have a "disproportionately negative impact on men of color and women."[20] Indeed, impressing on students the alleged racial and/or sexist bias behind these problems is one of the avowed aims of the course. Students are asked to grasp the "seriousness of these problems, *especially for men of color and women*."[21]

Another stated objective is to suggest social policies to address the problems. But the course seems concerned only with policies advocated by the political Left, such as affirmative action programs and pay-equity legislation. Instead of evaluating the merits of these policies empirically, the course seeks to justify them by associating them with vague concepts of "social justice" and the "common good."

Keeping the Sixties Alive: The Division of Rhetoric and Writing

Rhetoric Course: Non-Violent Rhetoric *RHE 309K*[22]

INSTRUCTOR: Margaret Syverson, Associate Professor of the Division of Rhetoric and Writing and Director of the Computer Writing and Research Lab

Notwithstanding its title, this is not a course in rhetoric; it trains students in the politics of nonviolent political action. Students "engage in various construction projects, both individually and collaboratively, developing a richer understanding of the theories and application of nonviolent action." In the service of this political agenda, students are asked to consider such leading questions as "How can theories of nonviolence be applied online?"

All the texts required for the course are ideological arguments for nonviolence. For instance, *The Unconquerable World: Power, Nonviolence, and the Will of the People,* by the left-wing journalist Jonathan Schell, is a revisionist history of nonviolence. The book makes no effort to evaluate the successes and failures of violent conflict; it dismisses violence as "a method by which the ruthless few can subdue the passive many." In contrast, Schell glorifies nonviolence as "a means by which the active many can overcome the ruthless few."[23]

Even more dubious is the author's utopian call for international "co-operative structures" to serve as the guarantors of peace. Schell inadvertently admits the weakness of his argument when he insists that these structures must play a role in the "enforcement of a prohibition against crimes against humanity"; obviously, such enforcement often requires force.

Is There No Other Way?, another book used in this course, similarly overstates the historical successes of nonviolent action.[24] The author, Michael Nagler, a professor emeritus of literature at the University of California at Berkeley, is neither a historian nor a political scientist. Other assigned texts include *Peace Is Every Step*, by the Vietnamese Zen Buddhist monk Thich Nhat Hahn and a collection of readings from Mohandas K. Gandhi. Whatever the merits of these books, they do not provide a balanced discussion of theories of nonviolence. This course is an exercise in advocacy.

Rhetoric of the 1960s *RHE309K*[25]

INSTRUCTOR: Erin Boade, Graduate Student in the Department of English

The first section of this course largely focuses on the radical black power movement and violent groups like the Black Panther Party. The second section focuses on "activism among white students," primarily the radical student organization Students for a Democratic Society (SDS). Assignments for this section require students to read a number of proclamations from radical student groups—including "The Port Huron Statement," the founding manifesto of SDS. It does not assign anything that is even remotely critical of such organizations, their political platforms, or their activities. The final section of the course, entitled "From NOW to Radical Feminism," is a survey of feminist politics and activism.

While this course purports to be a course in rhetoric, it is actually a course designed to inculcate a radical view of the 1960s. The instructor is not a historian and has no professional expertise for teaching this subject.

Rhetoric of Native Americans *RHE 309K*[26]

INSTRUCTOR: Tracey Watts, Graduate Student in the Department of English

This course is premised on the questionable proposition that "[i]n American rhetoric, Native Americans have become host to a variety of cultural presumptions that are usually inaccurate and frequently contradictory." The instructor, a graduate student, believes that Native Americans have never been portrayed accurately or fairly, but have only been "romanticized and demonized." This course has only one objective: to prove that assumption.

The course assignments have little to do with the rhetoric of Native Americans but a great deal to do with the radical views of the instructor on how the United States marginalizes "the other." One section, titled "The Rhetoric of Social Change," requires students to write about a 1975 shootout at South Dakota's Pine Ridge Indian Reservation between activists from the radical American Indian Movement and FBI agents. The course asks students to regard the incident from the perspective of one of the Indian radicals, Leonard Peltier, even though he is currently serving two consecutive life prison terms for the murder of two FBI agents.[27] That is to say, the instructor treats the convicted killer's claim that FBI racism triggered the events as if it were a fact rather than an unfounded and generally discredited conjecture. Reinforcing this sympathetic take on the Indian radical's actions, the syllabus announces its interest in describing "the context for Leonard Peltier's imprisonment" and advises students that in their writing assignments "you might argue that the FBI's treatment of Native Americans on the Pine Ridge reservation . . . demonstrated fascism or racism."

Marxism 101: The Department of Comparative Literature

Marxisms *CL 382*[28]

INSTRUCTOR: Katherine Arens, Professor of Germanic Studies

"Marxisms" could be a course in economics, or sociology, or political theory. But at the University of Texas it is offered in the Department of Comparative Literature, by a professor of Germanic Studies and Humanities. The course begins with readings by Marx and Friedrich Engels and continues on to derivative Marxist schools of thought that appeared throughout the twentieth century. Much of the attention of the course is directed at technical differences of interpretation between these schools of Marxism, while students are never assigned texts critical of Marxism itself.

Literature as Politics: The Department of English

Literature and Social Justice *E 360L*[29]

INSTRUCTOR: Barbara Harlow, the Louann and Larry Temple Centennial Professor of English Literature

Among the ostensibly literary works studied in the course is *Guantanamo,* a play by Victoria Brittain and Gillian Slovo, two left-wing activists who have charged, without evidence, that the United States commits "torture" at its detention facility in Guantánamo Bay, Cuba. Another text for the course, *Fighting for Human Rights,* is a collection of essays by leftist authors that equates "social justice" with the radical environmentalist movement, the International Criminal Court, and left-wing campaigns to ban the use of land mines. Under the theme of "social justice," the course also concerns itself with topics as disparate as genocide, AIDS, immigration, and war, all of which are considered through a political rather than a literary lens.

Socialist Playground: The Department of Communication Studies

The Department of Communication Studies has become a playground for associate professor Dana Cloud, whose clear political agenda in the classroom has somehow passed muster with the department. The radicalism seen in the course "Communications and Social Change" is just as evident in the four other classes she offers.

Rhetoric of Social Movements *CMS390*[30]

INSTRUCTOR: Dana Cloud, Associate Professor of Communications

This survey of "U.S. social movements from the 19th century to the present" focuses on movements consistent with Cloud's radical politics, such as the labor, antiwar, and feminist movements, the "lesbian rights movement," and the "global justice movement." The course does not regard these movements critically, considering their flaws as well as their successes. Instead, the required texts are written by leftists who actively support the movements about which they write. Emblematic of the required readings is Howard Zinn's *A People's History of the United States* (always a favorite of the academic Left), which defends "all the subordinate groups in a society dominated by rich white males."[31] Similarly, *Protest and Popular Culture: Women in the U.S. Labor Movement, 1894–1917,* is a sympathetic treatment of women's protest movements, particularly the feminist movement.[32] Still another, *Multitude,* is a political tract by the neo-Marxist theorists Michael Hardt and Antonio Negri.

Although the course purports to discuss the "conservative movement," no books about the movement or from a conservative perspective are included in the readings. The required text *The Social Movements Reader,* which discusses the civil rights movement, the "gay liberation" movement, the labor movement, environmentalism, radical feminism, and even the Iranian revolution, makes only passing—and negative—references to the "conservative antifeminist movement" and the "anti-abortion movement."[33]

This class amounts to an uncritical promotion of the causes of the political Left.

Communicating Gender in America *COM 370*[34]

INSTRUCTOR: Dana Cloud, Associate Professor of Communications

This is a course in radical gender politics masquerading as communications theory. The course discusses different analyses of "gender" and feminism, including transsexualism, radical and socialist feminism, black and "Chicana" feminism, and "liberal" feminism—but little by way of communications itself.

The assigned texts are explications of gender politics. In *Gendered Lives,* author Julia Wood explains that her status as "European American," middle-class, and heterosexual makes her "privileged," because her "race, class, and sexual orientation are approved by mainstream Western culture," but that as a woman, she belongs to an oppressed group, because "women are less valued than men in Western culture." Wood suggests no empirical evidence for either claim, and presumes them to be beyond challenge.[35]

Another assigned text, *My Gender Workbook,* is written by the transsexual performance artist Kate (formerly Albert) Bornstein. The book claims that gender is a social construction, lamenting that "we've bought into the biological imperative that has labeled genitalia as 'male' or 'female.'"[36] Unsurprisingly, the author evinces only contempt for science, sniping at the "old-guard scientists" whom she sees as a challenge to her political dogmas about gender.[37] "Who says penises are male and vulvas are female?" Bornstein demands.[38]

The curriculum encourages this notion that gender has no scientific basis. Students are asked to consider leading questions, such as "How have we been influenced by communication to adopt and perform particular gender identities?" "Communication," in other words, is understood to be a heteronormative element of the power structure that forces genders on the rest of us.

Twenty-five points of a students' final grade are determined by a "gender journal" they must keep throughout the course. In this journal, they are to include sections on "defining gender, identifying sources for gender in communication, questioning gender, questioning norms about sexuality, [and] understanding the ideas of gender critics," without—since no alternative views are provided similar respect—challenging them.[39]

Feminist Theory and Rhetorical Criticism *CMS390*[40]

INSTRUCTOR: Dana Cloud, Associate Professor of Communications

The purpose of this course, according to its description, is "to introduce students to a range of feminist political and critical theories and to explore the ways those theories can be combined with rhetorical critical methods to understand the gendering of public and cultural texts." The jargon is forbidding, but a representative section of this course, titled "Race and Sex and Class," illustrates the course's approach. In this section, students are asked to consider questions such as "What are postcolonial and third world feminisms?" "How do poststructuralist feminisms attempt to account for the disparate positions occupied by women?" "In what ways is queer theory a product of poststructuralism?"[41] These are all questions about radical theory—not one of them is critical of radical theory, and they do not address questions of rhetoric or issues in communications.

Rhetoric and Ideology *CMA 5.156*[42]

INSTRUCTOR: Dana Cloud, Associate Professor of Communications

Ostensibly a course *about* ideology, this is actually a course *in* ideology. Its main theme is to "explore Marxist contributions to rhetorical theory and criticism, with particular emphasis on a survey of the concepts of ideology and hegemony." The only texts used in the course are written by Marxist writers or feminist authors who embrace Marxism (while offering friendly amendments to help it rise out of the ashes of its global defeats). Nowhere in the course are students given the opportunity to review literature critical of Marxism. Instead, the course seeks to make rhetoric and ideology instruments of Marxism and affiliated schools of radical politics.

Propaganda Studies: The Department of Journalism

Social Justice and the Media *TC357*[43]

INSTRUCTOR: Robert Jensen, Associate Professor of Journalism

Robert Jensen is an associate professor of journalism. Yet this course is not about the craft of journalism and how it is, or should be, practiced. Instead, its subject is "social justice"—from an extreme left point of view. Students are required to read what Professor Jensen calls "exemplary journalistic works on social justice," in which distinguished category he seems to count only two books: *Common Sense,* by Thomas Paine, and *The Communist Manifesto,* by Karl Marx and Friedrich Engels. While the Paine pamphlet is the most moderate reading in the course, neither of these texts is journalistic. Both are revolutionary calls to arms. This is but one example of how Jensen's course exploits the classroom to carry out agendas outside the curriculum.

Jensen, whose own book is required reading in one of fellow radical Dana Cloud's courses, assigns his students a reading packet of essays mainly from Marxist and other radical theorists, whose views reflect the politics of the instructor. Like the main texts, the readings are not actually journalistic. For example, students are assigned to read a 1985 speech by Communist and black activist Angela Davis titled "We Do Not Consent: Violence Against Women in a Racist Society." In the speech, Davis rails against what she calls "the racist-inspired violence inflicted on Afro-Americans and other racially oppressed people here in the United States."[44] Racism is also the theme of "Racism Today: Continuity and Change in the Post–Civil Rights Era," by Professor Howard Winant. After asserting that race does not exist because it is "socially constructed," Winant nonetheless maintains that racism continues to thrive in the United States in the form of a "conservative discourse of individualism" that opposes affirmative action for minorities.[45]

To the limited extent that the readings in this journalism course actually treat the subject of media, they do so in the context of an obvious political agenda. A typical article is "A Propaganda Model," which is taken from the book *Manufacturing Consent: The Political Economy of the Mass Media,* by Noam Chomsky and his coauthor, Edward Herman. Deeply conspiratorial and obviously indebted to the authors' extreme views, this book claims that "money and power" filter the news to reflect their interests, and consequently that even in a democracy with a free press, reporting is a form of propaganda for the ruling class.[46] Unsurprisingly, the authors are especially troubled by what they call the major media outlets' espousal of "anti-Communist ideology."

Since the course features no alternative perspectives, students receive a profoundly one-sided understanding of these subjects, which in any case have little to do with the craft of journalism.

Dana Cloud was among the radical academics profiled in *The Professors,* written by one of the authors of this book. A closer investigation of the University of Texas curriculum reveals that while Cloud may be a particularly glaring example of a Texas professor who uses the classroom to train students in far-left politics, she is by no means the only example. Course after course, department after department—the trend is apparent throughout UT's curriculum. It raises a question with which we began the chapter: Will the University of Texas enforce its own academic standards, which distinguish between an academic course and a course in political propaganda?

The same question could be asked of another large state school in the Southwest: the University of Arizona.

6

Ideology Under the Sun

UNIVERSITY OF ARIZONA
TUITION: $5,046 IN-STATE
$16,281 OUT-OF-STATE

When the University of Arizona was first approved by the Arizona Territorial Legislature in 1885, it came as a considerable disappointment to the residents of Tucson, the school's planned home. Hoping that the $25,000 in funds set aside by the legislature for a university could be put to different use—perhaps for the building of a mental institution—Tucsonans entertained serious doubts that the university would ever take root in the sun-beaten Sonoran Desert.

Today, those concerns seem quaint. From the thirty-two students who attended the school's inaugural classes, the university's total enrollment now exceeds 36,000, while the original forty-acre campus now stretches to nearly four hundred. In the realm of academics as well, the school has exceeded early expectations: its science departments routinely place among the top in the country, and groundbreaking academic research has bolstered the school's reputation as one of the nation's leading public research institutions.

At the same time, a significant segment of the university's liberal arts curriculum offers a menu of courses that are political rather than academic, fails to observe professional standards, and violates the established canons of academic freedom. In a disturbing number of classes, there is not the slightest pretense of a scholarly approach to the subject or minimal respect for the academic rights of students.

Gender Oppression: The Political Science Department

V. Spike Peterson has an impressive academic résumé: a full professor of Political Science, she has been awarded a Fulbright scholarship, a writing and research grant by the MacArthur Foundation, and a fellowship from the Udall Center for Studies in Public Policy. But on digging deeper into her record, one finds that her teaching doubles as indoctrination in the extreme political viewpoints she endorses. A troika of courses she teaches through Arizona's Political Science Department reveals her radical ambitions.

Feminist Political Theory *POL 433/533*[1]

INSTRUCTOR: V. Spike Peterson, Professor of Political Science

Professor Peterson is the author of *Global Gender Issues,* which according to her website is "still one of the most widely used texts on gender and world politics." In this course, as in that book, she propounds a view we have seen so often in the Women's Studies courses we've analyzed: namely, the notion that gender is "socially constructed," or environmentally determined—a view announced as though it were a principle of Newtonian physics. Peterson's course description begins, "Because gender is socially constructed, it is instructive to study how gender ideologies—which profoundly shape today's intellectual inquiries and political realities—have been articulated in the form of political theory. In this course we will briefly review the tradition of Western political theory through a gender-sensitive lens and survey developments in feminist political theories."[2]

Are the traits associated with femininity and masculinity the sinister creations of a ruling patriarchy bent on oppressing women? Students in this course are expected, sheeplike, to embrace this questionable view, and from there to see the history of Western political theory from the perspective of radical feminism. Peterson declares that the "objectives of this course are to: 1) sensitize students to the social construction of gender and its implications for political theory; 2) enable students to identify gender bias in nonfeminist political theory; 3) familiarize students with debates and developments in feminist political theory; and 4) encourage students to make connections between theory and practice and understand how theorizing itself is political."[3]

To phrase these objectives more clearly, the professor intends to (1) indoctrinate students in the view that gender is socially constructed; (2) teach students that the entire Western tradition of political theory is a conspiracy against women; (3) immerse students in the world of feminist ideology; and (4) indoctrinate them in the view that all ideas are self-interested and political—a crude conclusion of Marxist ideology.

The assigned texts and readings in the course reflect its airless totalitarian nature: only one perspective is permitted. Among the assigned texts are *The Sexism of Social and Political Theory: Women and Reproduction from Plato to Nietzsche*; *The Disorder of Women: Democracy, Feminism, and Political Theory*; *Capitalist Patriarchy and the Case for Socialist Feminism*; *The Radical Future of Liberal Feminism*; *Talking Back: Thinking Feminist, Thinking Black*; *Segregated Sisterhood: Racism and the Politics of American Feminism*; and *Sexual Democracy: Women, Oppression, and Revolution*.

Gender and Politics *POL 335H*[4]

INSTRUCTOR: V. Spike Peterson, Professor of Political Science

Calling this class "Gender and Politics" suggests to the unsuspecting that it is an academic course that will view these controversial issues from more than one perspective, leaving students to draw their own conclusions. Nothing could be further from the truth. The course description makes this abundantly clear when it says that the class will examine "politics through the lens of gender hierarchy," with an "emphasis on how constructions of masculinity and femininity shape and are shaped by interacting economic, political, and ideological practices."[5]

Is there a "gender hierarchy"? According to Professor Peterson there is, and this contentious claim functions as the basis of the entire course.

The description goes on:

> This course is designed to examine gender, understood as a hierarchical, binary opposition of masculinity and femininity, and its intersection with power relations, understood as an expression of politics. We will examine how gender categories are constructed and how they shape our identities, our ways of thinking (concepts, worldviews), and our ways of acting (divisions of labor, institutions). We will examine how gender hierarchy is a *system* of differential power that intersects especially with ethnicity/race, class, and sexual orientation.

The claim that power relations are an expression of politics, and that they "intersect" with gender relations that are hierarchical, is hardly a consensus view outside of Women's Studies programs. Nevertheless, it, too, is presented as fact in this course.

The ideological agenda becomes even clearer from the stated course objectives:

> By examining power relations—politics—as gendered, the course illuminates 1) how the personal is political; 2) how we participate individually and collectively in the production, reproduction, and legitimation of power relations (social hierarchies); 3) how social hierarchies (of race, gender, class, ethnicity, sexual orientation, etc.) are interrelated; 4) how reflective, critical analyses are essential for achieving nonhierarchical social relations; 5) and how social transformation occurs, is impeded, and promoted.[6]

Every course objective listed is designed to promote the idea that American society is an oppressive hierarchy, and that there is a revolutionary alternative available to end its injustices. This is political propaganda, and not of a very high order.

Feminist and International Relations Theory *POL 461*[7]

INSTRUCTOR: V. Spike Peterson, Professor of Political Science

This is yet a third propaganda course taught by Professor Peterson. She states the course objectives as follows:

> To explore the implications for international relations theory of "taking gender seriously." Contemporary philosophy of science understands knowledge as socially constructed, with knowledge claims inescapably based upon experience and perspective. Historically, that experience has been primarily that of men (especially elite, white, Western men in regard to IR theory). There is now an extensive body of feminist literature documenting the "neglect" of gender (i.e., denying the significance of the sex/gender system in constituting social reality), the costs of that "neglect" for accurate understanding in the social sciences, and the need for re-constructing the very foundations of socio-political theory. Drawing upon that literature, we will take a "gendered" look at social theory and theorizing in IR.[8]

This short description is riddled with problems. For starters, there is no consensus among contemporary philosophers of science (or contemporary philosophers, for that matter) as to the nature of knowledge, let alone that it is "socially constructed." The nature-versus-nurture debate remains an unresolved philosophical/scientific issue. Moreover, virtually the entire field of neuroscience is devoted to the opposite view—namely, that the mind is not a blank slate on which society impresses its prejudices (see, for example, Steven Pinker's *The Blank Slate*). But students in this course will not even be made aware of these profound and unresolved differences, since no texts reflecting dissenting views are assigned, and since the very structure of the course is to train students in one sectarian doctrine favored by the instructor.

The Social Construction of Race: The African-American Studies Department

The Social Construction of Whiteness *AFAS 304A*[9]

INSTRUCTOR: Deborah Whaley, Adjunct Lecturer in African American Studies

So now whiteness, too, is socially constructed. In the judgment of this course, whites socially construct their own identity so that they can oppress others and enjoy—and appear to deserve—their privileges and power.

In fact, according to the syllabus, students in this course are expected to understand practically everything as "social constructions with material consequences"—"gender, race, sexualities, class, and ability." Students also must accept that there are "systemic race, class, and gender inter-relationships and hierarchies" as well as "dominant power structures."[10] To arrive at such conclusions, they are required to read texts by radical feminist ideologues such as Peggy McIntosh and bell hooks, and to watch a video by rapper Eminem that includes the image of a knife plunged into a photo of President Bush, and the lyrics "f**k Bush," "no more blood for oil," and "disarm the weapon of mass destruction that we call our president."

Oppressing the Natives: American Indian Studies

American Indian Studies: Asserting Sovereignty Through Cultural Preservation

AIS 595A and 485A, Section 3[11]

INSTRUCTOR: Nancy J. Parezo, Adjunct Associate Research Professor of Anthropology

This course is premised on two ideological claims. The first, discernible in the title, is that Native Americans and their culture remain captives of colonization. A key "research question" that students are asked to consider is "What are the ways that Native nations, communities and individuals (including scholars) can work toward sovereignty and decolonization?" But of course this is a leading question, based on the assumption that Native Americans in the United States are in fact colonized. To further encourage students in this politicized view of Native American culture, the course assigns texts such as *The Colonizer and the Colonized,* a critique of colonialism written by a Tunisian author in the wake of his country's independence from France in 1957, and *Voices of a Thousand People: The Makah Cultural and Research Centers,* which portrays American museums as instruments of cultural imperialism because they have supposedly "legitimated" some forms of knowledge at the expense of Native American traditions.[12]

The second ideological claim advanced by the course is that free-market capitalism is the enemy of Native American communities. This assertion is most conspicuously made in one of the assigned texts, *Who Owns Native Culture?* In this book, author Michael Brown writes that capitalism is designed to exploit "native" cultures.[13] Elsewhere in the book, he repeats the stock Marxist claim that capitalism is a form of "economic domination" that turns "local peoples into serfs."[14] As an example of a native tradition he admires, the author invokes the Zapatista National Liberation Army (EZLN), an armed Marxist insurgent movement in the Mexican state of Chiapas that Brown regards as a "potent symbol of grassroots resistance to the excesses of world capitalism."[15]

Socialist Feminism: The Women's Studies Department

Feminist Theories *Women's Studies 305*[16]

INSTRUCTOR: Kari McBride, Associate Professor of Women's Studies and the Undergraduate Director for the Women's Studies Department

A typical assignment in Associate Professor Kari McBride's "Feminist Theories" course instructs students to read "An Introduction to Marxism"—an uncritical account of Marxist thought written by McBride herself—and "two excerpts from Karl Marx's *Wage Labour and Capital:* 'What Are Wages?' and 'The Nature and Growth of

Capital.' "[17] The instructor's "Introduction to Marxism" explains that "a capitalist system is dependent on ideologies like meritocracy ('anyone can grow up to be president') that mask the realities of exploitation and privilege and keep the proletariat (working class) subjugated to the bourgeoisie (middle class) who grow rich on the surplus value of lower class labor."[18] Though McBride's degree is in English literature, the Arizona Women's Studies Department apparently considers her qualified to teach economic theory.

For another class session, the instructor assigns "A Socialist Feminist Manifesto for Cyborgs," written by radical feminist Donna Haraway—who, as we will see in Chapter 12, is a professor in the "History of Consciousness" at the University of California, Santa Cruz.[19] This sample from Haraway's "Socialist Feminist Manifesto" typifies the socialist views and political agenda of Haraway (and also of McBride's Feminist Theories course):

> Socialist feminists could do good work in alliance with the Congressional Black Caucus, and California Congressperson Ronald Dellums in particular, helping to formulate alternative budgets, national and international analysis of social meanings of biotechnologies and communications sciences, and agendas for race/gender/class sensitive science and technology policies to encourage wide public debate.[20]

Such readings offer little by way of academic analysis.

Feminist Theories and Movements *WS 539*[21]

INSTRUCTOR: Laura Briggs, Associate Professor of Women's Studies

The one "academic" publication to Laura Briggs's credit indicates how extreme her politics are. Her book, *Reproducing Empire: Race, Sex, Science, and U.S. Imperialism in Puerto Rico,* sees America as an imperialist power and describes the contemporary Puerto Rican family as "an axis of colonialism," since the island is a commonwealth of the United States.[22] Yet her harsh assessment of the "U.S. imperial project on the island" is shared by only a tiny minority of Puerto Ricans themselves, who, after all, enjoy the rights of Americans under the U.S. Constitution: in the most popular referendum, fully 96 percent of Puerto Ricans voted to affiliate with the United States as a commonwealth or as a state.[23]

Professor Briggs's course, "Feminist Theories and Movements," reflects her radical perspective. According to the description, the course aims to "provide a survey of some of the major issues, debates, and texts of feminist theorizing,"[24] but in reality it focuses on a narrow range of theories, all at the extreme left end of the ideological spectrum. It is not even a course in feminism but in radicalism. The most telling line in the description announces that the course seeks to "situate feminist theories in relation to a variety of other politically significant theories (including Marxism, post-structuralism, critical race theory and post-colonial theory)"—in other words, to "situate" radical feminism among other radical theories. Designed to indoctrinate students in feminist and radical views and activism, the course assigns only texts by radical feminists, radical race activists, and "queer theorists."[25]

Transnational Feminisms *WS 586*[26]

INSTRUCTOR: Laura Briggs, Associate Professor of Women's Studies

In another course offering, Laura Briggs admits that the chief concern of the class is the promotion of feminist politics. Her course description for "Transnational Feminisms" states:

> This field, to the extent that it is a field, takes up the contemporary challenge to think across national borders in relationship to feminist politics and the insights that feminist analysis offer. . . . At the same time, it is a field that has been provocatively engaged with political movements. To this end, the course will traverse complex theoretical as well as knotty political ground.[27]

The three assigned books cover a range of topics but are written from similarly radical perspectives. In Anna Lowenhaupt Tsing's *In the Realm of the Diamond Queen,* the author notes that her book, organized around "feminist critiques," is actually an attack on academic scholarship, particularly anthropology, which exists, in her conspiratorial view, to further the agenda of unnamed "senior male informants."[28]

Likewise, *Shattered Bonds: The Color of Child Welfare* is not a work of scholarship but a philippic against the U.S. child welfare system. In the book, author Dorothy E. Roberts purports to document what she describes as the "ugly reality that this system treats white families better . . . because they benefit from racial privilege."[29] Yet Roberts supplies no compelling proof for this inflammatory charge; instead she offers ideological statements presented as fair-minded analysis. In a typical passage, the author writes, "If you came with no preconceptions about the purpose of the child welfare system, you would have to conclude that it is an institution designed to monitor, regulate, and punish poor Black families."[30] The course assigns no alternative assessments of the child welfare system.

Radical historian Mary Renda's *Taking Haiti: Military Occupation and the Culture of U.S. Imperialism, 1915–1940* is an indictment of the American occupation of Haiti and the broader American foreign policy. As Renda sees it, the United States is an imperialist power that was "remade through overseas imperial ventures in the first third of the 20th century."[31] The inclusion of this book in a course on "transnational feminisms" may seem puzzling until one considers that one of the course themes is "the emerging history of U.S. imperialism." This of course presumes that the United States is indeed an imperialist country. In any case, the subject of American foreign policy seems beyond the academic expertise of a professor of Women's Studies.

Professor Briggs also asks students to read a chapter from the book *Cultures of United States Imperialism* in which author Amy Kaplan argues that American culture should be viewed through the lens of "European colonization, slavery, westward expansion, overseas intervention, and cold war nuclear power."[32] Of course, Briggs herself has argued that the United States is an imperialist power in her book, *Reproducing Empire.*

"Activism for Credit": The Department of Sociology

Collective Behavior and Social Movements *SOC 313*[33]

INSTRUCTOR: Jeff Larson, Graduate Student in the Department of Sociology

Jeff Larson is a graduate student, writing his Ph.D. dissertation on Che Guevara. He is apparently trying to prove himself worthy of his subject. Students enrolled in his course can earn points for participating in protest rallies or movement events and writing about them. Here is one of Larson's assignments:

> Activist-for-a-day (or two)
> October 27 (200 points)
>
> Here it is, activism for credit. Give four hours to a social movement organization and I'll give you 200 points. Of course, I also want to hear a little about what you've done, so you'll have to summarize your experience too. It's a small price to pay. What better way to learn about movements than to be in one?[34]

Larson says that he'll "leave it to you to choose a social movement organization (SMO) that interests you," but the suggestions he offers make no mistake about the kinds of politically minded groups he has in mind:

> Tucson has a bunch of great organizations that could use your help. For example, Wingspan has loads of things you can do for lesbians, gay men, transgendered and bisexual people right here in the Old Pueblo. Maybe you're more interested in endangered species and ecosystem protection—check out the Center for Biological Diversity, an important and influential organization that just happens to be based in Tucson. Consider the Brewster Center, Society of Friends (Quakers), Women's International League for Peace and Freedom, Border Action Network, Humane Borders, or Food Not Bombs. You might

look into campus SMOs or organizations listed on the Tucson Peace Calendar or Arizona Indymedia Center.[35]

The organizations recommended for 200 points of academic credit are radical groups whose agendas reflect the political prejudices of the instructor. Larson states those prejudices unapologetically on his website, where he announces that his "main interest is to knock the rich and powerful from their leather-lined perches and give the historically exploited and degraded a seat at the sustainably harvested, round table of autonomy."[36] Students must wonder: what exactly is a "leather-lined perch" or "table of autonomy"? Larson stopped mixing his metaphors on his professorial blog when he wrote in 2007, "Let's bomb the White House this year with calls to end this despicable war."[37]

This is an infantile course in infantile leftism, and is hardly appropriate for a taxpayer-supported institution or a modern research university.

Oppression Studies: The Individuals-and-Societies Requirement

The Politics of Difference: Ethnicity/Race, Class, Gender, and Sexualities *INDV 101*[38]

INSTRUCTOR: V. Spike Peterson, Professor of Political Science

To earn a degree, all undergraduates at the University of Arizona must complete a "General Education" requirement, which is ostensibly designed to help every graduate "attain the fundamental skills and the broad base of knowledge and understanding that all college-educated adults must have, whatever their specific areas of concentration."[39] Students must take courses within each of three different categories. Professor V. Spike Peterson's "Gender and Politics" course, described above, falls under one of these categories, which is designated as "Gender, Race, Class, Ethnicity, or Non-Western Area Studies." Meanwhile, another Peterson course, "The Politics of Difference," is included in a subcategory of courses known as "Individuals and Societies (INDV)."

On her syllabus, Peterson describes this course as examining "the *politics* (understood broadly as differential access to and control over material and symbolic resources) of *difference* (understood as institutionalized social hierarchies that oppress individuals)."[40] She does not seem to consider that this definition conflicts with her notion that race and gender are social constructions, which presumes that people are oppressed as *groups,* not individuals—women are oppressed as women, blacks as blacks, gays as gays, proletarians as proletarians.

The course pigeonholes individuals into four categories—"ethnicity/race, class, gender, and sexuality"—and then throws in the presumption that gender molds all of them: "We will pay particular attention to how *gender* dynamics shape individual identities, group structures, and the reproduction of multiple social hierarchies of difference." Even more breathtaking is the course's supposition that *all* categories—including "religion, physical ability, age, etc."—"constitute significant forms of oppression"[41]

The first objective of the course is to show students "empirical indicators of how individuals' lives are materially and symbolically marked by difference. Empirical evidence substantiates the asymmetrical power, that is, politics, of these markers."[42] But the fact that some people earn less money than others does not indicate—let alone substantiate—Peterson's claim that the source of this inequality is "asymmetrical power" based on "institutional hierarchies." Individuals are more than robotic members of groups; they are also individual actors in the social drama who have different skills and abilities that are more significant in determining their success or failure than their membership in groups. Are Barry Bonds and Michael Jordan multimillionaires because of asymmetrical power relations and institutional hierarchies that favor them? Are Warren Buffett and Bill Gates self-made billionaires, while tens of millions of white males are not, because of a socially constructed hierarchy? Is Oprah Winfrey a billionaire because she is the beneficiary of hierarchies constructed to benefit white males?

Unsurprisingly, Professor Peterson is not content merely to study radical theories about the "oppression" of women, minorities, and the poor. She expects students to "become more effective agents of social change" and to determine "how can we move beyond the oppressive dynamics of racism, classism, sexism, and heterosexism (homophobia)."[43] In short, this is a course in radical agendas, including the utopian delusion that "another world is possible"—a society that is classless, raceless, and gender-free. The quest for such a socialist utopia resulted in the murder of a hundred million innocents by radicals in the twentieth century, but students in this course will not be exposed to a cautionary point of view on these matters.

The "Fundamental Skill" of America Bashing: The Department of English

Freshman Composition *English 101*[44]

INSTRUCTOR: Sung Ohm, Graduate Student in the Department of English

As part of the General Education requirement, first-year students at the University of Arizona also must take a freshman composition course. General Education purports to teach "fundamental skills," and one might assume that the most important set of skills in a freshman composition course would be those involving grammar and composition. But one would be wrong. Instead, English 101 as taught by Sung Ohm, a doctoral student in English, is designed to equip students with a proficiency in anticapitalist and anti-American rhetoric.

Students, for example, are required to read a Howard Zinn essay on the Iraq War titled "An Occupied Country." In this essay, the well-known Marxist and anti-American polemicist writes, "The so-called war on terrorism is not only a war on innocent people in other countries, but it is also a war on the people of the United States: a war on our liberties, a war on our standard of living. The wealth of the country is being stolen from the people and handed over to the super-rich. The lives of our young are being stolen. And the thieves are in the White House."[45]

Students also are required to read an essay by another radical who thinks America's enemies should win the war in Iraq—University of

Texas journalism professor Robert Jensen: "The consequences of this imperial project have been grim for many people around the world—those who have been the targets of U.S. military power; those who have lived under repressive regimes backed by the United States; and those who toil in economies that are increasingly subordinated to the United States and multinational corporations."[46]

Another required text is an interview with Noam Chomsky, yet another radical with strong anti-American opinions (e.g., that America is "the world's greatest terrorist state").[47] How is an *interview* with a political activist a guide to *writing* skills? It isn't. And so it will come as no surprise that students are also required to read the *Communist Manifesto.*

English 101 is simply an opportunity for a nontenured radical to indoctrinate students in left-wing agendas. Every "alternative media website" that the instructor recommends to the class is on the left side of the political spectrum: AlterNet, Common Dreams News Center, Democracy Now News, Fairness and Accuracy in Reporting, the *Independent* (U.K.), Independent Media Center, *The Nation, The Progressive.* This list comes with gushing comments by the instructor: "Some of the best reporting on the war and terrorism"; "excellent, readable articles on the war and loss of civil liberties"; "immediate reporting of anti-war protests and resources for linking the current crisis to issues of global inequality."[48]

The University of Arizona's English 101 would be an appropriate introductory training course offered by any number of activist organizations on the left. But it is not a course that provides a needy freshman with instruction in becoming a more competent writer.

When we first compiled an analysis of the classroom indoctrination that goes on at the University of Arizona, we sent a copy to every administrator and faculty member at the University of Arizona. Considerable discussion on the university Listserv ensued, along with articles in the campus newspaper, mainly defending the courses under scrutiny.

Associate professor Laura Briggs, whose courses came under criticism, defended her ideological approach by claiming that "electives" and "graduate courses" are exempt from academic standards: "The classes that [Horowitz] mentions are electives and graduate courses, and these are courses that focus on one perspective. But that's what graduate courses are for."[49] Focusing on a single perspective is one thing: viewing it uncritically and as though it were scientific fact is quite another.

Karen Anderson, president of the University of Arizona Association for Women Faculty, accused the authors of "subliminal sexism," apparently for observing that, contrary to feminist dogma, the preponderance of scientific opinion suggests that there are innate differences between the sexes.[50]

The Graduate and Professional Student Council passed a resolution endorsing critical thinking and a free exchange of ideas—as though it were the authors rather than the courses analyzed in the article that threatened them.

The school newspaper, the *Arizona Daily Wildcat,* denounced the authors' criticisms and the proposal that academics should teach more than one side of controversial issues, and should observe academic principles, as "dangerous suggestions."[51]

Neither the faculty senate nor the university administration took any action to correct the problems documented in the original report and in this chapter. The problems endure at the University of Arizona, as they do up the road at Arizona State.

7

School of Inverted Values

ARIZONA STATE UNIVERSITY
TUITION: $4,688 IN-STATE
$15,847 OUT-OF-STATE

As the home of the Grady Gammage Memorial Auditorium, a grand columned structure that was one of the last designs of architectural great Frank Lloyd Wright, Arizona State University defies the bland stereotype of the public university. That's equally true in the province of academics. The school is required under Arizona law to grant admission to any applicant who satisfies minimal academic standards, but it has nevertheless built an impressive record of achievement. Among public schools, ASU ranks eighth in the country in the number of National Merit Scholars enrolled. Similarly, ASU's programs in evolutionary biology, industrial engineering, nanotechnology, and music are ranked among the top in their respective fields.

Arizona State's academic freedom guidelines, in place since 1982, grant professors a broad latitude in their research, but also include the following strictures in regard to their classroom conduct: "In the exercise of this freedom, the faculty member should be careful not to introduce controversial matters which have no relation to the subject matter of the course. The faculty member is also obligated to encourage the free pursuit of learning by students. The faculty member adheres to a proper role as intellectual guide and counselor. Every reasonable effort is made to foster honest academic conduct and to assure that evaluation of students reflects the true merit of their work."

In addition, the policy of the Arizona Board of Regents on "Political Activity" (section 6-905) states, "Employees . . . shall not allow their interest in a particular party, candidate, or political issue to affect the objectivity of their teaching or the performance of their regular university duties."

Unfortunately, an examination of the ASU liberal arts curriculum reveals a recurring pattern of ideological instruction, one-sided reading assignments, and politically motivated and unprofessional conduct that violates both the spirit and the letter of the university's guidelines.

View from the Left: The School of Justice and Social Inquiry

The School of Justice and Social Inquiry at Arizona State officially claims that it "is concerned with the empirical study of justice and injustice in contemporary societies."[1]

But there is no such thing as an "empirical study of justice and injustice." The question "What is justice?" is as old as Plato's *Republic* and has no consensus answer. Justice to some people is injustice to others. For example, the distribution of income in a market society from a conservative point of view is just, but to liberals and radicals it is unjust. The school's official claim that justice and injustice are matters of "empirical study" is a subterfuge that allows it to assert a sectarian ideology as if it were fact. Not surprisingly, its required texts are devoted to the exposition of this sectarian ideology as provided by such polemicists as Howard Zinn, Angela Davis, and Barbara Ehrenreich.

Also, the school expresses its ideological agenda—more specifically, its left-wing agenda—on its official website, which describes the "three broad foci" of its academic program:

- Economic Justice—particularly the global dimension of changing economic relations.

- Social Justice, Law and Policy—focusing on environment, immigration, welfare, crime, and other policies that inspire justice concerns, particularly around race, class, and gender.
- Cultural Transformation and Justice—especially the role of the media and new technologies in changing perspectives on justice.[2]

Both "Economic Justice" and "Social Justice" are ideological terms associated with the political Left, generally referring to redistribution of income and resources. The third focus—"cultural transformation"—is a left-wing action program: using media to advance an agenda of social change.

The School of Justice frames other central concepts ideologically as well. According to the departmental curricula, for instance, the terms "criminal" and "terrorist" have been devised by ruling classes to define political dissent as social deviance and to repress subordinate ethnicities, genders, and classes. Social welfare programs are described and analyzed exclusively as means of keeping "oppressed" classes in line.

The analysis that follows only scratches the surface of the courses offered by the School of Justice and Social Inquiry, but it accurately reflects the intellectual principles that govern its educational program. This program is more appropriate to a political party or sect than an academic institution. It violates the academic freedom standards set by the Arizona Regents and the American Association of University Professors.

Wealth Distribution and Poverty *JUS 321*[3]

INSTRUCTOR: H. L. T. Quan, Assistant Professor in the School of Justice and Social Inquiry

Assistant professor H. L. T. Quan teaches several courses in the School for Justice. Her faculty biography, posted on the departmental website, is that of a political activist, not a disinterested scholar. It notes that her teaching interests are "Race, Gender and Social

Protests, Race, Gender & Justice, Theories of Development, Community Research, Feminist Methodology, and Radical Political Thought," while her research interests include "Black Consciousness, Race, Gender & Global Cities, Black capitalism, and Women of Color & Feminist Epistemology." Her bio adds that "Professor Quan is currently writing a book about savage developmentalism and its tendencious [*sic*] propensity to secure order and capitalist expansion."

Quan clearly signals her ideological agenda in her course description for "Wealth Distribution and Poverty," which begins:

> "An imbalance between rich and poor is the oldest and most fatal ailment of all republics." —Plato
>
> More than two millennia after Plato made the above observation, extreme economic inequality continues to be a fatal source of civil strife and a major impediment to the pursuit of life, liberty and happiness. An investigation of wealth distribution and poverty is imperative for all inquiries into questions of economic and social justice.[4]

The description goes on to say that the course "will provide an introduction to the ways in which race and gender interact with class stratification." Professor Quan introduces these concepts through three required texts, all written from a left-wing—and generally a far left-wing—point of view. The nonscholarly agendas of the first required text, *America Unequal,* are made clear in the publisher's description: "*America Unequal* demonstrates how powerful economic forces have diminished the prospects of millions of Americans and why 'a rising tide no longer lifts all boats.' . . . *America Unequal* challenges the view, emphasized in the Republicans' 'Contract With America,' that restraining government social spending and cutting welfare should be our top domestic priorities."[5] This isn't an accurate summary of the Republican position, but the general description of the text certainly reflects the political agendas of the authors.

Social Class and Stratification, the second required text, is described in an enthusiastic review posted on its publisher's site as "a welcome contribution to renewal of interest in class as the decisive force behind social inequalities." A second reviewer describes the book as "politically engaged" and notes that its strength "is the incorporation of non-class based inequalities—specifically race and gender." In other words, this is Marxism updated by the incorporation of modern feminist and left-wing race theories.

The third required text, *Regulating the Poor,* argues that welfare is an instrument of social control of the poor for the benefit of the rich. Coauthor Frances Fox Piven is a well-known Marxist who is the architect of a strategy to bankrupt the welfare system by overloading the welfare rolls, thereby creating a social crisis that would pave the way for revolution. Her National Welfare Rights Organization nearly succeeded in this mission in New York City, until Mayor Rudy Giuliani introduced reform measures that removed the overload from the welfare rolls.[6]

Students in Quan's course are also required to read selections by Cedric Robinson, a proponent of "black Marxism"; Howard Zinn and James and Grace Lee Boggs, all Marxist pamphleteers; Ruth Wilson Gilmore, an activist in Angela Davis's movement against the "prison-industrial complex"; socialist writer Barbara Ehrenreich; and Maoist William Tabb.

There seems to be nothing "empirical" about this course.

Social Protest, Conflict, and Change *JUS 430*[7]

INSTRUCTOR: H. L. T. Quan, Assistant Professor in the School of Justice and Social Inquiry

Nor does Professor Quan attempt anything like a dispassionate academic inquiry in "Social Protest, Conflict, and Change." Her course description reads as follows:

> In this course, we will investigate concepts, theories, and cases that sought to illuminate protest as a social and historical phenomenon, and which sprung countless policy changes, social

> reforms, and even economic and political revolutions. We will investigate the underlying causes and sources of protest as well as its ultimate impact on society at large. We will also ask the following questions: What is the role of social protest in a democratic society? And, what is the relationship between social protest and a human existence that holds justice dear?

What the course will not ask is whether social protest movements actually advance the cause of "justice," or any other question critical of the political Left. And what it will not examine are social protest movements that do not reflect Professor Quan's political preferences. The description announces that "race, gender and class will serve as a critical prism to gauge the complexities of individual motivation, policy impact and societal change," and specifically cites "the U.S. 20th century Civil Rights movements, the labor movements, the anti-war protests, the women's movements," placing special emphasis on "the poor people's movements and women and radical protests."

This is pretty clearly a course in celebrating and emulating the Left. Sure enough, the required readings include two collections of essays written by left-wing radicals to advance their causes—*The Social Movements Reader: Cases and Concepts* and *No Middle Ground: Women and Radical Protest*—and another manifesto by Frances Fox Piven and her coauthor, Richard Cloward: *Poor People's Movements: Why They Succeed, How They Fail.*[8]

Introduction to Justice Studies *JUS 105*[9]

INSTRUCTOR: Judson S. Garrett, Graduate Student in the School of Justice and Social Inquiry

This course, which is required for all Justice majors, purports to "provide an introduction to the study of justice from a social science perspective." But the course description quickly gives the lie to that claim:

> Ancient theorists on justice, such as Plato and Aristotle, viewed justice as both a matter of social harmony as well as personal

> virtue. *Today, we are more inclined to perceive justice as a calculus for the fair distribution and exchange of goods,* primarily focusing on concerns regarding private property and individual liberty. *This sense of justice is expressed in such terms as "economic justice" and "social justice."*[10] [emphasis added]

Although the "we" in this description deceptively implies that justice conceived as "the fair distribution" of goods is now conventional wisdom, it is of course only the "wisdom" of the socialist Left. The Nobel Prize–winning economist Friedrich Hayek wrote an entire book called *The Mirage of Social Justice* to dispute this concept, and of course there is a large body of literature describing the redistribution of goods according to political designs as a great *injustice.* In short, the question of whether economic distribution through the free market is fair and just is hotly contested, and deciding the issue by arbitrarily labeling one side of the argument "justice" is not an intellectually responsible position. But predictably, students in this course are not exposed to alternative viewpoints. Instead they are required to read Barbara Ehrenreich's *Nickel and Dimed: On (Not) Getting by in America* and feminist Debra DeLaet's *The Global Struggle for Human Rights: Universal Principles in World Politics.*

To instruct students in this fashion is itself a form of pedagogical injustice. But instructor Judson Garrett goes even further, declaring that if American society is seen to be "unjust" because income is unequally distributed, then America's entire criminal justice system is illegitimate, because its equal protections enforce an unequal distribution of goods and rewards. Garrett's course description states, "Based on a notion of retributive justice, or imposing a penalty that in some sense balances the harm inflicted by the offense, 'criminal justice' seeks to maintain the equilibrium that already exists in society. But what if society is not already just? If justice dictates that people have a legal and moral right to maintain and develop the advantages they possess over others (e.g., wealth, intelligence, heredity, etc.), then we are . . . forced to . . . ask, 'Is justice simply the interest of the stronger?' "[11] The one required text that deals with the American criminal justice system is titled, tellingly, *The Politics of Injustice: Crime and Punishment in America*.

The course turns the concept of criminality on its head, viewing the definition of what is criminal by the American court system as an instrument of social control to keep in line the classes that receive a smaller distribution of goods and rewards. This is anything but an inquiry into, or a scholarly presentation of, the subject of justice.

Mass Media, Propaganda, and Social Control *JUS 294*[12]

INSTRUCTOR: David L. Altheide, Regents Professor in the School of Justice and Social Inquiry

According to Professor Altheide, the ruling powers and authorities in society artificially construct crises through the media—which they own and dominate—spreading fear in order to control the subordinate classes. In his course description he says that students are expected to "develop a critical understanding of the production, use and consequences of propaganda for social life, and to develop some research, writing, and analytical skills for media investigation. . . . A research project will focus on the characteristics of propaganda in recent wars, including 'terrorism' and the War in Iraq."[13]

The scare quotes around the word "terrorism" are no accident. Altheide's book *Fear and Terrorism* argues that the Bush administration used the 9/11 attacks to "launch a sophisticated propaganda campaign" whose goal was "to scare the American people into giving up civil liberties as well as supporting the war in Iraq."[14] And in the course, he poses the question "Is There Such a Thing as a Good Terrorist?" The point of view of the course is that the term "terrorist" is an instrument of social control used to demonize oppressed people who resist their oppression. Put another way, the Bush administration invented the War on Terror not to fight actual terrorists but to oppress the American masses. Thus students are required to read not only Professor Altheide's own book *Creating Fear: News and the Construction of Crisis,* but also *War, Media, and Propaganda: A Global Perspective,* by Nancy Snow and Yahya Kamalipour. Snow echoes

Altheide's views; the title of her latest book is *Information War: American Propaganda, Free Speech, and Opinion Control Since 9/11.* Kamalipour, meanwhile, is an Iranian leftist who refers to the American government as "the warlords of the global village."[15]

Like so many other courses offered in Arizona State's School of Justice and Social Inquiry, "Mass Media, Propaganda, and Social Control" is itself propaganda.

All About Activism: The Department of Women's Studies

All About Feminism *WS 191*[16]

INSTRUCTOR: Mary Logan Rothschild, Retired Professor of Women and Gender Studies and History

This introductory course on feminism is, in practice, a defense of feminist activism, and illustrates the extent to which the values of political activism have superseded those of scholarship in the Department of Women's Studies (at Arizona State as at so many other institutions). Students in this course are required to read only one text, *Listen Up: Voices from the Next Feminist Generation.* It is not an academic textbook but a collection of first-person political essays by feminist authors who explain and promote "feminist values" (with none offering a critical perspective on feminist politics).

The course instructor, Mary Logan Rothschild, is a feminist activist who sees her academic role as an extension of her political agendas. On a faculty website she describes herself as a "tireless advocate for women's issues and gender equity" and also "dedicated to the retention and promotion of female faculty."

Women in Contemporary Societies *WST 300D*[17]

INSTRUCTOR: Dr. Jill A. Fisher, Assistant Professor of Women and Gender Studies & Consortium for Science Policy and Outcomes

Notwithstanding its claims to the contrary, the "critical thinking" this course endorses is not a healthy skepticism for passionately held ideas, but rather an embrace of them. The course promotes a number of theories informed by feminism, since it deals with "the complex interactions of gender with other variables, such as race, class, age, ethnicity, sexual preference, etc."[18] Once more we see a Women's Studies course based on the familiar claim that differences between the sexes are not natural biological facts but a "social construction"—expressions of a patriarchal system that oppresses women. (One section of the course is titled "Social Construction, Patriarchy, and Feminisms.")

Far from providing a "critical" perspective on feminist theory, the course requires students to read only radical feminist authors, including Angela Davis, Barbara Ehrenreich, Joan Wallach Scott, Naomi Wolf, bell hooks, and Rigoberta Menchu (whose "autobiography" continues to be read in university classrooms long after it was exposed as a Marxist fable and a fraud).[19]

Feminist Voices of Color *Women's Studies 394*[20]

INSTRUCTOR: Dr. Lisa Anderson, Associate Professor of Women and Gender Studies

What the course calls "feminism" is really a species of identity politics, which is outlined and explained in the readings that promote "black lesbian feminism" (*Sister/Outsider*), American Indian feminism (*Off the Reservation*), and Chicana feminism (*Massacre of the Dreamers*). Not one of these can be described as a work of academic scholarship. "Critical race theory," another focus of the course, is yet another ideological construct of the political Left, applying Marxist categories to race. Blacks and other "persons of color" function as the Marxist proletariat in this schema, and because they lack institutional "power," they cannot have racist views or even, in extreme versions, commit crimes.

According to the syllabus, the course considers questions such as: "About what do feminists of color theorize? What have feminists of color contributed to feminism? How does making race and ethnicity explicit change feminism? How do feminists of color deal with issues of sexuality?"[21] These questions might be appropriate to consider on Feminists of Color Pride Day, but they do not have the academic integrity required of a college course.

"Free Peltier!": The American Indian Studies Program

Political activism is also the central focus of the courses in Arizona State's American Indian Studies Program. In the course catalogue, the program is described as emphasizing "scholarly expertise" and grounded in a "broad knowledge of American Indian nations and peoples." In its programmatic goals, however, political rather than scholarly agendas rank high. Some of its goals are to "establish courses and other forms of curriculum, including basic interdisciplinary coursework for the purpose of establishing sensitivity to and enhancing knowledge of cultural diversity in the general student body" and to "identify and more adequately serve the needs of community, Indian nations and organizations."[22]

American Indian Rights: From the American Indian Movement to the Present *American Indian Studies 494*[23]

INSTRUCTOR: Susan A. Miller, Assistant Professor of American Indian Studies

This course is described as a "chronology of American Indian rights advocacy from the early 20th century to the present." What makes the course a noteworthy example of intellectual corruption is that it not only studies political activism but engages in it as well.

To this end, the course includes a section, called "Colonial Justice and the Turn to Diplomacy," that encourages the view that present-day America is an imperialist society and Native Americans are its chief victims. This section focuses on the case of Leonard Peltier,[24] the same American Indian activist and convicted killer who is a subject of the "Rhetoric of Native Americans" course at the University of Texas. Instead of presenting a balanced presentation of the facts of Peltier's case—including that he was convicted and imprisoned for life for the execution-style murder of two FBI agents on the Pine Ridge Reservation in South Dakota—the course requires students to read tributes to Peltier from a number of activist websites that uniformly portray him as an innocent victim of white racism and demand his release. Among them are the crusading sites www.freeleonard.org and www.freepeltier.org.[25] None of the assigned readings provides a fair journalistic, let alone academic, treatment of the case or indicates the basis for Peltier's conviction and repeated denial of parole.

Another section of the course has no obvious connection to American Indians at all, and seems to have been selected primarily for its accordance with the radical political views of the professor. Titled "Indigenous Diplomacy on the International Stage," this section requires students to read the writings of Subcommander Marcos, the onetime leader of Mexico's Communist Zapatista guerrilla movement. Not only are students provided no readings critical of Marcos, but the course description designates the Zapatistas as a "resistance" movement, rather than, for example, a terrorist force.

"Education as a Revolutionary Act": The Department of Chicana and Chicano Studies

The American Indian Studies Program is not the only Arizona State curriculum to reject professional instruction in favor of advocacy for revolutionary Marxist ideals. Courses taught by associate professor John Jota Leaños revolve around his political commitments, which are described in his departmental biography:

> Mr. Leaños is an artist whose main research interests are in studying Digital Culture from Xicana/o, Latina/o perspectives as well as investigating how the university functions as a corporate-paramilitary institution. Mr. Leaños is also interested in the history and study of public art in the form of Xicana/o resistance, Tactical Media, and interventionism.[26]

These themes may be appropriate for a political performance artist, which is what Leaños is—he also has a master's degree in photography from San Francisco State University—but they don't suggest rigorous academic inquiry. And one wonders how Leaños justifies accepting a salary from a university he regards as a "corporate-paramilitary institution."

Chicana/Chicano Popular Culture *CCS 111*[27]

INSTRUCTOR: **John Jota Leaños, Assistant Professor in the Department of Chicana/o Studies**

This course is a good example of the transparently ideological manner in which Leaños teaches. The course description states:

> We will study predominant as well as marginalized theoretical trends of popular culture that will assist us to reflectively engage the social significance and political impact of popular culture. We will examine the influence popular culture has on forming identity, shaping culture and as a mode of revealing, producing and reproducing ideology and political struggle.[28]

Apart from his lack of academic qualifications to assess themes so wide-ranging, Leaños promotes his extreme political views, including the notion that Hispanic culture is actively "marginalized." He also declares that his "approach to teaching is grounded in the ideas of" the Marxist "liberation educator" Páolo Freire, author of *The Pedagogy of the Oppressed,* who "believed that students must be directly engaged in their education as a revolutionary act in a 'quest for mutual humanization.' "[29] In short, Leaños admits that his philosophy of teaching is the Marxist idea that the educator's role is not to impart knowledge but to "liberate" his students from the influence of an oppressive dominant society.

Sympathy for "The Other": The Department of Social and Behavioral Sciences

Im/Migration & Culture *ASB 340; SOC 331; SBS 450*[30]

INSTRUCTOR: Kristin Koptiuch

An equally blunt example of political activism is provided by the course "Im/Migration & Culture" in Arizona State's Department of Social and Behavioral Sciences. This course purports to draw on "empirical research" in order to provide an expansive survey of the social, economic, and political aspects of immigration. But as a list of topics discussed in the course demonstrates, it is actually a radical critique of capitalism and globalization, and its methodology is primarily political. Following are the topics discussed in the course:

- how options to migrate are socially constituted, and examine [*sic*] the recent emergence of "transmigrants" whose lives cut across national boundaries.
- how both long-standing and recent structural processes and international connections underlie contemporary migrations: colonialism, war and military occupation/intervention, development, globalization of labor recruitment and economic interactions, global flows of technology, information, media, and culture.
- major cities as strategic sites in the postcolonial global economy where a multiplicity of migrants, cultures, and identities that have been deterritorialized from local settings all over the world are reterritorialized in urban centers.
- how migrants are situated in and navigate through social processes of migration.
- how migrants negotiate their contradictory experience of being caught between the nation and the globe, and manipulate their diasporic identities to adjust to their shifting positioning.

- how migrants resist their devaluation as Other within nations of settlement, and their subordination within a transnational capitalist system that increasingly depends on their labor even as this contribution appears devalued.
- discourses about im/migration, by policy makers, citizens, and migrants in public and popular culture.
- local, national, and global immigration debates, with an eye to how the cultural hybridity of diasporic communities has challenged native citizens worldwide to re-imagine their own national communities in this transnational era.[31]

These are manifestly not "empirical" approaches. The very notion that there is a "postcolonial global economy" is an ideological construct, and also a logical impossibility in that not all parts of the globe have a recent history of colonial rule. The claim that immigrants constitute a social "Other" and have suffered "devaluation" by the "capitalist system" is little more than left-wing jargon. But more than simply indoctrinating students in left-wing biases—and these only tangentially related to actual immigration, which is driven mainly by opportunities omitted from the subject field of this course—the professor requires them to participate in a field trip intended to reinforce her politics.

The "full-day excursion" takes the class to Nogales, Mexico, across Arizona's southern border. There, students experience an "interview with the US Border Patrol or Grupo Beta (Mexican Border Patrol); visit to a migrant shelter/community center; lunch with families in a *colonia* squatters' settlement; visit to a maquiladora [factory]; exercises such as a market basket survey comparing cost of living on both sides of the border; [and] discussions with migrants and US and Mexican experts and officials about migration issues."[32]

The class travels with BorderLinks, a group the instructor characterizes as a "non-profit educational organization." But BorderLinks is in fact a left-wing advocacy group that, under the rubric of supporting "economic and social justice," blames the plight of Mexican migrants on free-trade agreements between the U.S. and Mexican governments, and on U.S. companies and economic development. The group also publicizes what it claims are "human rights abuses and unconstitutional searches by Border Patrol officials" in the United States. Requiring students to participate in the trip that transparently has more to do with instilling the anticapitalist convictions of groups like BorderLinks than with exposing students to scholarly viewpoints on immigration is the very opposite of what an academic course should do.

"Inherently Political": The Department of African and African-American Studies

Introduction to Ethnic Studies *APA 210/294*[33]

INSTRUCTOR: Karen Kuo, Doctoral Candidate in the Department of English at the University of Washington

Like many courses in Arizona State's Chicano and Native American programs, this introductory course in Ethnic Studies, offered by the Department of African and African-American Studies, makes no effort to conceal an essentially political orientation. The course description asserts that after taking the class students are expected to be "familiar with the various methodological and disciplinary approaches to studying minority communities, *and understand the inherently political nature of such scholarship* [emphasis added]."[34]

The description also notes that "in the context of this course, the term 'ethnic minority group' refers to African Americans, Asian/Pacific Americans, Chicanos/Latinos and American Indians." That "context" omits Jews, Irish, Sri Lankans, Uzbeks, and any number of other ethnic minority groups that the Left has not designated as "oppressed"—or that have not pressured universities into creating Ethnic Studies programs.

A final problem is that the course instructor, a doctoral candidate in English literature, has no academic background in the anthropology, sociology, history, or economics of ethnic groups and hardly seems qualified to lecture on the complex sociohistorical themes on which the course is based.

Minority Group Politics *AFR 494*[35]

INSTRUCTOR: Michael J. Mitchell, Associate Professor of Political Science

A course in "Minority Group Politics" offered through the African and African-American Studies Department might be expected to provide a broad overview of black Americans' historical successes as well as their struggles. Instead, this course promotes an ahistorical assessment that regards the history of African-Americans as one of unrelieved oppression. To this end, the course covers topics such as "Pan-Africanism, Black Nationalism, Marxism, Black Power, Garveyism, Race and Class, Governance, Political Economy, Democracy, Feminism, and Civil Rights." It also elevates radicals with no serious claims to scholarship—such as Huey Newton, a gangster;[36] Stokely Carmichael, an anti-Semite and icon of the racist Nation of Islam;[37] and Angela Davis, winner of the "Lenin Peace Prize"[38]—to the status of important thinkers. All of these "authorities" claim that American blacks are the oppressed victims of institutional racism.

With the exception of Booker T. Washington and A. Philip Randolph, who lived in the era of segregation, the course does not include a single thinker who is not a leftist (and generally an extreme leftist). It includes no black intellectuals such as Thomas Sowell or John McWhorter, who have written extensively on the condition of America blacks but express views that differ widely from those the course prefers.

This is not a course in "Minority Group Politics." It is course in left-wing views of left-wing politics.

(Un)Ruly Voices of African American Women Post Harlem Renaissance *AFH 394*[39]

INSTRUCTOR: Lynette D. Myles, Doctoral Candidate in the English Department

This course is predicated on the assumption that African-American women are dominated by white Americans and by men generally (including black men), and that those "dominant forces" work to " 'silence' and 'erase' them culturally." Black females "have not been heard," according to the course description.[40]

The course focuses on language but is tone-deaf. By encouraging students to analyze language for its political "agency" rather than its literary qualities, the instructor encourages a form of philistinism that is contrary to the very idea of studying literature in the first place.

If the shape of this course were not so predetermined by the instructor's political agendas, it might recognize the tremendous cultural breakthroughs of the past half-century that have resurrected the writings of Zora Neale Hurston and afforded recognition to Toni Morrison (oddly enough, two authors whose works are featured on the course reading list). But such a view would confound the political program that requires blacks and women to function as symbols of racial and gender oppression. One may well ask if there is not something racist in the fact that universities such as Arizona State regard it as acceptable to deny students in African-American and other Ethnic Studies programs a quality academic education but provide them with embittered political boilerplate instead.

Women, Ethnicity, and Equality: Searching for Global Justice *AFS 393*[41]

INSTRUCTOR: Angelita Reyes, Professor of African and African-American Studies and English

The very title of this course reflects its programmatic political agenda. So does the course description, which states that the class "seeks to present, identify and explore," among other things, "injustices linked to gender-oriented struggles for justice and equality."

The course description also says that the class examines "topics that are related to feminisms and women of color cross-culturally through the social constructions of gender, class, ethnicity, critical race theories, and human rights." It is, of course, a cliché among radical academics to say that race, class, and gender are "social constructions," but Professor Reyes's claim for the course description says, "The term 'race' as it is currently used and applied will be challenged through scientific paradigms of current research investigations."[42] But in fact the course includes no scholarship critical of these radical theories, and nothing in Reyes's academic background—she earned her doctorate in Comparative Literature—indicates that she is qualified to lecture on such "scientific paradigms."

Even Professor Reyes's self-described interests—as summarized on her university website—seem more like political passions than areas of study: "Dr. Reyes is particularly interested in the issues of race, class, gender, sexuality and ethnicity—intersectionality. Blending the personal and the historical, the practical and the theoretical, her recent book *Mothering Across Cultures: Postcolonial Representations* explores mothering as a paradigm of progressive feminisms." *Intersectionality* is a mystery. Not so Professor Reyes's intention to subject students to her ideological tics in this course.

Designated Oppressed: The Asian Pacific American Studies Program

Ideology also makes up the core of the Asian Pacific American Studies Program at Arizona State. Although the school describes the program as "interdisciplinary," the disciplines discussed in its courses are little more than the ideological safe houses of the political Left. Symptomatic of this approach is a course titled "Asian Pacific American Genders and Sexualities,"[43] which, according to the course catalogue, is an "exploration of gender and sexuality issues as they relate to Asian Pacific American experiences, including interracial relationships; stereotypes, feminism, queer theory." There is much evidence of ideological perspectives in this course, but very little evidence of scholarship.

Special Topics: Asian Pacific American Legal History

APA 394[44]

INSTRUCTOR: John P. Rosa, Assistant Professor of Asian Pacific American Studies

The catalogue description notes that this course is a "social/cultural history" that "examines immigration laws, civil rights legislation, and popular trials regarding Asian Americans and Pacific islanders since 1790." The description then reveals that this is not an academic course about history or law, but an undisguised exercise in political proselytizing, since it states that the class "draws upon progressive legal scholarship dealing with race, personal legal narratives, and documentary films in order to study a range of 'API' [i.e., Asian Pacific Islander] experiences within the larger framework of racial paradigms in the U.S."[45] That is to say, the course treats left-wing "progressive" legal theories as authoritative, and individual opinions as the equivalent of scholarship.

Does the "Asian Pacific Islander" category include Japanese-Americans, who have long been the second-richest ethnic group in America, exceeding in average income White Anglo-Saxon Protestants?[46] Of course not, because the category, like the course, is political and was specifically designed to create a "disadvantaged" and therefore "oppressed" group.

Although the Arizona Board of Regents explicitly forbids university employees from allowing their interest in a particular "political issue to affect the objectivity of their teaching," this injunction is routinely ignored at Arizona State University, whose classrooms are plagued by problems of left-wing radicalism and political indoctrination. Such problems are similarly evident far to the east, at Temple University in Philadelphia.

8

Temple of Conformity

TEMPLE UNIVERSITY
TUITION: $10,859 IN-STATE
$19,878 OUT-OF-STATE

Temple University is a rare bright spot in the troubled "city that loves you back." Even though Philadelphia has one of the highest murder rates in the country, some 34,000 students flock to this commuter school, situated in one of its urban centers, because of its distinguished academic record. Recent surveys place Temple ahead of top public schools in Pennsylvania and neighboring New Jersey. Among its many successes is the Fox School of Business and Management, which is the largest business school east of the Mississippi and which offers one of the leading entrepreneurship programs in the country.

In 2005, when the Pennsylvania legislature created a Select Committee on Academic Freedom to study the state's public universities—including Temple—it declared academic freedom to be "indispensable to American colleges and universities" and that such freedom is "likely to thrive in an environment of intellectual diversity." These are nice sentiments, but at Temple this "indispensable" freedom is conspicuously lacking, and its academic programs reflect lockstep thinking rather than intellectual diversity.

Consider, for instance, the "writing-intensive two-year course sequence" called "Intellectual Heritage" that Temple requires all students to take. On the program's web page professors post some thirty different sample exam and study questions under the title "Faculty Perspectives on Marx."[1] Every one, without exception, prompts students to explain what Marx said in the way one might explain the theories of Copernicus, whose hypotheses have been confirmed by real world experiments. In contrast, all Marxist experiments in the real world have failed—in fact, they have caused the economic impoverishment of whole continents, man-made famines, and human suffering on an unprecedented scale—and yet not one of the professors contributing to the Intellectual Heritage guides bothers to note this historical fact.

In one sample guideline, a professor writes: "Marx presents an astute understanding and critique of Capitalism. Is it convincing?" The question does not say, "Marx analyzed capitalism. Is his analysis convincing?" That would have been educational. Instead, the student is effectively told what to think: *Marx wrote a wise critique of capitalism. Are you stupid enough to disagree with him?* What if the student is not convinced and encounters that question on an exam? Since he has been forewarned that the professor thinks Marx is "astute," will the student risk saying that Marx was catastrophically wrong, that his unfounded attacks on capitalism led to the creation of regimes that were among the most oppressive and destructive in human history, and that his professor is living in an intellectual Never-Never-Land? Or is he going to humor the professorial prejudice and maximize his chances of getting a decent grade?

Another Intellectual Heritage professor, who is also the chairman of the Political Science Department, provides an extensive study guide that denies in so many words that the awful acts committed in the name of Marx have anything to do with Marx or his ideas. "The collapse of authoritarian communism," he writes, "means the death of Marxist-Leninism [which] has little to do with classical Marxism." This would be news to millions of very intelligent people—including Lenin himself and such intellectual luminaries as Gyorgy Lukacs, Antonio Gramsci, Louis Althusser, and Eric Hobsbawm—who thought authoritarian communism was Marx's plan. At the very least the relationship between classical Marxism and Marxism-

Leninism is a much-debated issue. It is, therefore, an issue worthy of academic inquiry, not of a sweeping, unsupported statement that the two had "little to do" with each other.

The faculty guides to Marx on the Intellectual Heritage website fail in every respect to live up to the standards of basic academic inquiry. They offer no critical literature on Marx and Marxism, no writings by von Mises, Kolakowski, Sowell, Malia, Richard Pipes, or any other scholarly critics of Marxism. Nor do they confront the connection between Marx's ideas and the vastly destructive effect of Marxist societies, which murdered 100 million human beings and created unimaginable poverty on a continental scale.

Only two Intellectual Heritage professors suggest even the slightest critical approach to Marxist theory. Professor Stephen Zelnick's guide indicates how capitalist societies have responded to Marx's challenge in a way that reflects positively on their flexibility, and negatively, therefore, on Marx's "astute" analysis. And Professor Marc Stier has also provided a guide, called "Failure of Revolutions," that addresses the fact that Marx's predictions about revolution have been refuted by history.

But this is the way Professor Stier sets up his discussion and defines how it will proceed: "We can understand the failure of a revolution to occur as Marx predicted in Marx's terms. The conditions that Marx expected to bring about a revolution did not arise. And we can give a powerful social class-based explanation of the failure of those conditions to arise." In other words, even though Marx was wrong, and catastrophically wrong, he was actually right—because the proper conditions for the revolution he prescribed did not exist. Not to worry, then: we can still be Marxists—or neo-Marxists—and employ "powerful social class-based" explanations of historical events.

An intellectually defensible discussion of Marxism, one suited to an academic classroom, might include the following question, "If Marx failed to foresee the conditions that would end capitalism correctly, might not his entire theory of capitalism be false, including the 'powerful social class-based explanations' of capitalism he offered?" But the Intellectual Heritage Program has ruled a truly academic discussion of

Marx out-of-bounds from the start. As the Political Science Department chairman explains, "One of the main problems in studying Karl Marx is that most contemporary theorists interpret Marx in their way—the point is to interpret Marx in his way." In other words, students are to approach Marx not as critics of Marx but as acolytes of Marx.

Like the Intellectual Heritage Program, another general requirement at Temple, the First-Year Writing Program, fails to observe basic academic standards. The program, run by the English Department and taught mainly by graduate students, is designed "to provide Temple students with a comprehensive experience of writing to learn and learning to write." The "writing to learn" part of the course has less to do with teaching students to master the English language than with instilling radical views on gender, and to a lesser extent, on race. The required texts for the program are ideological in nature.

The official course handbook candidly acknowledges that the sociological topics covered in the class are complex: "We will be using gender (and gender roles in American culture) . . . because it is both relatively simple (everybody has one) and extremely complex in terms of how gender impacts people's lives and identities, feelings, and behaviors." But if this is "an extremely complex" subject, why is it being taught by instructors of English Literature, amateurs who have no professional training in the subject, and why do the readings overwhelmingly reflect only one (radical) perspective on what is admittedly a controversial issue? If the task is to teach students how to write, the texts should be composed of writers who know how to write, not writers picked for the presumed correctness of their political views—namely, radical feminists and radical agitators.

Still another required program that fails to meet basic tests of intellectual diversity and academic professionalism is the summer reading program for all incoming freshmen. Between 2002, when the summer reading requirement was instituted, and 2007, five of the six texts Temple assigned its freshmen represented radical left-wing viewpoints, while the other fit fairly comfortably within a left-wing frame of reference.

In 2002, for example, Temple's required summer reading book was *Fast Food Nation*, by Eric Schlosser. The author was invited to campus to speak to students and was paid a substantial fee for doing so. *Fast Food Nation* is an assault on the fast-food industry by a left-wing ideologue at war with the free-market system. It was selected by the *Guardian,* England's left-wing daily, as one of the top ten "anti-capitalist books." While there is nothing wrong with assigning an anticapitalist text on a reading list, there is no excuse for requiring all incoming freshmen to read only one side of such a controversial subject.

The required book for 2003 was *Lies My Teacher Told Me*, by James Loewen, who also was invited to Temple to speak and was part of a panel sponsored by the History, Social Studies, and Education Departments. As noted in Chapter 4, this book is a radical diatribe against the United States, arguing that "we are all dupes, manipulated by elite white male capitalists who orchestrate how history is written."[2] Again, the problem is not assigning a book, even one as historically illiterate and malicious as this one. The problem is that it was the only book Temple freshmen were required to read that year with the imprimatur of the institution.

In 2004 the required book was *Caucasia,* a novel by Danzy Senna told from the perspective of an African-American girl named Birdie in the 1970s who is dealing with the racial issues of the time. The official theme for Temple freshmen that year was "Color and Character," so not only was Senna invited to campus, but also forty professors led first-year students in small discussion groups on the topic during the first three weeks of the fall semester. *Caucasia* reflects a narrowly left-wing viewpoint, with the main characters advancing the book's political agendas. Birdie's mother is an anticapitalist radical on the run from the FBI, and her father is a "Black Power" intellectual. A main character says, "We got to raise our children to know how to fight. There's a war going on . . . we got pigs in the White House, and pigs patrolling the streets."[3] Birdie's mother describes immigration authorities as "Fascist murderers, monsters,"[4] and excoriates television news for "spreading lies about Castro."[5] She justifies terror, praising the actions of a radical who blew up a police car, saying, "We live in disgrace. We slaughter our own and we slaughter people overseas who don't think or look like us . . . and the only way to get people's attention is to do something drastic."[6] Birdie herself says, "My mother swore that I'd be the first child raised and educated free of racism, patriarchy, and capitalism."[7] The extremist views in this book parallel—perhaps even exceed—the left-wing ideas of Loewen's and Schlosser's texts.

In 2005 Temple assigned its incoming freshmen *West of Kabul, East of New York,* an autobiographical account of the writer Tamim Ansary's experiences in a biracial family—his mother Caucasian, his father an Afghan. This book is not ideological like the others, but neither did it provide much-needed intellectual diversity to the program.

For 2006, Temple chose *When the Emperor Was Divine,* by Julie Otsuka. Here is the school's description: "This piece depicts the struggle of a Japanese-American family sent to an internment camp during World War II. Otsuka has received praise for her poignant and personal prose describing an 'uncertain time' in American history. As you read, you are forced to consider your own cultural and ethnic identity, as well as your responsibility to the community and to your understanding of citizenship."

In other words, citizenship is to be learned by reviewing a dark chapter in American history when, during war conditions, the United States took steps to intern Japanese nationals and Japanese-Americans who it was feared would be loyal to the emperor—something every other Allied power did, including Canada. Fair enough. But aren't the sacrifices that Americans made in the war itself—rescuing all of Asia from the horrors of Japanese imperialism and military occupation, establishing democracy in Japan—also important in considering one's own cultural and ethnic identity, as well as one's responsibility to the community and "understanding of citizenship"? Where is the assigned reading about America's "greatest generation," and why are students consistently being exposed to only one side of the argument on matters as important and controversial as these?

In 2007, the selection was *Black Ice,* a 1991 memoir by black author and activist Lorene Cary. The book expresses Cary's longtime conviction that America's white communities harbor latent feelings of racism against blacks. Although the book's narrative, centering primarily on the author's time at a prestigious and mainly white boarding school in New England, to which she was awarded a generous scholarship, might suggest that racism has greatly receded as a social force, the author insists that the opposite is the case. Everywhere at the school she detects signs of veiled racism, and considers her very presence there a betrayal to her black culture. As she recounts in a typical section, "One teacher, by way of correcting a young student's paper, commented on the pattern of grammatical errors and warned the boy that he'd have to overcome his black English. We suspected, after reading several papers, that our teachers typically judged black 'errors' more harshly than others, and that once obsessed by idiom they lost sight of black students' ideas."[8]

Thus, for Cary, even teachers' attempts to teach proper grammar become evidence of racial bigotry. Similarly, when interviewed about her book, Cary described it as "part of a tradition that starts with the slave narratives," as though her privileged life and mostly imagined grievances were somehow a continuation of the real oppression once borne by black Americans.

A generous interpretation of Temple's freshman summer reading program would hold that the university chooses radical texts merely to provoke stimulating discussion. But if that were the case, wouldn't critical questions about the books be formally included in the syllabus? Wouldn't critics of the books also be invited to campus along with the authors to stimulate such a discussion? It seems that intellectual dialogue is precisely not what the administrators of this program are looking for.

A contributing factor to this problem is that at Temple University, as at so many other colleges, professors with a conservative or libertarian viewpoint appear to be a rare breed. A number of recent scientific studies have shown that nationwide, the ratio of liberals to conservatives in the liberal arts professoriate ranges from 10 to 1 to 30 to 1.

Professor Stephen Zelnick, a former vice provost at Temple and former chairman of its English Department, testified at Pennsylvania's academic freedom hearings about the stunning lack of intellectual diversity at his school: "As director of two undergraduate programs, I have had many opportunities to sit in and watch instructors. I have sat in on more than a hundred different teachers' classes and . . . have rarely heard a kind word for the United States, for the riches of our marketplace, for the vast economic and creative opportunities made available for energetic and creative people (that is, for our students); for family life, for marriage, for love, or for religion."[9]

A careful investigation into the Temple University curriculum shows that Zelnick was not exaggerating.

Liberating the Race: The Department of African-American Studies

If a German American Studies Department at Temple taught its subject exclusively from an "Aryan perspective" and instructed students that Aryans were a global community bound by blood, and that Germany was the center of world history, what would be the reaction? Suppose that this same department had an introductory course required of all majors, which stated its teaching philosophy in these words:

> As Aryan people, our strengths are found in the creation of communities. Whether these communities are on Broad and Erie [in Philadelphia], in Mesopotamia, on South Street or the classroom, we are building Aryan communities. *Our energy, spirit and blood bond us as an Aryan community.* As an Aryan community, during this course, we will engage many topics that will aid us in the further liberation of Aryan people. The goal, first and foremost, is to *allow* these experiences to contribute in our growth and development as Aryan people. The classroom is the community, the reading materials are our map, and Aryan consciousness is our guide. Let us continue the process of Aryan liberation!

Of course, Temple has no German-American Studies Department. The above paragraph is the "teaching philosophy" of the introductory course in "Afrikan American Studies" at Temple University. The statement actually reads, "We are building Afrikan communities . . . the reading materials are our map, and Afrikan consciousness is our guide. Let us continue the process of Afrikan liberation!"[10]

This is the program of a political and racial movement (complete with the eccentric spelling "Afrikan"). Forging a blood community across continents is anything but an academic or scholarly mission.

Temple's Department of African-American Studies has long been notorious for its ideological narrowness, its racism, and its lack of credible scholarship—all present from the moment it was conceived as a department. The department's central doctrine is "Afrocentricity," which the eminent classical scholar Mary Lefkowitz, the Andrew W. Mellon Professor in the Humanities (emeritus) at Wellesley College, characterizes as the teaching of "myths disguised as history."[11] As noted in Chapter 2, Professor Lefkowitz's book *Not Out of Africa* is a devastating indictment of the fraudulent nature of Afrocentric "scholarship." In that book she writes; "There is little or no historical substance to many of the Afrocentrists' most striking claims about the ancient world. There is no evidence that Socrates, Hannibal, and Cleopatra had African ancestors. There is no archaeological data to support the notion that Egyptians migrated to Greece during the second millennium B.C. (or before that). There is no reason to think that Greek religious practices originated in Egypt. . . . Other assertions are not merely unscientific; they are false. Democritus could not have copied his philosophy from books stolen from Egypt by Anaxarchus, because he had died many years before Alexander's invasion [of Egypt]. Aristotle could not have stolen his philosophy from books in the library at Alexandria, because the library was not built until [fifty years] after his death. There never was such thing as an Egyptian Mystery System (which is a central part of Afrocentrist teaching)."

Lefkowitz specifically cites Temple University professor Molefi Asante, the individual most responsible for bringing Afrocentricity into both the public sphere and the classroom. An "African-American liberationist," Asante served as chair of Temple's African-American Studies Department from 1984 to 1996 and remains a professor in the program. He acknowledges that when he designed the African-American Studies graduate program at Temple—the nation's first Ph.D. program in African-American Studies—he built the curriculum around Afrocentric theory: "There already existed Masters programs [in African-American Studies] at Cornell University, Ohio State University, UCLA, Yale, SUNY-Albany, and Atlanta University. What was different in my conception was the elevation of the Afrocentric paradigm as the instrument to guide programmatic development."[12]

In his book *Kemet, Afrocentricity, and Knowledge* (1990), Asante writes that the achievement of Afrocentric theory was to free people of African descent from their dependence on Eurocentric frames of reference. Asante argues that "the objectivity of knowledge referred to by European scholars could not be separated from the consciousness of the social-cultural world and that Europeans brought that consciousness with them whenever they discussed Africa." This, as Lefkowitz observes, is a form of intellectual racism: "Asante appears to be saying that no one need believe anything that any European says about Africa."[13]

The Temple department that Asante shaped not only promulgates Afrocentric theory but also provides a home for political activists. For instance, the department until recently offered a course called "Mass Media and the Black Community," which was described as an "examination of the peculiar role mass media plays in the African American community." The course was taught by Professor Ella Forbes, since retired, whose apprehension of the media's role may well be described as peculiar: she believes that American media outlets are institutionally biased against blacks and promote solely the interests of whites. "From our own experience of oppression we've developed a much greater skepticism of the government," Forbes has said. "The major media outlets are seen as just further extensions of the government and a puppet of white public opinion." Professor Forbes is certainly entitled to her opinion; she is not entitled to make it the theme of her course, as the course description for "Mass Media and the Black Community" suggests that she did.

Temple's African-American Studies Department is also busy credentialing the next generation of professors to spread its cultic thinking to other schools. One of the department's products is Karanja Keita Carroll, who taught "Introduction to African American Studies," "Dimensions of Racism," and "Psychology of the African American Experience" at Temple while earning his doctorate in the department. Carroll subscribes to many of Afrocentrism's racist theories. For example, he has written in defense of the "melanin theory" used by some of the more extreme Afrocentrists to make a pseudoscientific claim for the racial supremacy of blacks. A grotesque distortion of the scientific literature, this theory posits that melanin, a pigment responsible for skin color, also endows blacks with a wide range of superior genetic traits and abilities. Accordingly, Carroll has written that melanin is responsible for making African blacks "spirit-focused," while Europeans are "material-focused" and "patriarchal."[14] In addition to the racist idea that skin color—the lack of melanin—leads to white patriarchy, the idea that African cultures are somehow not patriarchal (or less patriarchal) is so astonishingly ignorant as to take one's breath away.

Carroll also adheres to a distinctly conspiratorial view of the field of psychology. In particular, he considers psychology to be a form of "Western oppression" used to subjugate the "Afrikan diasporic community."[15] Consequently, carrying this view to a racial extreme, he believes that to study psychology from anything other than an "African perspective" is to do the bidding of these oppressive forces: "If you aren't studying from the African perspective, then just whose perspective are you using?"[16] Carroll claims that the psychology of blacks is fundamentally different from that of whites: "There is no such thing as an Oedipus complex for African people. It comes from a distinctive cultural perspective that we simply don't have."[17] Carroll has also claimed that the roots of the word "psychology"—often and accurately attributed to the Greek word "psyche"—actually come from African culture. "But they aren't going to tell you that in a traditional psychology class," he has said.[18] Notably, Carroll has no prior academic background in psychology. But that has not kept him from teaching courses on "black psychology" at the State University of New York at New Paltz, where he is now a lecturer in the Department of Black Studies.

It was Carroll whose syllabus for "Introduction to African American Studies" implored students to "continue the process of Afrikan liberation!" The course focused on "Afrikan American Studies within an Afrikan conceptual framework (i.e. the Afrikan worldview) via the paradigm of Afrocentricity." Carroll required students in this class to read *Introduction to Black Studies,* by Maulana Karenga.[19] A self-proclaimed "African socialist," Karenga founded the 1960s militant black power organization the United Slaves and spent four years in prison after being convicted of torturing two of his female disciples. He also created the holiday Kwanzaa and its underlying philosophy, called Kawaida. According to Karenga, Kawaida, which is covered in the text required for Carroll's course, borrows from "early Chinese and Cuban socialism," with Kawaida practitioners believing that one's race "determines life conditions, life chances and self-understanding." In the preface to *Introduction to Black Studies,* Karenga admits that the text is "self-consciously Afrocentric," and "demands that Black Studies root itself in the African experience."

Carroll indoctrinated Temple students in Afrocentrism in "Psychology of the African American Experience" and "Dimensions of Racism" as well. He began the syllabus for each class (in different semesters) with a quote from Afrocentric psychologist Amos N. Wilson:

> I have to warn my students time and time again that when you enter my classes you are not going to be comfortable. . . . I am here to make you suffer because, if you are in any class, particularly a social science class and you are comfortable, chances are that you are being lied to. It is in these classes that you must attain a confrontation with yourself, with reality and where you must attain a confrontation with the lying world that has created you in terms of who and what you are now. You must confront the nature of this *beast* called *education,* of which you are a part,

> and how it is going to transform you into a beast; how you then must become conscious of what it is doing to you, and against you, so that you may escape its planned destiny for you.[20]

For "Dimensions of Racism," Carroll required students to read a book authored by Wilson titled *Falsification of Afrikan Consciousness: Eurocentric History, Psychiatry, and the Politics of White Supremacy*. The objective of the book is to expose "the role Eurocentric history-writing plays in rationalizing European oppression of Afrikan peoples and in the falsification of Afrikan consciousness." It contends that "the alleged mental and behavioral maladaptiveness of oppressed Afrikan peoples is a political-economic necessity for the maintenance of White domination and imperialism."[21]

While Carroll has moved on from Temple, he continues preaching his Afrocentrist gospel—as do former colleagues who are still teaching Temple University students.

Egyptian Language and Culture *AAS 415*[22]

INSTRUCTOR: Molefi Kete Asante, Professor in the Department of African-American Studies

According to the syllabus he has provided for the graduate-level course "Egyptian Language and Culture," Professor Asante seeks to address "the language and culture of ancient Kemet [Egypt]" by advancing "[a]n Afrocentric methodology applicable to an Africological interpretation of cosmological, epistemological, axiological and aesthetic phenomena." His course description states:

> Ancient Egyptian Language and Culture is not strictly a language course but rather an Afrocentric experience in ferreting out the interstices between language and action in a Nile Valley culture. . . . Students completing this course should have a general overview of the history of ancient Kemet, . . . and an appreciation of Kemet's place as one of the classical civilizations of Africa.[23]

But as the syllabus makes abundantly clear, the course goes far beyond a "general overview" of Kemet culture. The essential foundation of the course is the much-disputed claim that Kemet was really an African civilization; mainstream classical scholars regard Kemet as an Ancient Egyptian and Greek civilization, but students are nevertheless expected to share the professor's controversial view:

> It is important that Kemet be placed in its African context otherwise almost none of the concepts that we discuss in this course will make any sense to you as they did not make any sense to many of the early European Egyptologists. Indeed, as we shall see, many contemporary European writers on Kemet have little understanding of what they see because they have refused to see Kemet for what it was, an African civilization.[24]

Apart from its dubious debt to history, the identification of Kemet with Africa is also grammatically suspect, as Robert Morkot, an archaeologist specializing in Egypt, has noted in his book *The Egyptians*: "Kemet means 'black' and is generally taken to mean the land that is covered by silt during the inundation of the Nile. Many Afrocentrist writers have argued that Kemet defines Egypt as 'the land of the black people,' but this is a grammatically incorrect reading. That Kemet means the land rather than people is further confirmed by its use in contrast to D*e*SHR*e*T, the 'red,' a term for the areas beyond cultivation, continuing into the deserts."[25]

Asante's course actively excludes such alternative scholarly perspectives, in effect stifling students' capacity to reach independent conclusions. This is the very definition of indoctrination.

Activists Unlimited: The Institute for the Study of Race and Social Thought

As counterparts to the Department of African-American Studies, Temple University also administers several research institutes through its College of Liberal Arts. Although nominally apolitical, these institutions in both the scope of their research and the nature of their organized events resemble nothing so much as left-wing political groups. The Institute for the Study of Race and Social Thought, for instance, was founded in 2005 by Temple philosophy professor Lewis Gordon, whose academic research interests include "Africana philosophy, philosophy of human and life sciences, phenomenology, philosophy of existence, social and political theory, postcolonial thought, theories of race and racism, philosophies of liberation, aesthetics, philosophy of education, and philosophy of religion."[26] Under Professor Gordon's leadership, the center has become a university-sponsored outlet for his ideological prejudices, not least his determination to make political activism an integral part of Temple's academic curriculum.

The institute's inaugural symposium, in the spring of 2005, was titled "Transgressing Racial and Sexual Boundaries in the 21st Century," and aimed to "engage both theorists and activists on the importance of racial and sexual intersections in a trans-global economy and the necessity for building partnerships." Also in 2005, the institute held a conference titled "Black Civil Society in American Political Life." Organized around the polemical theme that blacks in America remain victims of societal injustice requiring radical social change, the conference was made up exclusively of academics, such as Martin Kilson and Cornel West, who supported the ideological claims that racial and class oppression were determining factors in the life of black Americans.[27]

In 2006, the institute dispensed altogether with the pretense of scholarship and played host to Ewuare Osayande. According to a description provided by the institute, Osayande was an "independent scholar and activist" and a "central figure in the social justice movement" in Philadelphia. In fact, Osayande has never written a work of scholarship and is best known as a member of the Black Radical Congress, a Communist group. Osayande is somewhat notorious for his views that the United States is the "axis of evil," that racism is "inherent" in the American system, and that the current U.S. government is guilty of the "re-enslavement of the African American community."

Casting additional light on its nonacademic agendas, the institute hosted "Heretical Nietzsche Studies." The event centered not on the merit of the nihilistic philosopher's work but on his influence on various movements associated with the American Left. It concentrated on "Nietzsche's political thinking, his views on religion, his relation to feminism and the critique of gender, his growing impact on race and postcolonial studies, and his ongoing contributions to French post-structural thought." At no point has the institute included academics whose views on racial, social, or political issues do not accord with those of Professor Gordon. Consequently, although the institute's mission statement states that it "supports and conducts inquiry into the dynamics of race and its relations to the social world," in practice it blocks real academic inquiry.

Racism Is "Like Smog in the Air": The Department of Sociology

Urban Society: "Race," Class, and Gender in the City

GUS R055[28]

INSTRUCTOR: Professor Melissa Gilbert, Associate Professor of Geography

The syllabus for this course makes plain its intention to promote a radical perspective in which race, class, and gender hierarchies constitute the central structures of society, making the conclusion that American society in general and white people, and free-market capitalism in particular, are oppressive. The course then instructs students that radical activist movements are the solution to these systemic oppressions.

The first section of the course is called "The Social Construction of 'Race': Racism and White Privilege." Its central idea—really a radical academic cliché—is that white oppressors have created the concept of "race" in order to oppress nonwhite people. The assigned texts exclusively subscribe to this view. Among them is an essay titled "Defining Racism: 'Can We Talk?'," by Beverly Daniel Tatum. Its central argument is that racism is omnipresent in American society and that any suggestion to the contrary is a function either of ignorance or of white racism. Here is a representative passage:

> Prejudice is one of the inescapable consequences of living in a racist society. Cultural racism—the cultural images and messages that affirm the assumed superiority of Whites and the assumed inferiority of people of color—is like smog in the air. Sometimes it is so thick it is visible, other times it is less apparent, but always, day in and day out, we are breathing it in.[29]

This ideological message is reinforced by another reading assignment, Peggy McIntosh's "White Privilege: Unpacking the Invisible Knapsack":

> It seems to me that obliviousness about white advantage, like obliviousness about male advantage, is kept strongly inculturated in the United States so as to maintain the myth of meritocracy, the myth that democratic choice is equally available to all. Keeping most people unaware that freedom of confident action is there for just a small number of people props up those in power and serves to keep power in the hands of the same groups that have most of it already.[30]

The views expressed in these assigned texts are themselves racist—and crudely so, given their refusal to provide tangible evidence for their malicious charges against whites. Moreover, they have nothing at all to do with the course's nominal subjects—geography and urban studies—and their inclusion in this course is a testament to the political agendas of its instructor, Professor Melissa Gilbert.

It is on the foundation of such transparently political and ideological claims that the entire course stands. The next section of the course is headed "The Social Construction of Gender and Defining Racism and Sexism." Here the class lessons advance that old chestnut of Women's Studies programs nationwide—the ideological claim that differences between men and women are "constructed" by society with the aim of oppressing women. Students are accordingly compelled to read texts making the case for the "Social Construction of Gender" and the "Social Construction of Sexuality" as well as more polemical essays that assert the oppression of women in American society as an established fact. The opening sentence in one of these essays, "Oppression" by the feminist author Marilyn Frye, declares, "It is a fundamental claim of feminism that women are oppressed."[31]

Professor Gilbert's course moves on to "The Social Construction of Class Inequalities and 'Race,' Gender, and Class as Interlocking Systems." Only then does it get to the "urban" subject matter that is supposed to be the subject of the course: "Internal Structure of U.S. Cities: Institutional Racism." The lessons are buttressed by readings that portray the American educational, health-care, and justice systems, American employers, and American municipal structures as "racist" and oppressive toward women and nonwhites. As Professor Gilbert's website notes, she approaches her subject through the frameworks of "feminist geography" as well as "feminist and critical race theory."

Urban matters are then left behind for an aggressively one-sided discussion of—or more accurately, attack on—globalization (i.e., international capitalism). Reading assignments for this section include an essay called "The Real 'New World Order': The Globalization of Racial and Ethnic Relations in the Late Twentieth Century," in which author Nestor Rodriguez describes slavery as an example of "historical capitalist influence on inter-group relations" and claims that "the racist ideological foundations laid by northern European white males continue to frame issues of race relations today."[32] All the other required texts are critical of globalization as well, and in case some students have difficulty with written texts, they are also required to watch *Roger and Me*, an anticorporate propaganda film by Michael Moore.[33]

The indoctrination continues with assignments that promote left-wing activism. After watching the documentary *Poverty Outlaw,* which is premised on the claim that insufficient welfare payments are the driving cause of urban poverty, students are required to read

"Building Coalitions Among Communities of Color: Beyond Racial Identity Politics," by Columbia University professor Manning Marable, the Marxist activist who serves as a member of Angela Davis's American Communist Party splinter group the Committees on Correspondence.[34] Another piece of radical political propaganda students are required to read is the article "Interrupting the Cycle of Oppression: The Role of Allies as Agents of Change," by social activist and self-described "anti-racism educator" Andrea Ayvazian, who despairs of the "many forms of systemic oppression" that have left people "immobilized, uncertain about what actions we can take to interrupt the cycles of oppression and violence that intrude on our everyday lives."[35] In addition, students must read an article by socialist Harold Meyerson that praises the Service Employees International Union, the largest labor union in the AFL-CIO, because it "has understood that the only real power of the poor is the power to disrupt. And no other union has channeled that disruption in so brilliant and productive a way."[36] And finally Gilbert assigns a piece whose title telegraphs its political perspective—"Sweats and Tears: A Protest Is Sweeping U.S. Campuses to End the Use of Sweatshops to Produce College-Endorsed Clothes."

Professor Gilbert has made clear that she is not interested simply in having students read about left-wing political activism; like many other radical professors, she is a proponent of making "service learning" a key component of the curriculum. For Professor Gilbert this means encouraging her students to join "community organizations," particularly those committed to "grassroots efforts at social transformation."[37]

Sociology of Race and Racism *Sociology RO59*[38]

INSTRUCTOR: Anne Shlay, Professor of Sociology, undergraduate director of the sociology program

In its description this course repudiates ideology in principle only to promote it in practice:

> In the U.S., we think we know race and ethnicity because we can see different skin colors, hear different languages, and have been told that our "people" came from either here or there. But this type of knowledge is really ideology—a set of ideas that comes from a particular social vantage point, not truth per se. And it is the sociology of race and ethnicity that can add layers of understanding about ever changing ideas about difference and identity.

So according to the course instructor, Professor Anne Shlay, an obsessive concern with race and ethnicity will discover the truth that a simplistic ideology based on race and ethnicity will not. America's pluralistic ideologies of diversity and equal rights are really masks for racism.

The description of this supposedly nonideological course goes on to state that the American society is built on a "social hierarchy defined by race and ethnicity" that "validates patterns of privilege and disadvantage, and therefore, makes race and ethnic inequality seem both appropriate and valid." The course does not explain how such a hierarchy could be "defined" by race when de jure racial hierarchies were outlawed by the Thirteenth, Fourteenth, and Fifteenth Amendments and eliminated in practice by the Civil Rights Acts of the 1960s and the agencies, such as the Equal Employment Opportunity Commission, created to enforce them. There are no institutional hierarchies based on race, because any institution that supported them would be sued by the NAACP, the ACLU, and a dozen other groups and would be prosecuted by the Department of Justice.

According to this course, race itself is "socially constructed and politically utilized" by the white racist rulers of this hierarchy to oppress the ruled. Students in this class, in addition to examining "the construction of racial and ethnic identities, the roots of different forms of prejudiced thinking, [and] the historical record on discrimination," learn about "how religion and ethnicity have blended to create a new racial concept—Whiteness." The course description explains that the class will "examine the concept of White privilege." This concept of "white privilege" is also an ideological claim. What white privilege protected the Duke lacrosse players from being crucified for a year by their own school, the American court system, and the national media?

This course is a textbook example of indoctrination, in which a fringe ideology is drilled into a captive and defenseless student audience as a truth beyond dispute: the professor's dubious claims concerning racial hierarchies and white privilege are the only views taught. Indeed, all three required books echo the professor's ideological and political premises. From *Rethinking the Color Line: Readings in Race and Ethnicity,* students must read essays by Marxist anthropologist Marvin Harris, pro-Castro educator Jonathan Kozol, Marxist historian Howard Zinn, former Black Panther Angela Davis, and radical law professor David Cole.[39] From the second book, *White Privilege: Essential Readings on the Other Side of Racism*, Professor Shlay assigns readings by radical feminists Peggy McIntosh and bell hooks, Marxist journalism professor Robert Jensen, and radical race activist Tim Wise.[40] And the third required text, *Racial and Ethnic Groups*, by Richard Schaefer, is a sociology textbook that treats the experience of racial and ethnic minorities in the United States as one of unremitting subjugation. Typical sections in the book bear titles like "Exploitation Theory," "Trends in Prejudice," "Hate Crimes," "The Mood of the Oppressed," "Understanding Discrimination," and "White Privilege."[41]

Confronting the "American Nightmare": The Department of History

Dissent in America *HIST 184*[42]

INSTRUCTOR: Ralph Young, Senior Lecturer in the Department of History

Much as the study of geography and urban studies has become, under Professor Gilbert's direction, a left-wing political project, so too has the study of history in the classroom of Professor Ralph Young. An antiwar activist who has staged department-wide teach-ins to protest the Iraq War, Young uses his classes to promote his interest in what he calls political "dissent" but which is actually radical causes of an extreme nature. In a 2004 interview, when asked how Communist folk singer Woody Guthrie would view contemporary American politics, Young replied, "Above all he'd be sickened over American policy (both foreign and domestic) today. He was against 'Hitlerism and fascism homemade and imported,' and I'm sure he'd think what we're suffering through right now is 'Homemade Hitlerism.' "[43]

Young's course is not so much a study of dissent, therefore, as it is an immersion in radical paranoia with the idea of creating radicals from among his students. Among the subjects the class touches on are: the antiwar movement in its opposition to various American military engagements; the feminist movement in its opposition to American patriarchy; radical and communist movements in their opposition to American capitalism; and gay liberation movements in their opposition to American heterosexism.

In the final section of the course, titled "Contemporary Dissent," students are required to study musical groups distinguished by their vocal opposition to American society—including the nonmusical rantings of bands such as Rage Against the Machine, Mos Def, and Public Enemy ("Fight the Power"). Students are introduced to the allegedly heroic stances of antiwar organizations like Veterans Against the Iraq War, left-wing special interests like the ACLU and Amnesty International, and even the environmental terrorist organization the Earth Liberation Front.

One might easily conclude, after completing this course, that there is nothing commendable or even defensible in America's founding, and that the authentic American tradition is that of anarchists, communists, and other nihilistic opponents of its founding principles. The course description asks, "Why is it that some people never 'buy into' the 'American Dream' perceiving it not as a Dream, but more like a Nightmare?" The answer is "Perhaps because they have taken courses with Professor Young."

History of the United States Since 1877 *History C068*[44]

INSTRUCTOR: Ralph Young, Senior Lecturer in the Department of History

Not surprisingly, this Ralph Young course has an identical focus. The only assigned text is *Created Equal: A Social and Political History of the United States,* Volume II, a history textbook that Professor Young notes he has selected for its special attention to the following topics:

> Political Corruption and the Decline of Republican Idealism; American Imperialism; Radical Politics and the Labor Movement; Marcus Garvey and the Persistence of Civil Rights Activism; Colonialism and the Cold War; The Impact of Nuclear Weapons; Who Is a Loyal American?; White Resistance, Black Persistence; Boycotts and Sit-Ins; Mobilizing for Peace and the Environment; From Civil Rights to Black Power; The New Left and the Struggle Against the War; Cultural Rebellion and the Counterculture; Women's Liberation; The Many Fronts of Liberation; "Reaganomics" and the Assault on Welfare; An Embattled Environment; The Rise of the Religious Right; Dissenters Push Back; The Widening Gap between Rich and Poor; Labor Unions; The War in Iraq.[45]

What all these themes have in common is that they are grossly inappropriate for any history course aspiring to be more than a training course in radical politics.

20th-Century U.S. History *History 271*[46]

INSTRUCTOR: Ralph Young, Senior Lecturer in the Department of History

Though the title of this course would seem to indicate a broad survey of America over the last century, Professor Young's curriculum reduces the complex history of the United States to a narrative about the heroic opponents of the American "power structure." Far from dispelling myths about American history, the course manufactures its own. Here, for example, are the areas of concentration in the course:

> Workers' Rights; Anti-War sentiment during the Filipino Insurrection, WWI, WWII, Vietnam, Iraq; The Women's Movement: From Suffragist to Feminist; The Struggle for Civil Rights; Cultural Dissent: The rise of a counterculture from Beatniks to Hippies; Right Wing Dissent: From the KKK to Paramilitarism; Environmentalism; Gay Pride, AIM, La Raza Unida.[47]

As any serious historian would recognize, these assorted movements together represent only a minuscule and mainly marginal chapter in the epic narrative of America's history in the twentieth century. Not only does Young exaggerate the importance of these movements, he also does not examine them in a way that could be remotely described as scholarly or academic. For instance, this is how the syllabus describes an important "oral history" assignment:

> Each student is to interview someone (relative, friend, acquaintance, former teacher) who participated in some way in any form of activism: the civil rights movement, the anti–Vietnam war movement, the counterculture, feminism, gay pride, environmentalism, anti–Iraq war demonstrations. Often we are surprised, and deeply touched, by what we learn from these interviews.[48]

While the assignment stipulates that students can interview someone who participated in "any form of activism," from the laundry list of examples it seems obvious that the professor has in mind *left-wing* activism. One wonders how the professor would respond to a student who felt "deeply touched" by interviewing, say, a pro-life activist.

This course misleadingly frames issues from a leftist perspective, and in so doing it clearly subverts the academic enterprise in favor of political activism.

For those concerned about the issue of academic freedom, it was an encouraging sign that the Pennsylvania legislature appointed a Select Committee on Academic Freedom to study Temple and the state's other public universities. As the preceding investigation indicates, Temple University has nothing close to the "environment of intellectual diversity" that the legislature affirmed to be "indispensable."

It was even more encouraging that the committee—unlike so many professors at Temple—actually accepted and listened to a variety of viewpoints, including the testimony of one of the authors of this book. That testimony was circulated among administrators and trustees at Temple. As a result the Temple administration decided to reorganize the Freshman Summer Reading Program. In 2008 no book was assigned while the program was being reconfigured. At a time when so many universities steadfastly refuse to make any changes when presented with overwhelming assaults on academic freedom, the fact that Temple considered making even slight adjustments could be taken as a sign of progress. At the same time, no changes in the regular Temple curriculum were made.

A similar radicalism is entrenched at Miami University in Ohio.

9

Mobilize U

MIAMI UNIVERSITY (OHIO)
TUITION: $11,443 IN-STATE
$23,875 OUT-OF-STATE

Miami University in Ohio has long inspired praise. Upon seeing its classic Georgian architecture and its bucolic location beneath the shade of beech, cherry, and oak trees, the poet Robert Frost is said to have called it "the prettiest college that ever there was." Today, official rankings regularly count the school's undergraduate business and accountancy programs among the top in the country. In the 1980s, the school was grouped among the original "Public Ivies," state institutions distinguished by their elite-quality educations.

The first academic experience a student will have at Miami is through the Summer Reading Program, which is required of all incoming freshmen. The university catalogue describes the significance of this program:

> Participation in the Summer Reading Program is your first assignment as a university student. Your willingness to take the assignment seriously and to participate actively in group discussions in August may have important influences on your subsequent achievements as a Miami Student.[1]

Like Temple, Miami University assigns only one book for the summer, and students are expected to discuss it in freshman classes.

The author of the book is invited to campus to address a freshmen assembly and discuss his or her work. Authors are paid as much as $15,000 for the visit.

In 2006, the assigned book was *Ahmad's War, Ahmad's Peace,* a critical examination of the Iraq War by Michael Goldfarb of National Public Radio. Goldfarb hosts the series "Pax Americana," which compares America to the Roman Empire and other empires in history. Part One of the series is called "Imperial Intentions," and its description ends with these words: "Why do they hate us? We aren't an occupying empire, are we?" The series description informs listeners that America's "expansion" is "not accidental."[2]

On a subject as volatile and contested as the war in Iraq, not to mention American "imperialism," how is it academically appropriate for Miami University to assign one left-wing text to impressionable freshmen and to invite to campus just one author who is not only critical of the war but regards it as an expression of America's unquenchable thirst for world domination? How is this compatible with the ideas of disinterested inquiry and intellectual pluralism? Why would an educational institution not assign two texts with differing views on these subjects, unless its intention was to persuade students to adopt a particular point of view?

This assignment is not an anomaly in the Miami freshman reading program. Invariably, when the program assigns texts on controversial political subjects or cultural issues, only one side—the left side—of these controversies is represented. Not all the assignments in the program fall into the category of controversial issues: the reading in 2005 was about a woman who died young from a disfiguring cancer, while the previous year it was a novel about slavery. But in 2003, the assigned book was *Nickel and Dimed,* Barbara Ehrenreich's socialist polemic that has become such a favorite of the academic Left. Ehrenreich, of course, has no academic credentials to support her radical views on the subject of low-wage jobs in America or to make her anecdotal evidence particularly educational for university freshmen. Even so, this could have been an educational opportunity if a second text representing an opposing point of view had been assigned for comparison. No such text was assigned.

In 2002, the required text was *The Things They Carried,* a book about Vietnam by Tim O'Brien, whom one reviewer described as someone who "went to a war [he] didn't believe in." Again, a controversial issue, and again, only one side represented.

In 2001, the book was *Dead Man Walking* by anti–capital punishment activist Sister Helen Prejean. Again, the university assigned only a left-wing perspective on a matter that is subject to considerable, and serious, debate.

The one-sided nature of these assignments reflects a troubling institutional attitude. Does Miami University have so little concern for its own academic freedom principles and for the pluralism of ideas that it cannot bring itself to provide more than one preferred side of a contentious issue?

"Activism" and "Genderqueers": The Women's Studies Department and the Women's Center

As at many other schools, the Women's Studies Department at Miami University is the most prominent example of a political program masquerading as an academic field. The political self-conception of Women's Studies at Miami University is hardly concealed. The Women's Studies departmental website even features a section called "Activism,"[3] as the logical consequence of the ideology the curriculum inculcates. Because Women's Studies has forty affiliated professors who teach in departments ranging from history to anthropology, sociology, literature, and law, its political agendas are not quarantined within its own territory but exert a corrupting influence throughout the Miami liberal arts curriculum.

The "Activism" link on the Women's Studies website directs students to the university's Women's Center and to this explanation for its presence: "How does the Women's Studies Program connect with the Women's Center? Here at Miami, these two entities are distinct but highly cooperative. While the Women's Studies Program is primarily academic, the Women's Center is an academic support services program which places women at its center. The Center focuses on support, education and advocacy."[4] The Women's Studies Department does not acknowledge that a focus on advocacy might transform the very nature of the education offered. Advocacy groups have a vested interest in *not* exploring both sides of controversial issues, which is the key to proper academic inquiry. To seriously consider other views would hamper their advocacy mission.

The Women's Center explains its attitude toward "Gender Issues," which are central to the Women's Studies curriculum, in these terms:

> *Gender* is a socially constructed system of classification that ascribes qualities of masculinity and femininity to people. An aspect of all known cultures, gender is continually being reinterpreted and varies greatly from culture to culture. Words that refer to gender include: woman, man, feminine, masculine, transgender and genderqueer. *Transgender* is an umbrella term referring to behavior and attitudes that challenge conventional gender roles, responsibilities and relationships. The term *genderqueer* describes people who purposely blur gender lines, challenge gender norms and often adopt androgynous personas.[5]

In other words, at the Women's Center—and in dozens of courses at Miami University—gender is regarded not as a fact of nature but as an artificial construct that society imposes on individuals or that individuals choose for themselves. Thus "genderqueers," according to the Women's Center, are individuals who *choose* to be androgynous or homosexual in order to challenge the status quo.

The university website provides no indication that this might be a controversial point of view. Nor does the Women's Studies website in describing its academic program: "Women's Studies raises questions about gender as a *social construction,* and the ways in which those constructions affect disciplinary knowledge, the experiences of women and men, our social fabric, the arts, creative writing, institutions, intimate relationships, and the workplace [emphasis added]."[6]

This is the description of an all-inclusive ideological theory, along with a program to indoctrinate students in that theory. Courses that adopt this disputed viewpoint as their fundamental, unquestioned assumption violate the code of professional ethics established by the American Association of University Professors, which says that a faculty responsibility is "informing students of the generally accepted conclusion on the subject matter of the course when those conclusions differ from the conclusions of the instructor." Yet the courses offered by the Miami Women's Studies Department train students in this ideology exclusively.

The department makes clear the fact that radical theory is its real mission. The department website declares that "Women's Studies courses are organized around contemporary feminist research and theory." Meanwhile, the department requires students to complete a senior thesis in order to earn a Women's Studies degree, and the first requirement for the senior thesis is that it "must incorporate feminist and/or womanist perspectives and critiques."[7] This would be like insisting that a history thesis about American politics incorporate a conservative perspective or one about the Soviet Union a Communist perspective. It is entirely alien to the spirit and purpose of a modern research university.

The following four courses exemplify the department's attempts to train students in radical feminist theory instead of examining feminist theory with scholarly detachment.

Women and Difference: Intersections of Race, Class, and Sexuality *WMS 301*[8]

INSTRUCTOR: Madelyn Detloff, Assistant Professor of English and Women's Studies

From the start, this course locks students in to certain categories of analysis and in so doing predetermines the results of the analysis. The course description states that the class employs "interdisciplinary theoretical approaches to the interplay of race, class, gender, sexual orientation, and other aspects of social identity in women's lives," analyzes "the ways social difference is defined, used, and experienced," and emphasizes "feminist and womanist theories that take into account the interdependence of multiple categories of social difference."[9]

Every aspect of this course is framed as an exposition of feminist ideology. Thus, categories relevant to individual identity—such as nationality, culture, physical characteristics, and ancestry—are eliminated at the outset because they don't fit radical schemata and presumably don't lead, in an inexorable manner, to demands for "social change."

Black Feminist Theory *WMS/BWS 425*[10]

INSTRUCTOR: Gwendolyn Etter-Lewis, Professor of English, Black World Studies, and Women's Studies

This is another example of a course that rather than examining a theory in an academic manner, merely promotes the theory. The course description says that the seminar "examines black feminist theory from a variety of perspectives," but that "variety" does not seem to include any perspectives that are critical of the theory.

The description telegraphs the course's biases when it notes that the class "samples a diversity of texts by theorists in the U.S. and African diaspora."[11] The term "African diaspora" is a misappropriation of a concept from Jewish history, which refers to the expulsion of an entire people, bound by a common language, a common history, and a common religion, from their homeland and their dispersal for thousands of years. Large numbers of Africans were transported from Africa to foreign lands. But their enslavement was at the hands of other Africans, and they did not speak a common language or have a common history or a common religion. The use of the term "diaspora" in this context is political, not analytic, and is meant to appropriate sympathy, not illuminate a problem.

As we have seen so often before, the radical theory of "social construction" extends not only to gender but to race as well—the idea being that society's alleged ruling groups use such constructions to "oppress" their subjects.

Feminist Literary Theory and Practice *WMS/ MPT 368*[12]

INSTRUCTOR: Yvonne Keller, Visiting Assistant Professor of Women's Studies

This course purports to be an "introduction to feminist literary theory." But the description quickly adds that the class "deals with how feminism has shaped reading and interpretive practices, and develops some practical strategies for literary study"—a clear indication that the course's true interest is not in "introducing" students to feminist literary theory, but in training them to become devoted practitioners of the theory.

Race Politics: The Black World Studies Department

The class Black Feminist Theory in the Women's Studies Department is cross-listed with BWS 425, signifying that it is also a course in the Black World Studies Department. The latter department explains its mission as being to engage students "in the discovery of historical and contemporary production of the Black Experience(s)" and to stress "changing constructions of race and its implications regarding global relations of power and inequality."

In other words, the Black World Studies Department shares with the Women's Studies Department a radical view of race as a "social construction." The required introductory course to the Black World Studies curriculum is described in these terms:

> BWS 151—Introduction to Black World Studies (4)—Introduces the Afrocentric perspective as it has developed in anthropology, history, political science, geography, sociology, religious studies, mass communication, theater, art, etc. Covers theories, research, mythologies, and practice of African studies. Students

develop historical and contemporary understanding of the African Diaspora.[13]

Thus this course accepts the ideological term "African Diaspora" and proposes to teach students to understand it. It also uses as its intellectual framework "Afrocentrism," which, as noted, is a tendentious and racialist theory of the "black experience"—and allows for historical facts to be simply ignored when they don't conform with the ideological perspective. Notably, the Black World Studies Department hosted as the keynote speaker at its fall 2005 symposium the chief prophet of Afrocentrism, Temple professor Molefi Asante.[14]

Equally troubling is the department's connection to the activist Miami University Center for Community Engagement in Over-the-Rhine, which mirrors the connection between the Women's Studies Department and the Women's Center. Over-the-Rhine is a disadvantaged community in urban Cincinnati that was the scene of race riots and multiple slayings connected to those riots in 2005. Both the riots and their aftermath continue to be the focus of political battles pitting radical leftists against law enforcement officials, city fathers, private-sector entrepreneurs, and conservatives.[15]

The director of the Black World Studies Department, Rodney Coates, has indicated that there is a direct link between the department curriculum and the activism of the center. In an interview that appeared in *Compass* magazine, an annual publication of the College of Arts and Sciences, Coates said, "I believe that black world studies is the dialogue not only in racial justice, but in social justice. Social justice is the next adventure in intellectual and creative endeavors. . . . "Implicitly, this [social justice] is part of all of our courses. Social justice has its roots in the very essence of human justice movements. It is a theme that is timeless."[16] The *Compass* article added that "the black world studies program hopes to bring social justice into real-life experiences," and to that end created the Miami University Center for Community Engagement in Over-the-Rhine.

The term "social justice" favored by Coates is a political concept incorporating anti–free-market, redistributionist policies; it is an agenda of left-wing movements advocating greater government intervention in the private sector. Thus it is entirely inappropriate for the concept to play a vital role in "all" an academic department's courses, as Coates claims is the case with the Black World Studies Department. It is even less appropriate for a public university to set up a center, financed by Ohio taxpayers, to carry out sectarian political agendas in its municipal districts and to recruit college students for this purpose.

The Miami University Center for Community Engagement in Over-the-Rhine is in practice an extreme political movement rather than an academic project, as is made clear on its own website.[17] The home page features several menus, including one titled "Engagements"—as in engagements in issues affecting Over-the-Rhine. Clicking on "Engagements" leads to a section titled "Agit-Prop" (a term that originated in Communist Russia, a shortened form of "agitation and propaganda"), which contains games and exercises with names like "Anti-Gentrification" to engage students on one side of the policy disputes affecting Over-the-Rhine. How training students in left-wing propaganda constitutes an academic activity, the site fails to explain.

Another menu on the home page is labeled "Discussion Papers." But these papers are not intended to prompt "discussion"; like the agitprop exercises, they advocate on one side of key policy controversies. One paper, coauthored by the head of the center, Thomas Dutton, is titled "Gentrification—It Ain't What You Think." Neither in grammar nor in substance is this article an academic inquiry into the problems of Over-the-Rhine. It is instead a manifesto in favor of publicly subsidized housing ("equitable community development") as opposed to what it terms a "market rate housing based development strategy." Dutton is listed in the university catalogue as a professor of Architecture and Interior Design—hardly an academic credential for assessing economic development policies. He also cowrote an article on the Cincinnati riots in the left-wing magazine *The Nation* with the Reverend Damon Lynch, a local demagogue and firebrand during the riots.[18]

Another "discussion paper" coauthored by Dutton is devoted entirely to the idea of political activism. Titled "The Futures of Community Organizing: The Need for a New Political Imaginary," the piece states, "Political analysis and practice are always linked, and a limited analysis will limit possibilities for action, but also for political imagination as well." Dutton and his coauthor rail against "the globalization of production and consumption, the near-conflation of governments and the multinational corporate sector, and . . . the world banking system, WTO, World Bank, and the IMF." They also portray community organizers as "modern day Davids confronting the Goliath of world conditions."

The Miami Center's website also features a "discussion paper" titled "Labor Against Empire: At Home and Abroad," written by Robin D. G. Kelley, a well-known Marxist professor and member of the Communist Workers Party.[19] Kelley is the author of *Hammer and Hoe,* a history of the Communist Party in Alabama, and *Yo' Mama's Disfunktional,* a collection of polemics. In October 2003 Professor Kelley facilitated a conversation at the Miami Center called "Hip Hop, Culture, and Urban America."

A representative sample from Professor Kelley's "discussion paper" reveals just how remote it is from anything that might be called a scholarly discourse:

> Anti-imperialism has been fundamental to black radical politics in the past, and we need to make it central to contemporary labor struggles—not just black labor. Today we face an American Empire more powerful than ever, and certainly as ruthless as in the days of Haiti's occupation. Under the Bush administration's global war, we are witnessing the suppression of self-determination for nations of the Global South and the real possibility of re-colonization; massive poverty and the disappearance of viable welfare states in the face of structural adjustment policies; privatization of the commons, resulting in imperialist control over indigenous resources; unbridled corporate destruction of the environment resulting in global warm-

ing, droughts and epidemics; and the suppression of radical movements for social justice and transformation.

Kelley's entire paper is devoted to the alleged depredations of America's global "empire"—which in his view relates to the problems of Over-the-Rhine, because "a place like Cincinnati represents colonial domination in its raw, naked form. The city entered the world stage in a big way in April of 2001 when police fatally shot Timothy Thomas, a 19-year-old African American, in the predominantly black neighborhood of Over-the-Rhine. Police pursued Thomas, who was unarmed, because they had a warrant out for his arrest because of unpaid parking tickets. His murder sparked a massive insurrection in Over-the-Rhine and in other parts of Cincinnati that forced the Mayor to impose a state of emergency and compelled the Governor to send in National Guard troops. Thomas's murder was just the tip of the iceberg."

Professor Kelley's view that the Cincinnati police are murderers and that the race riots were a "rebellion" is also the official view of the center. Indeed, Thomas Dutton coauthored still another discussion paper that summarized the riots as follows: "April 7, 2001 will be forever etched in the minds of Cincinnati residents: at about 2:20 a.m., Timothy Thomas was shot and killed by police officer Stephen Roach in a dark alley in the Over-the-Rhine neighborhood. Mr. Thomas—a teenager who was unarmed—was the fifteenth person to die at the hands of the police since 1995; all were African American men. Mr. Thomas' death triggered several days of protest and rebellion that the media continues to reduce to 'the April riots.' "[20]

Actually, Thomas, who had *fourteen* outstanding warrants for offenses, including resisting arrest, led police on a chase through a drug-ridden and violent neighborhood in the middle of the night. He was reaching for his waistband when he was shot, not "murdered." Kelley's suggestion that the fifteen felons killed by police were innocent men murdered because they were black is also remote from any reality. As Heather Mac Donald reported in *City Journal*, "In fact, the list of the 15 police victims shows the depraved nature not of Cincinnati's cops but of its criminals. Harvey Price, who heads the roster, axed his girlfriend's 15-year-old daughter to death in 1995, then held a SWAT team at bay for four hours with a steak knife, despite being Maced and hit with a stun gun. When he lunged at an officer with the knife, the cop shot him. Jermaine Lowe, a parole violator wanted for armed robbery, fled in a stolen car at the sight of a police cruiser, crashed into another car, then unloaded his handgun at the pursuing officers. Alfred Pope robbed, pistol-whipped, and most likely fired at three people in an apartment hallway, just the latest assault by the vicious 23-year-old, who had already racked up 18 felony charges and five convictions. He then aimed his handgun at close range at the pursuing officers, and they shot him dead in return."[21]

Mac Donald's article, of course, is not included in the Miami Center's "discussion papers," so students are left to believe that that the fifteen were victims of police racism. Nor has the university invited Mac Donald or any other commentators to present divergent views on the volatile questions the center addresses. Instead, students in the Miami program are relentlessly indoctrinated in views that can only inspire anger at white people generally and law enforcement officials in particular. In this program they are taught that felons are "rebels" and that the law enforcement agencies of a vibrant democracy are brutal murderers and racist oppressors.

Even before students attend their first class at Miami University, the administration sends them a clear signal about the only side of the political landscape it is willing to tolerate, with its summer reading program for incoming freshmen. The situation does not improve once students arrive on campus, either. When academic departments are formally aligning with university-sponsored activist centers to support left-wing causes, it is a sure sign that a school has forgotten its mission.

Another university, several hundred miles west of Ohio, has also slipped its academic moorings.

10

Politically Correct U

UNIVERSITY OF MISSOURI
TUITION: $8,172 IN-STATE, $18,828 OUT-OF-STATE

When it was founded in 1839, the University of Missouri–Columbia—familiarly known as "Mizzou"—made history. It was the first public university built west of the Mississippi River and the first in the territory acquired as part of the Louisiana Purchase, an apt symbol for the expansion of American civilization into the new frontier. The school's trailblazing tradition continues today. With an enrollment of over 28,000 and a curriculum comprising some 265 degree programs, the school is Missouri's largest public research university. Its programs in journalism and creative writing are considered among the most competitive in the country, providing the school a reputation as the "writing university." Medical programs, such as the Sinclair School of Nursing, have added luster to its reputation.

In a democracy, the presumption underlying all public education is that students are taught how to think, not what they should be thinking. The hundred-year tradition of academic freedom in higher education is based on this principle, which has long since been incorporated into the academic policies of most American research universities, including the University of Missouri's. Yet Mizzou's course offerings, like those of the other schools profiled in this book, regularly fail to meet these standards.

Leftist Mantras: The Women's and Gender Studies Program

The Women's and Gender Studies Program at Missouri declares in its "Mission Statement" that it is "committed to the interdisciplinary, feminist study of the social, cultural, and historical processes that gender human identity."[1] This is in effect a doctrinal proclamation—a clear statement that the department recognizes feminism as the only approach to the study of women, and that gender is (despite scientific evidence to the contrary) presumed to be the product of "social, cultural and historical processes."

The mission statement continues, "Central to the program's mission is the conviction that the study of cultures, knowledges, and representations cannot be separated from the study of women and gender, and that gender and sexuality are fundamental categories of analysis in all disciplines." The claim that gender and sexuality are fundamental categories of knowledge would come as a surprise to mathematicians, physicists, and molecular biologists, among other specialists in the hard sciences. The mission statement's description of this extreme view as a "conviction" that is "central" to the program underscores the anti-intellectual and ideologically narrow approach the Women's and Gender Studies Program takes toward its subject.

Specialization and expertise in a discipline—cornerstones of modern scientific knowledge—presume certain limits in the field of study. No such limits restrain the faculty of the Women's and Gender Studies Program, which subscribes to an ideology that is global in scope: "In recognizing that the construction of these categories is contingent on time and place, the program stresses scholarship and teaching that are broadly comparative and range across multiple cultures, national and transnational contexts, and historical moments. Its faculty employ a broad range of theoretical approaches and methods that help students to integrate women's, gender, and/or queer studies with analyses of race, ethnicity, religion, spirituality, nationality, and class, and to think critically and synthetically about the multiple axes of power through which sexual and gendered identities are constructed."[2]

This is an invitation to speculate within an abstract ideology that cannot be anchored in empirical findings or evaluated by professional expertise. The theoretical boundaries of these speculations, on the other hand, are narrowly defined. Thus, the "broad range of theoretical approaches" referred to in the mission statement includes only variations in feminist ideology. It is as if a program in Marxism were to claim a "broad range of theoretical approaches" when it merely promoted Maoism and Trostkyism alongside Stalinism but never studied critiques of Marxism from non-Marxist perspectives.

The program's agenda of political indoctrination is made clear in the concluding declaration of the mission statement: "Courses encourage students to analyze the world in which they live, in order that they might act to transform it." The possibility that the world should not be transformed, or cannot be transformed, is simply excluded from consideration. Evidently, the idea that such possibilities exist is politically incorrect.

The official website of the Women's and Gender Studies Program even provides students with links to the political organizations to which it seeks to recruit them. These include the Feminist Majority Foundation and the National Organization for Women. How is the promotion of sectarian political groups an appropriate function of a modern research university or a taxpayer-funded institution such as the University of Missouri?

The program also promotes on its newsgroup a University of Missouri "Diversity Initiative" entitled "White on White: Exploring Racism: A Workshop on White Privilege." The obvious presumption of this workshop is that white students—and only white students—belong to a racist group whose members have difficulty talking about their racism:

> Many White people interested in learning more about race, privilege and social justice have difficulties finding safe spaces for such conversations.
>
> - Are you racist?

> - Does racism only affect people of color?
> - How can you confront racism in your community?
>
> These workshops provide an opportunity for White people to talk honestly about racism in the company of other White people.[3]

This workshop is one of the most flagrant and offensive examples of indoctrination we have encountered in this survey of college curricula. It is a cardinal assumption of the radical Left—but no one else—that only whites can be racists. Yet that is the assumption of the Women's and Gender Studies Program at the University of Missouri. A program designed to indoctrinate students in a radical worldview—whether that view is situated to the right or the left on the political spectrum—violates the most fundamental standards of scholarship of a modern research university, as well as the established principles of academic freedom.

Bodies, Cultures, and Nations

WGST 1120 (formerly Introduction to Women's and Gender Studies)[4]

Since the Women's and Gender Studies Program is frankly political and ideological, it is not surprising that this introductory required course is specifically a course in "feminist politics" and not an academic exploration of the subject of women. According to the course description, this survey of "a century of feminist politics and theory" asks students "to think critically about the diverse ways in which human identity is gendered, and the historical development of gendered inequalities." The description goes on to say that the course pays "particular attention to the importance of race, ethnicity, class, and sexuality in the cultural construction of sexual difference."[5]

Yes, there it is again: the ideologically inspired and scientifically controversial claim that sexual differences are "constructed" culturally. This course will entertain no challenges to this causal explanation;

indeed, the entire program is committed to it with almost totalitarian finality.

The introductory course also assumes the politically charged claim that free societies such as the United States feature "oppressive social conditions." No dispute is going to be raised about that either. The course description expressly states that the class considers only radical "feminist and gender theories" that "contest" these "oppressive social conditions in the United States and throughout the world."

The Female Experience: Body, Identity, Culture

WGST 1360/Sociology 1360[6]

INSTRUCTOR: Kendra Yoder, Sociology Graduate Student

This course, according to its description, "examines institutions in U.S. society that exert social control over women's bodies, especially the media, the legal system, and the medical professions."[7] The course makes this extreme claim without acknowledging that the assertion is contestable, especially given that the United States is a democracy whose Constitution and laws forbid discrimination; that it is characterized by a bewildering array of media institutions, privately and publicly controlled; and that it has a similar array of public and private medical institutions and systems of delivering medical services. The radical view represents the fundamental assumption of the course itself, so there is little chance that students will be exposed to alternative perspectives.

Feminist Theory I *WGST 2020*[8]

INSTRUCTOR: Catherine Holland, Associate Professor of Political Science and Women's Studies

The Women's Studies courses examined in this book are not scholarly examinations of feminist theory but training courses *in* feminist theory. Missouri's "Feminist Theory" class is yet another example of this sort of indoctrination. The course description states that it "introduces central themes and problems within feminist thought, including consciousness-raising, motherhood, class, race, sexuality, nationalism and transnational feminism." It adds, "By surveying a series of debates critical to second-wave feminism, we will examine the difficulty of articulating what Simone de Beauvoir called the feminine 'we' and move to the more recent articulation of the feminist (if not quite feminine) 'we' by feminist theorists of transnational politics."[9]

Such indoctrination is no more appropriate to a university than would be a course to examine the doctrines of conservatism from an exclusively conservative perspective, or Intelligent Design theory exclusively from a religious point of view. Moreover, like so many other courses in this program, its declared field of study is so broad—"consciousness-raising, motherhood, class, race, sexuality, nationalism and transnational feminism"—that it is outside the realm of any instructor's specific (and credentialed) expertise.

This course is merely an exercise in radical political ideology.

Women in Popular Culture *Women's and Gender Studies*[10]

INSTRUCTOR: Evelyn Somers Rogers (Ph.D. in Literature)[11]

"This course seeks to fulfill the program's mission," explains the syllabus for "Women in Popular Culture." The program's mission is inseparable from the inculcation of feminist ideology: "Drawing on the theoretical framework created by feminist scholars, this course investigates the ways women are portrayed in today's media." Take away the first half of this sentence, and this is an appealing academic course on women in the media; add it, and this is a course in feminist indoctrination.

The course description contained in the syllabus also reveals the class to be an internal discussion among feminists, not an academic review of feminist controversies:

> We will begin by looking at how second-wave feminism labeled femininity a tool of self-oppression. From there we will move to a review of third-wave feminist and post feminist the-

> ories that see femininity in a more friendly light, as flexible and creative. Along the way, we will examine a wide variety of feminine identities in contemporary popular culture.[12]

Reflecting the uncritical approach the course adopts, the description makes claims that appear subjective and without empirical support. For example, it asserts that "most studies of women in popular culture focus primarily on adult women of childbearing age and in doing so reinforce the belief that women's primary function is reproductive." This unsupported claim props up the notion that popular culture contains oppressive stereotypes about women that only feminist theory is competent to analyze.

The assigned texts buttress the radical viewpoint. One of two required texts is *Feminism, Femininity, and Popular Culture*, by Joanne Hollows, who describes herself as a "student of feminism." Hollows's aim in the book, she explains, is to "theorize" a relationship between feminism and popular culture. To that end she examines several feminist works but never casts a critical glance at feminist claims. While discussing filmmaking, for instance, Hollows considers the role of women in the films under review but also "introduce[s] some of the key themes of feminist film theories," which "should be understood in relation to both second-wave feminist activism . . . and feminist film making." Put another way, her interest in this book is to promote feminist ideas. This is also the intention of the course.

Outlaw Genders *WGST 2080*[13]

INSTRUCTOR: Elisa Glick, Assistant Professor of English and Women's and Gender Studies

The premise of this course is that "male" and "female" are artificial categories produced by a patriarchal culture, and not based in any order of nature or reality:

> What is gender and how do we define its boundaries? How are "male" and "female" bodies and identities produced by culture?

> How do "outlaw genders" challenge our understanding of (and experience of) sex, gender, and sexuality? What does gender freedom look like? These are a few of the questions we will explore in this cross-cultural course on gender and sexual diversity.[14]

Here, as in countless other Women's Studies courses, the dubious claim that male and female genders are "produced by culture" is simply rammed down students' throats, as the class assigns no texts that include scientific findings that show profound masculine and feminine characteristics rooted in nature.

The intellectual quality of the course is previewed by the clotted jargon that the instructor uses to describe it. The description states, for example, that the class "will study the diverse lives of gender variant people" and "will pay particular attention to those systems of gender-based oppression that suppress multiple gender identities and expressions." Once more, the course simply declares *ex cathedra* that questionable premises are true—in this case, the idea that a ruling patriarchy imposes "gender-based oppression." No other point of view is represented in the course as a viable alternative to this radical perspective.

A student will emerge from this airless classroom not empowered by critical thinking but bowed down by propaganda.

Feminist Research and Criticism *WGST 4110/Sociology*[15]

INSTRUCTOR: Mary Jo Neitz, Professor of Sociology and Women's Studies

This course frankly describes itself as a training course for radical feminists in radical feminism. There appear to be plenty of feminist critiques of social science made available to students, but no critiques of feminism or the feminist perspective:

> This course is centrally concerned with how feminists in the social sciences produce knowledge, what we do with that knowledge, and if the process is any different because we are feminists. We will examine feminist critiques of social science

> research methodologies, questions of feminist epistemology, and how feminists struggle with those questions in our work. We will be reading exemplars from anthropology, history, political science, psychology and sociology.[16]

Feminist doctrines, feminist exemplars, and feminist problems add up to a sectarian tour of a sectarian subject.

Feminist Political Science

Women's and Gender Studies 4880[17]

INSTRUCTOR: Kitty Holland, Associate Professor of Women and Gender Studies and Political Science

According to its catalogue description, this course is premised on the feminist refrain that the "western tradition of political thought" represents women as "as inimical to change and to public life." The course makes a point of excluding all perspectives that might clash with a feminist agenda. The assigned texts are all authored by "feminist political theorists who write both to contest the premature foreclosure of women from politics, and also to establish a theoretical ground from which women may speak politically." It is abundantly clear what "theoretical ground" is being prepared by this course so that women can "speak politically"—not a broad ground of thought but a narrowly radical one.

Social Perspectives on Women, Race and Class

Women's and Gender Studies 1332[18]

INSTRUCTOR: Sam Bullington, Assistant Professor, Geography and Women's and Gender Studies

The catalogue states that this course "examines the processes of differentiation which create social categories such as gender, race, and class around which social life is built." How many times does a student majoring in Women's and Gender Studies have to hear a detailed exposition of this scientifically questionable theory as a central part of the course content? What is the justification for such repetition? What fresh viewpoint or new knowledge will they ever be exposed to? Are the designers of this program so fearful that their majors will forget—or stray into alien ideological fields of thought—that they must drum it into the student at very available opportunity?

This time the mantra about the social construction of gender and race comes from a professor of Geography. What is his academic expertise on such a topic? What professional knowledge does he have regarding this subject other than the narrow ideological formulas espoused in every other course in the program?

One section of the course "highlights the efforts of individuals and social movements to resist and reframe dominant meanings of such categories, as well as to ameliorate their material effects." Again, what academic expertise does a professor of Geography bring to this topic? What, professionally speaking, does he know about it? Professor Bullington is not a specialist in the fields of sociology, economics, or anthropology and thus has no professional credentials to expound on the complexities of class and race or on their "dominant meanings." His only qualification is a commitment to what the department obviously regards as its party line.

Women and Health from a Transnational Perspective

Women's and Gender Studies/Nursing 4600[19]

INSTRUCTOR: Srirupa Prasad, Visiting Assistant Professor of Sociology

A reasonable expectation for a course on women's health is that it be taught by an instructor with an expertise in the subject of medicine or public health. But Professor Prasad is a professor of sociology, and her research interests run to such ideology-infused topics as the "relationship between health, culture, colonialism" and "the impact of globalization and neo-liberal capitalism."

If one looks at Professor Prasad's academic website, one finds only a single research project that deals in detail with an actual illness (tuberculosis), and it is only its social impact with which she is concerned. Her focus, moreover, seems to emanate from her impression that western nongovernmental organizations are not providing medical help to Indian women in a manner she considers politically correct. More typical is this project: "I am involved in a third project with Amit Prasad to study medical tourism, medical transcription, and drug testing in India. We are analyzing how three transnational processes assign different identities to people, which very often translates to and are effects of unequal rights of different social groups in the context of neo-liberal globalization." The term "neo-liberal globalization" is a left-wing argot for "international capitalism"; it is unclear whether by "unequal rights" Prasad refers to actual legal inequalities or is making some meta-claim that the market system *causes* inequalities.

In this course, Prasad examines "health and medicine from a gender-sensitive perspective" and explores "how notions of disease, sickness, and healing are gendered as well."[20] In accordance with this "gender-sensitive perspective," the course claims that the spread of liberal markets ("neo-liberal globalization") has adversely affected women, exacerbating allegedly pervasive inequalities in women's health care. Instead of inquiring as to whether this is in fact the case, students are instructed to answer such leading questions as "How has globalization created a transnational system where such inequalities are further strengthened?" An even more politically directed question asks, "Can a feminist intervention change such a scenario?"

This is self-evidently a course in feminist and anticapitalist propaganda; it is not an intellectual inquiry to determine the facts.

Psychology of Women

Women and Gender Studies/Psychology 4830[21]

INSTRUCTOR: Rebecca Martinez, Visiting Assistant Professor in the Department of Psychological Sciences

"Psychology of Women" is predicated on two ideological claims about gender and women. The first—big surprise—is the claim that gender roles are "constructed" by society. The course description asks, "How is it possible to socialize and enculturate human beings into becoming 'women' or 'men' and playing out the myriad roles which differentiate males from females in nearly all cultures of the world?" Note the quotation marks around the terms "women" and "men," indicating that these categories are not real, or biologically based, that they are alterable social constructs.

The second ideological claim is that psychology as a discipline is based on "an androcentric [i.e., male-centered] view of behavior, assuming that normative behavior can be identified by studying male behavior and that female behavior can be studied to examine how it differs from 'the norm.'" Note again the quotation marks, which question the very idea that there is a "norm." This is part of the course ideology that human beings are blank slates who can be engraved with messages that suit the agendas of an ideological movement. Professor Martinez presents as fact the claim that psychology as a discipline is male-centered, failing to acknowledge that many of its leading practitioners are women. There is no evidence to suggest that the course would subject this or any other feminist claim to critical scrutiny—not when the professor excludes critical perspectives from discussion.

Senior Research Seminar in Women's and Gender Studies

Women and Gender Studies 4990[22]

INSTRUCTOR: Kitty Holland, Associate Professor of Women and Gender Studies and Political Science

After spending three years in a program dedicated to indoctrinating students in feminist perspectives, seniors will be perfectly prepared for this final-year seminar. It is frankly presented as a course not in research methods appropriate to the study of women and/or gender, but in *feminist* methods of conducting such research. "The goal of this seminar," the course description states, "is twofold: first, to think critically about what it means to do interdisciplinary feminist research, and second, to do it."[23] The program offers students no course in alternative research methods.

Internship in Women's and Gender Studies *WGST 4940*[24]

INSTRUCTOR: Jessica Jennrich, Associate Director of the Women's and Gender Studies Program[25]

This is a course to recruit students to feminist political causes. The title clearly indicates as much, and the course description elaborates that students will be directed: to "professional experience in appropriate feminist related agency or organization."[26] What is this course doing in a university? Would there be no objection to a course whose purpose was to get students to act as interns for the Republican Party? Or the Democratic Party?

"The Social Construction of Cruelty": The Peace Studies Program

The Peace Studies Program at the University of Missouri is another classic example of politicized training rather than academic education. Its political agenda is evident from its mission statement, which defines "peace" as synonymous with left-wing social programs and environmentalist activism. Peace, it states, "is more than the absence of war. It is also the presence of justice. Peace is providing the basic necessities of life for every human being; eliminating violence, oppression, greed and environmental destruction; and working through conflict at home, at work and between nations."[27]

"Peace is providing the basic necessities of life for every human being"? This sentence makes no sense. It certainly does not state a scholarly mission; rather, it promotes the socialist agendas of Missouri's Peace Studies Program. In any case, governments that have sought to realize such utopian schemes as providing "basic necessities of life for every human being" and reengineering human nature to eliminate "violence, oppression, [and] greed" have in practice been among the most violent, oppressive, and economically catastrophic regimes in history.

Although the Peace Studies Program indicates that its students "pursue the concepts and realities of peace, war, violence, and justice from a variety of perspectives,"[28] the perspectives actually listed in the mission statement reflect the heavily slanted view that war is the result of social injustice and other inequities. Like the Women's and Gender Studies Program, the Peace Studies Program takes the view—which it shares with Communist and socialist totalitarians—that human beings are blank slates and that conflict is rooted in internal social structures. The program thus ignores the dominant schools of thought in political science and international relations studies, in which scholars emphasize that conflicts are caused not by "social injustice" but by the actions of states within a harsh environment of international anarchy. From the syllabi available, it appears that the program also discounts the idea that a strong military might be a surer guarantor of peace than the promotion of pacifist movements.

Introduction to Peace Studies *Peace Studies 1050*[29]

INSTRUCTOR: C. Michele Martindill, Adjunct Professor of Sociology

This introductory course reflects the one-sided approach of the Peace Studies Program. An examination of the required reading list tells the story: with the exception of a single text—Elie Wiesel's *Night,* a novel on the Holocaust—the reading for this course is entirely drawn from the far left of the political spectrum.

In fact, students are required to read two favorite authors of the radical Left: James Loewen and Jonathan Kozol. On her syllabus, course instructor C. Michele Martindill describes Loewen's sloppily researched diatribe against the United States, *Lies My Teacher Told Me,* as explaining "how we traditionally learn about war and peace; how minds are numbed; why we don't ask questions." Meanwhile, she says that Kozol's *The Shame of the Nation: The Restoration of Apartheid Schooling in America* shows "How and why schools perpetuate conflict and social injustice." She does not explain what the subject of

American education has to do with international conflict. Perhaps Kozol's radical politics accounts for his inclusion in the course reading: the author is famous for his praise of the school system of totalitarian Cuba.

Professor Martindill also assigns Dalton Trumbo's antiwar novel *Johnny Got His Gun,* describing it as a "WWI story that was published at the onset of WWII . . . and then removed from the shelves" and claiming that the book shows "how organizations and institutions can silence certain voices." Martindill's description makes no mention of the fact that Trumbo was a well-known Communist writer, or that *Johnny Got His Gun* lays heavy blame on capitalists and corporations for causing unnecessary wars. Nor does it mention that the American Communist Party promoted Trumbo's book in the 1930s when the party was in its antiwar phase—that is, when it supported the Hitler-Stalin Pact and denounced the Allied coalition against Nazi Germany as just another agent in an imperialist war. But after Hitler attacked the Soviet Union, thus transforming the war back into a "war against fascism," Trumbo himself suppressed the book and turned over to the FBI the names of people who had asked him for copies of *Johnny Got His Gun.* Insofar as the book was concerned, any "silencing" was done by the Communist Party and Trumbo himself.

Another title on the required reading list—the first title, in fact—establishes the central premise of the Peace Studies Program: that social inequality causes war. Martindill characterizes this book, Allan G. Johnson's *Privilege, Power, and Difference,* as a look at "how sociologists view the differences or inequalities that can lead to conflict or peace."

Martindill requires students to read on a subject that would not obviously be associated with peace studies: animal rights. But in this course, students are encouraged to accept the theory—common to the more extreme elements of the animal-rights movement—that eating animals is not only inhumane but also a cause of war. The sole text assigned on this subject, David Nibert's *Animal Rights/Human Rights: Entanglements of Oppression and Liberation,* is written from such an extreme perspective. Nibert, a self-described socialist who has defended animal liberationist terrorist organizations, asserts that various groups—including women, gays, blacks, people with disabilities, and "nonhuman animals"—are victims of "capitalism." He argues that "the frenetic pace of global capitalism, as promoted by economic and political elites in the United States and like nations, is tantamount to war against the earth and the vast majority of its inhabitants."[30] There is no indication that Missouri students are made aware of just how extreme Nibert's views are; the class is certainly not assigned readings that might challenge such views.

Still another required book deals with animals: *Regarding Animals*, by Arnold Arluke and Clinton R. Sanders. Professor Martindill, in her description of this text, demonstrates how the Peace Studies Program has appropriated the Women's Studies obsession with "social construction"; she writes that the book examines "the social construction of cruelty."

Quite noticeably, this reading list contains no works from the vast literature on the relationship between war and interstate relations by eminent political scientists. This lacuna is evidence not merely of ideological closed-mindedness but of academic incompetence as well.

Introduction to Peace Studies *Peace Studies 1050*[31]

INSTRUCTOR: Colin Wark, Graduate Student in Sociology

This is a second section of the introductory course for the Peace Studies Program, and in its course description it reveals itself to be a program of indoctrination in radical ideologies: "This course will deal primarily with issues related to peace building and social justice. . . . Hopefully the student will consider the ways in which phenomena such as poverty, racism, sexism and violent conflict are closely intertwined with one another as well as linked to human suffering generally."[32]

The required texts for this course have little bearing on the causes of war and peace but are principally texts designed to inundate students with radical viewpoints. For example, students are assigned *The Power of Nonviolence: Writings by Advocates of Peace,* a collection of essays by antiwar writers and activists. In the introduction, Howard Zinn, who has called America the world's greatest terrorist state, writes, "We need to be resolute in our decision that we will not go to war, whatever reason is conjured up by the politicians and the media, because war in our time is always indiscriminate, a war against innocents, a war against children. War is terrorism, magnified a hundred times."[33] Zinn has never expressed such sentiments in regard to wars waged by Communists, Islamic terrorists, or any nation besides the United States. Another required text telegraphs its ideological perspective in its title: *The Rich Get Richer and the Poor Get Prison: Ideology, Class, and Criminal Justice.*

While being fed a radical perspective, students are also required to work for organizations that are integral to the political Left. The syllabus states that all students must complete a "peace practice," meaning that they are required to volunteer for sixteen hours at a nonprofit organization. The professor specifies the kinds of organizations that fulfill the "peace practice" requirement: "homeless groups, progressive groups, anti-war, anti-death penalty, anti-draft groups, 'grassroots organizing for affordable housing,' and environmental projects."

Why should the taxpayers of Missouri foot the bill for such a political training and recruitment program? Why does the university administration approve it?

Literature as Political Dogma: The Department of English

Major Women Writers, 1890–Present *English 4189*[34]

INSTRUCTOR: Karen Piper, Associate Professor of English

The title of this course is deceptive. Its catalogue description shows that it has a far narrower focus than major women writers since 1890—and a much more political agenda. The description begins:

> *"Imperialism and Gender."* This class will examine women's role in modern warfare, particularly looking at imperialist wars and postcolonial rebellions of the twentieth century. We will look at the way in which women either felt confined or liberated by war, as well as examine the alternatives to warfare that women have created through writing. The connections between "nationalism," "patriotism," and masculinity will also be called into question.[35]

The scare quotes around "nationalism" and "patriotism" telegraph the instructor's views, as does her blanket characterization of "imperialist wars." Such wars apparently include the conflict in Iraq, since the final assigned reading is *Love My Rifle More Than You,* the memoir of Kayla Williams. Williams is an odd choice for a course allegedly about "major women writers," because she is not even a writer by profession but rather a disgruntled Iraq War veteran.

In fact, the only author studied in the course who is generally considered to be a "major writer" is Virginia Woolf. The course description, noting that "we will draw conclusions about the place of women in contemporary warfare," recounts the books that are studied in the class:

> Starting with *Imperial Leather,* we will discuss the way gender definitions shifted under British imperialism. We will then read the South African and British novels: Olive Schriener's *Story of an African Farm,* and Virginia Woolf's *Mrs. Dalloway,* discussing the impact of colonization on white women at home and abroad. Then will we read African, Indian, and Caribbean novels by Bapsi Sidhwa *(Cracking India),* Tsitsi Dangarembga *(Nervous Conditions),* Jamaica Kincaid *(A Small Place).* Finally, we end with the memoir of Kayla Williams, an American soldier in Iraq, called *Love My Rifle More Than You.*

Williams's memoir serves as a pretext for discussing the course's real theme—what Professor Piper views as American "imperialism." This course is a mockery, abusive both to students who pay tuition in order to receive expert instruction and to Missouri taxpayers who underwrite the transaction.

Criticism and Theory *English 8060*[36]

INSTRUCTOR: Karen Piper, Associate Professor of English

In this course, another offering with a misleadingly neutral title, Karen Piper focuses even more resolutely on so-called American imperialism. The catalogue description reads:

> This course focuses on "empire," looking specifically at texts that chart the course of empire from the nineteenth to the twenty-first centuries—including Edward Said's *Culture and Imperialism*, Arundhati Roy's *An Ordinary Person's Guide to Empire,* and Antonio Negri and Michael Hardt's *Empire.* First, however, we will discuss the history of the field of "post-colonialism," as well as the history of the decline of European colonialism in the mid-twentieth century. Then, we will look at some of the field's main terms: decolonization, neocolonialism, hybridity, black atlantic, double consciousness, settler societies, and globalization.

Note in this description how political jargon ("neocolonialism," "hybridity") provides the "main terms" of the recently created field of "post-colonialism," a Marxist school of theory. The term "neocolonialism," in fact, is a Marxist coinage designed to impute imperialistic designs to industrial nations that have no colonies. The claim is controversial, to say the least, but the texts students are required to study treat it as fact and do not challenge its assumptions:

> We will read Leela Gandhi's primer to the field, *Postcolonial Theory,* which looks at theoretical connections with Marxism and feminism as well as giving a concise overview of the field, and selections from *Colonial Discourse/Postcolonial Theory* and Robert Young's *Postcolonialism: An Historical Introduction.* Finally, we will talk about empire in all its contemporary permeations,

including Negri and Hardt's amorphous sense of the term. This course is useful for anyone interested in becoming more fluent on issues of race and globalization.[37]

The entire focus of this course is "empire," as seen through a Marxist lens. Remember, this is a course offered by the Department of *English.* Karen Piper is not a trained historian, sociologist, political scientist, or economist, but she pontificates on economic, sociological, and political subjects.

Likewise, the texts she assigns—which are decidedly not literary works, despite this being an English class—are not written by qualified experts. For example, Michael Hardt, whose book *Empire* attempts to construct a Marxist theory of the modern world, is a professor of Comparative Literature; his coauthor, Antonio Negri, was a professor of Political Philosophy before being convicted in an Italian court for terrorist activities.[38] The late Edward Said,[39] author of *Culture and Imperialism,* was not a historian but a Professor of Comparative Literature, a fact that is all too apparent, as many critics have noted, from his often factually flawed writings on imperialism. Arundhati Roy is a writer of fiction and a far-left political activist, and her book *An Ordinary Person's Guide to Empire* is not a work of scholarship but a crude polemic against what she calls "neoliberal capitalists," and "the project of corporate globalization," which she portrays as a sinister conspiracy to "subvert" democracy.[40]

Piper has assembled a roster of amateurs and ideologues and doesn't bother to provide students with any works by scholars who might offer an opposing hypothesis.

Sexuality and Gender Theory *English 3080*[41]

INSTRUCTOR: Elisa Glick, Assistant Professor of English and Women's and Gender Studies

This course and its instructor, Elisa Glick, provide an example of how ideologues from Women's Studies have invaded the wider academic curriculum. The course description makes no pretense of being about English language or literature, and is frankly political. It begins:

> *"Sexuality Studies: Theory, Culture, and Politics."* Debates about the politics of sexuality have been at the forefront of contemporary efforts to rethink concepts of identity, desire, and the body. This course seeks to provide a theoretical and cultural context for such debates by investigating the complex and often contradictory relationship between sexuality and society. After tracing the historical emergence of the modern sexual self, we will survey contemporary theories of sexuality and sexual representations, particularly as they intersect with systems of race, class, and gender. Topics will include sexuality and desire under capitalism; feminist theories of sexuality and the feminist "sex wars"; cultural representations of HIV/AIDS; racialized sexualities; sexual and gender diversity; gender performance; the politics of embodiment.

That an *English* Department should offer such a course is but another illustration of the debasement of academic standards.

The Colonial Encounter in African Fiction *English 4170*[42]

INSTRUCTOR: Christopher Okonkwo, Assistant Professor of English

Like other courses in the English Department, this one is misleadingly presented as a course in fiction, specifically African fiction. Closer examination shows that its actual subject matter is the ideological views of Professor Okonkwo. The professor's interest in "postcolonial theory" informs the tendentious political theme of the course: that the Western world holds a "disparaging" belief about Africa that "has yet to completely depart Western consciousness even as we enter the twenty-first century." Professor Okonkwo attributes this allegedly pervasive belief to the history of Western colonialism in Africa and devotes much of the course to a discussion of the negative effects of colonialism. For instance, students are asked to consider such themes as "colonial destabilization of native cultures; the colonizer's religion, education, and language; land and economic exploitation; identity, gender, and class politics; 'race' and interracial relationships; violence and decolonization, and the post-colonial condition."

Professor Okonkwo, however, is not a historian, let alone a historian of colonialism. He brings no observable academic expertise to bear on the subject. Moreover, while there is nothing inappropriate about examining the influence of colonialism on African fiction, the demonstrable aim of this course is to promote a one-sided critique of the Western world and its colonial history—an objective that would be unprofessional for a history course and is even less justifiable in a course taught by a professor of English.

Africana Theory and Literature Criticism *English 8410*[43]

INSTRUCTOR: April Langley, Assistant Professor of English

This course is not remotely connected to the study of English literature, and in fact is the same course as Women and Gender Studies 8005. It is conceived entirely within the framework of a radical viewpoint, as demonstrated by the ideological idiom in which the course description is written:

> *"Black Feminist/Womanist Thought, Theorizing the Dilemma of Race and Gender."* This course will investigate political, cultural, and historical aspects of a range of gender theories from the African Diaspora—from 18th- and 19th-century pre-womanist and feminist works to contemporary ones. Accordingly, race and gender will be studied as occupying shared and intersecting positions from the margins, periphery, and center. Thus, while the course will deal with theories of gender, we will do so with the understanding that both "womanist" and "feminist"—as

> descriptive, delimiting, and liminal terms—constitute a central component of the dilemma posed by debates in which theories of "race" and "gender" are simultaneously engaged. Importantly, neither womanist nor feminist is fully representative of the constructed and constitutive nature of race and gender as it applies to women of African descent and their struggles against multivalent oppressions—which include but are not limited to race, class, and gender.[44]

The required reading for the course reinforces the instructor's political approach, as the reading list represents an excursion in the ideological mindset of the radical Left.

Africana Womanism *English 4420*[45]

INSTRUCTOR: Clenora Hudson-Weems, Professor of English

Professor Hudson-Weems is the author of *Africana Womanist Literary Theory* and *Africana Womanism;* indeed, she is the inventor of the term "Africana Womanism," which seems to have attracted few disciples. According to her course description, this class is "specifically designed to broaden one's scope in the area of issues, recurring themes and/or trends in modern Africana women fiction." The professor requires students to examine "the lives and selected works" of five leading "Africana women writers"—Zora Neale Hurston, Mariama Bâ, Toni Morrison, Terry McMillan, and Sister Souljah—in order to learn "an authentic theoretical concept and methodology, Africana Womanism."[46]

Unfortunately, there are numerous similar courses in the Missouri English Department. They exist alongside perfectly legitimate courses like "Introduction to English Literature," "Introduction to American Literature," and "Introduction to Medieval Literature: The Age of Chaucer." But the sampling above suffices to show how far afield and outside any conceivable academic standard many courses have been allowed to go.

"Utopistic" Wool-Gathering: The Black Studies Program

Introduction to Black Studies *Black Studies 2000*[47]

INSTRUCTOR: David L. Brunsma, Associate Professor of Sociology

Professor Brunsma makes no secret of his activist agendas. In his faculty biography, he writes that he is "committed to investigating and initiating ways in which scholarship can be actively used to combat structural racial injustices." He describes his own preferred brand of pedagogy as "utopistic sociology" and suggests that a key focus of his teaching and scholarship is to reduce "inequalities" in society. But such goals are incompatible with true scholarship, which by its very nature is disinterested, allowing the facts to determine the conclusions and not the other way around.

This introductory course reflects Professor Brunsma's political outlook as well as his antiwhite bias (according to his website, he has written a "critical autoethnography" entitled *White Lives as Covert Racism*).[48] According to its catalogue description, the course goal is "[t]o begin to understand the social, cultural, and economic underpinnings of privilege and the structures and processes of race, racism, prejudice, and discrimination both historically and contemporarily."

The claim that certain "structures" in American society perpetuate racial "privilege" is a controversial one that a professional academic course should be expected to examine critically, not assume. But without exception, the course texts reinforce Professor Brunsma's extreme views. One text, *Beyond the Down Low: Sex, Lies, and Denial in Black America,* is a polemical attack on the "racism, sexism, classism, misogyny, homophobia, heterosexism, and cultural imperialism" that, according to the author, characterize American society. This text, written by political activist Keith Boykin, repeatedly claims that Americans judge blacks on the basis of negative "preconceived perception[s]" rather than as individuals—in other words, that white America is racist.[49] Similar themes inform *Black Looks: Race and Representation,* by the radical feminist bell hooks, and *Let*

Nobody Turn Us Around: Voices of Resistance, Reform, and Renewal: An African-American Anthology, which takes a sympathetic view of criminal organizations like the Black Panther Party and assorted radical black activists, including the convicted murderer—and radical icon—Mumia Abu-Jamal.[50]

Graduate Seminar on Race Relations

Black Studies/Soc 8087[51]

INSTRUCTOR: Professor David L. Brunsma, Associate Professor of Sociology

A graduate seminar taught by Professor Brunsma is marked by the same ideological agenda as Black Studies 2000. The seminar is a forum for the professor to expound his views on critical race theory, the radical school of thought whose central contention is that minority groups remain "marginalized" and "oppressed" in a feudal America with "hierarchies" based on race and class. Students are required to accept this one extreme school of thought uncritically. Accordingly, they are instructed to accept the validity of "critical race knowledge and read the past through its lens" in order to arrive at an "understanding of race and racism in the United States and the World System at large."

A required text for the course is *White Supremacy and Racism in the Post-Civil Rights Era*, which argues that since the 1960s a "racial structure—the new racism, for short—has emerged that accounts for the persistence of racial inequality."[52] This book is not a work of scholarship but a crude polemic. Rather than giving due consideration to the wide range of arguments at odds with the work's thesis, the author characteristically dismisses them as "representing the conservative view on race in the United States."[53]

Another assigned text, *Black Feminist Thought: Knowledge, Consciousness, and the Politics of Empowerment,* claims that "African-American women's experiences as mothers have been shaped by the dominant group's efforts to harness Black women's sexuality and fertility to a system of capitalist exploitation." It is filled with categorical condemnations of the United States and semiliterate rants about the "dominant White society," "White male control of the marketplace," and "racist and sexist ideologies" that have "become hegemonic."[54] Similarly, the book *The Wages of Whiteness: Race and the Making of the American Working Class* is a Marxist text that disparages the white working class and sets out to document what the author calls the "the racist thought of white workers."[55]

All of the assigned texts paint an extremely negative portrait of white Americans, and some of them can be reasonably characterized as racist diatribes. For example, students are asked to read "Somebody Blew Up America," a notoriously anti-Semitic poem by the radical black activist Amiri Baraka, which blames Jews for 9/11.

This seminar resembles a jihad more than a college course. It is therefore not surprising that assignments are designed to encourage students to be racial activists. A "community engagement" component of the course "merges scholarship and activism," requiring students to regularly engage in such activities as "volunteer work, thinking about departmental policy, writing letters to the editor of the *Columbia Tribune,* attending a rally/protest, etc."

The "utopistic" Brunsma betrays the ambitions not of a scholar but of a political activist.

At the University of Missouri, the assaults on academic freedom are widespread—evident not only in new, politically correct programs like Peace Studies but even in traditional, well-respected academic units like the English Department. The offenses against the fundamental principles of higher education are egregious, and it is disturbing that the university has allowed them to proceed for so long.

The citizens of Missouri should be concerned about the radical agendas that their tax dollars are supporting. But such attacks on academic standards are endemic to private universities as well, as the case of the University of Southern California demonstrates.

11

Trojan Radicalism

UNIVERSITY OF SOUTHERN CALIFORNIA
TUITION: $35,810

While visiting California at the end of the nineteenth century, travel writer Emma Hildreth Adams noted the following about the University of Southern California, founded just a few years earlier in 1880: "It has the confidence of the community and looks forward to success."[1] More than 120 years later, the community's confidence would seem well placed. Indeed, it is unlikely that Adams would recognize what has become of the aspiring school she saw set in the humble frontier town. Like the town itself, which is today Los Angeles, the school has vastly outgrown its origins. While there were 53 students and 10 teachers in the school's inaugural class, today 33,000 students and some 3,200 full-time faculty now call the school home. With a 25 percent admissions rate, USC is one of the most selective universities in the country.

The university is fond of touting its "intellectual vitality," and its business and law schools validate the claim. But an examination of its liberal arts curricula suggests that, as at other schools, less is there than meets the eye. Several USC divisions, like the School of Social Work and the Department of Gender Studies, are well-developed training programs for left-wing activists, mired in the dogmas of the politically correct. Other departments, like English Literature, infuse their courses with radical agendas that make a mockery of their pretensions to academic stature.

Literary Marxism: The Department of English

Theories of History, Ideology, and Politics *ENGL 503*[2]

INSTRUCTOR: Anthony Kemp, Associate Professor of English

Though it is offered in the English Department, this is not a course in literature. The title of the course suggests it would be better situated in any one of several other departments—history, sociology, political science. Its real focus, however, is not any of those fields but, more simply, left-wing propaganda.

The course centers on the radical claim that society is a façade for sinister class interests. The subject of ideology has been addressed by many writers from many angles, but this course chooses only one—Karl Marx—to provide its organizing concept. Thus the official course description states: "Ideological thought posits that the conscious and semi-conscious idea-systems of a society are manifestations of false-consciousness, a covering, concealing, mystifying, containing screen for the reality of social relations, that is, for privileged, exploitative interests of material and economic power."

The texts for this course are works of politics—mainly Communist politics. Primarily students read texts written by Marx and Engels, but also included are works by the anarchist Simone Weil and the Maoist and postmodernist Michel Foucault. The course instructor's academic training, however, is in comparative literature, which means that USC students are paying $40,000 a year to learn Communist politics under the guise of an academic inquiry conducted by an amateur.

Studies in Gender *ENGL 630*[3]

INSTRUCTOR: Judith Halberstam, Professor of English

The professor for this course, Judith Halberstam, counts among her academic specialties "theory, feminist and gender studies, [and]

postmodernism," and this course is a forum for her preferred ideological agendas. Though it is offered in the English Department, its focus is "queer scholarship that situates the study of sexuality at the intersection of questions of race, nationalism, globalization and militarism." The course is also concerned with the "new framing of queer studies" that "powerfully challenges the white normativity of some earlier strands of sexuality studies, and the implicit hetero-normativity of some strands of U.S. ethnic studies and postcolonial studies."

That is to say, this is another professor teaching her ignorance in the fields of sociology ("race"), political science ("nationalism" and "militarism"), and economics and geopolitics ("globalization"). This professor is also an ideological extremist who thinks that normality ("normativity") is an ideological construct. According to Halberstam, even in such extremely left-wing academic fields as ethnic studies and postcolonial studies, left-wing heterosexuals oppress gays through the imposition of hetero-normative concepts and standards.

19th-Century British Literatures and Cultures: Feminism and the Form of the Novel *ENGL 540*[4]

INSTRUCTOR: Hilary M. Schor, Professor of English

This course at least has a literary dimension, although it is subordinated to an ideological agenda: to impose a feminist politics on the interpretation of the Victorian novel. The course description observes that "the connections between 19th century British Feminism and the realist novel are abundantly clear—in fact, it may well be that they are all too clear." So rather than exploring and questioning the extent of the relationship between feminism and realism in literature, this course assumes that the connection is beyond debate and compels students to consider the novels under discussion from a feminist perspective.

How would this professor react if a parallel course forced students to interpret a century's worth of fiction exclusively from a contemporary Christian perspective? Or a "neoconservative perspective"?

Multicultural Literary Studies: "Our Daily Bread": Race, Gender, and Genre in the Americas *ENGL 650*[5]

INSTRUCTOR: Teresa McKenna, Associate Professor of English

Drawing on the work of the Stalinist poet Pablo Neruda, the course is designed to "explore Neruda's sense of the poet in the world as emblematic of the writing of a number of contemporary feminist writers who as poets and essayists have brought their work to the public in an effort to forge community and to transform society's views of social and sexual relations." Put more simply, this is a course in merging feminist and Communist doctrines, while vulgarizing literature in the process.

Apart from a few books by respected authors, such as Joyce Carol Oates and Toni Morrison, the class consists predominantly of works by feminist activists like bell hooks, the "Chicana" feminist Cherríe Moraga, the Mexican journalist and left-wing political activist Elena Poniatowska, and the feminist poet Audre Lorde. The catalogue description also refers to the course's interest in "expression related to the formation of feminist communities." This is not a survey of literature but an exercise in radical narcissism.

Change the World: The School of Social Work

USC's School of Social Work is a political program disguised as an academic enterprise. In its mission statement, the school explains that its main purpose is to "to prevent and mitigate severe social problems which challenge the viability of culturally diverse and complex urban settings." In the service of this goal, students are expected to "master critical research and analytical skills and focus attention on how factors such as cultural and class differences, age, race, gender, and sexual orientation impact the field and practice." In short, students are expected not only to become social activists but also to absorb uncritically the school's ideological claims that class, race, gender, and sexual orientation are crucial to understanding poverty, family dysfunction, substance abuse, and other social problems.

Social Work in Educational Settings *Social Work 614*[6]

INSTRUCTOR: Ron Avi Astor, Professor in the School of Social Work

This is a training course in political activism. Two of the key themes for this course, and evidently for the field of social work as a whole, are "social justice and social change." The official course description notes that "social workers in educational settings strive to maximize educational opportunities for individuals, groups, neighborhoods, and regions, and promote progressive local, state, and national policy."[7] In other words, the goal of social work is to promote "progressive" (i.e., left-wing) political policies.

This sectarian agenda is reflected in the one-sided reading list provided to students. One of the principal texts is yet another book by Castro acolyte Jonathan Kozol, *Savage Inequalities: Children in America's Schools*. Here Kozol argues that the failures of American education, and especially of urban public schools, can be explained by a lack of adequate funding. Although this is a widely disputed thesis, since the worst schools in the country (in Washington, D.C.) have the highest per-pupil spending ratio, while urban schools with modest funding but expanded accountability for teachers have been able to improve their academic performance, it is a dogma for the "progressive" Left. Not surprisingly it goes unchallenged in this course.

After taking this class, students might reasonably conclude that being a social worker is synonymous with being a left-wing political activist. Indeed, the course description says so: it explains that the books used in the course, including Kozol's, "fit the ideal of what school social workers could be striving to reach."

Institutional Inequality in American Political and Social Policy *Social Work 200*[8]

INSTRUCTOR: Marcia R. Wilson, Adjunct Associate Professor in the School of Social Work

This is a crude—but not exceptional—attempt to pass off a left-wing political agenda as an academic course of study, and to offer it as a course in Social Work at that. The course description claims that "a variety of groups" in American society "experience inequality in status and opportunity, including African-Americans, Asian-Americans, Latinos, Native Americans, women, gay men and lesbian women and other special populations." The claims that these groups are all victims of inequality is not only an ideological prejudice but demonstrably false. For example, although Asian-Americans make up only 5 percent of the total American population, they have the highest median income of any other racial demographic, a statistical reality difficult to square with the course's orthodoxy.[9]

Similarly dubious is the instructor's operating premise that inequality is the result of structural flaws in American society. The course description states that students "should acquire" an "understanding of institutionalized disadvantage and inequality in American life" and "how political, economic and social policies have been shaped by institutional inequality." This is a radical point of view, not a scientific datum, but students are required to accept it.

Each section of the curriculum instills the course's radical doctrines. One examines how American westward expansion played a "role in institutionalizing the view of minority groups as exploitable persons." A section on immigration employs "paradigms of the American immigrant experience that reveal discrimination and unequal positioning of different ethnic groups." Still another section, presented under the tendentious title "The Empowerment of the Corporate Industrial Complex and Its Effect on Inequality," is specifically designed to counter the "myth" of immigrant success in the United States, of "making it in the promised-land." This section concentrates on the "rise of nativism and the persistence of racism and sexism."

LGBT Psychological, Social, and Political Issues

Social Work 599[10]

INSTRUCTOR: Ian Stulberg, Part-Time Lecturer in the School of Social Work

The primary goal of this course is to encourage students to think as advocates of identity politics. Its curriculum focuses on the "experience of lesbian and gay individuals" and "bisexual and transgender people." Upon completing the course, students are expected to show they have absorbed its instruction in "homosexual identity formation," understand "internalized homophobia" (i.e., that gays who do not subscribe to the instructor's point of view are self-hating), and can "identify the consequences of societal homophobia on the psychological development of lesbian and gay people." Instead of examining these issues academically, students are required to "deepen their self-awareness regarding the role sexual orientation plays in their lives." Because of the course's relentless ideological agenda, understanding bisexuality as a personal choice—to take one example—does not appear to be an option for students in Social Work 599.

The principal text assigned, *Psychological Perspectives on Lesbian, Gay, and Bisexual Experiences,* reinforces the course's doctrinal orthodoxies, stating in its introduction that the book is written from a "gay-affirmative perspective" and that "an understanding of sexual orientation will enhance psychological research and practice by reducing heterosexist bias." Like the course itself, this text makes the assumption that the prevalence of "heterosexist bias" in society is a fact rather than a hypothesis.

Managing a Diverse Workforce in a Global Context

Social Work 599[11]

INSTRUCTOR: Michàl E. Mor-Barak, Professor in the School of Social Work

"Managing a Diverse Workforce in a Global Context" is one of a number of courses that promote "diversity" in the workplace. One section of the course, titled "Global Legislation and Public Policies Towards

Diversity," is devoted to legislation seeking to expand "diversity related employment legislation around the world, social policies and affirmative/positive action programs." The sole assigned book, *Managing Diversity: Toward a Globally Inclusive Workplace,* is written by the professor herself. In it, Professor Mor-Barak complains that "corporate leaders" are insufficiently supportive of "workforce diversity" and that corporate managers have an "unfortunate inability" to "divest themselves of their personal prejudicial attitudes, and creatively unleash the potential embedded in a multicultural workforce." The commitment to "diverse" hiring practices is so pronounced that the course doesn't seem to consider that employers might value other qualifications, such as a demonstrated record of accomplishment, over concerns about skin color and ethnicity.

Feminist Theory, Social Action, and Social Work in the Philippines Seminar *Social Work 599*[12]

INSTRUCTORS: Annalisa Enrile and Valerie Richards, Clinical Assistant Professors in the School of Social Work

In addition to its regular courses, the School of Social Work offers seminars that are also training programs for political activists. The stated aim of "Feminist Theory, Social Action, and Social Work," is to provide "students with a broader understanding of the feminist perspective in social work and its influence in facilitating social change." Having completed the seminar, students are expected to exhibit a "keener awareness of gender issues and the feminist perspective in social work practice." Professor Enrile serves as the national chair of the GABRIELA Network, a self-described "Philippine-US women's solidarity mass organization" that "functions as training ground for women's leadership, and articulates the women's point of view."

As part of the seminar, students travel with Professor Enrile to the Philippines to take part in the annual Women's International Solidarity Affair. To get a sense of the political tenor of this conference, consider that in 2004 it resolved to condemn the wars in Iraq and Afghanistan as a "genocidal attack by the U.S. and its allies" and specifically rejected the "label 'terrorist' to demonize people, groups and organizations who struggle against globalization, militarism, imperialism, and for national liberation," an unmistakable reference to Islamic terrorist groups.[13]

Enrile's seminar, too, is a "training ground."

Branded: The School of International Relations

The School of International Relations at USC is in many ways a lengthened shadow of its current director, Laurie Brand. In her off-campus life, Brand is best known for her antiwar and anti-Israel activism. In 2002, she signed an academic petition charging that Israel was engaging in an "ethnic cleansing" campaign against neighboring Palestinian Arabs. Not one to leave her political commitments at the classroom door, Brand has in the past called for professors to embrace what she calls a "special responsibility," which in practice seems to consist of criticizing American society from the left while celebrating the "complexity and the richness of societies beyond these borders." An analysis of the courses offered through the school indicates that this political agenda is a pervasive part of the international relations program, not least in the courses taught by Professor Brand.

Middle East International Relations: Colonialism, Nationalism, and Identity *IR 581*[14]

INSTRUCTOR: Laurie Brand, Professor of International Relations; Director, School of International Relations

Presented as a historical survey of nationalism and colonialism, this course is organized around Professor Brand's pro-Arab views of the Israeli-Palestinian conflict. Three full sections of the course are devoted to a one-sided analysis of the Israeli-Palestinian issue. The section "Israel/Palestine: Contested Histories" supplies abundant evidence. All of the texts assigned have an anti-Israel point of view, assailing the justice of Israel's creation and questioning the legitimacy of its existence as a majority Jewish state. *From Haven to Conquest,* by the Arab author Walid Khalidi, asserts that the history of Israel is really the history of the violent dispossession of the Palestinians by colonialist Zionist settlers. The course does not assign the work of scholars who call such claims into question, pointing out, for instance, that much of the land at the time of Israel's creation was controlled by absentee landowners rather than the resident Arab population, that Jewish settlers had no monopoly on violence, and that the entire region was part of the Turkish empire for four hundred years prior to these disputes and not in the possession of any Arab peoples.

Instead, the course assigns such books as *Sacred Landscape: The Buried History of the Holy Land Since 1948,* in which left-wing author Mêrôn Benveništî, pretending to speak on behalf of Israelis, asks, "Have we transformed a struggle for survival into an ethnic cleansing operation, sending people into exile because we wanted to plunder their land?" To this loaded question, Benveništî provides an unambiguous answer in the form of another question: "Is there not something we must do now to assuage the burning sense of injustice, however one-sided, of the uprooted?" In short, according to the author, it is the Arabs who are the victims in the Middle East conflict despite the fact that they have waged three aggressive wars against Israel since its founding, and have called for its obliteration.

In addition to these books, the course requires students to consider a series of articles by the Haifa University professor Ilan Pappe.[15] Pappe, an Israeli citizen, is associated with the "post-Zionist" school that denies Israel's right to exist as an ethnic Jewish state (but has no problem with other ethnic states). Pappe, whose views about Israeli history are far removed from the scholarly mainstream, claims that Israel's existence can be explained as a "Jewish ethnic cleansing operation against the indigenous population."

In interviews, Professor Brand has rejected using classrooms for purposes of political indoctrination. "I don't think indoctrination serves anybody's purpose, whether it's indoctrination of center, right or left," she has said.[16] But like everyone else, she should be judged by what she does not by what she says.

Gender and Global Issues *IR 316*[17]

INSTRUCTOR: Ann Tickner, Professor of International Relations

This course is premised on several controversial claims. One is that "women have not been major players in the foreign policies of states or in international organizations" and have been "marginalized from foreign policy-making." This assertion flies in the face of the obvious counterexamples: Israeli prime minister Golda Meir, Indian prime minister Indira Gandhi, British prime minister Margaret Thatcher, German prime minister Angela Merkel, Pakistani prime minister Benazir Bhutto, and American secretaries of state Madeleine Albright and Condoleezza Rice.

Another claim is the feminist trope that the prevalence of men in positions of power and their influence over foreign policy explains the recurrence of war throughout history. To reinforce this conclusion, the course examines whether national security is "gendered masculine" and "[h]ow might this affect states' foreign policies." Less subtly, the course description asks, "Why have wars been fought primarily by men?"

Instead of being critically analyzed and debated, these claims are underscored by the assigned readings, which consist largely of radical feminist texts. The political agenda of one of these books, *Women in Developing Countries: Assessing Strategies for Empowerment*, is evident from its title. In another, *The Curious Feminist: Searching for Women in a New Age of Empire,* the author expressly declares her interest in "activist-minded scholarship" and proceeds to argue that all political events are, at bottom, "deeply gendered."

Culture, Gender, and Global Society *IR 509*[18]

INSTRUCTOR: Ann Tickner, Professor of International Relations

Here Professor Tickner reduces the complexities of geopolitics to feminist identity politics. The course aims to explain how "cultural, gendered, and social identifications" shape "global patterns of political and economic conflict and cooperation." It is far from clear that "gender" plays any significant role in any of these areas. That the course nonetheless advances the theory as conventional wisdom is an example of the kind of political curriculum that the School of International Relations regards as appropriate.

Ecological Security and Global Politics *IR 422*[19]

INSTRUCTOR: Frederick Gordon, Part-Time Lecturer in the Department of Political Science

This is a course in left-wing environmentalism. The description warns of the "[g]rowing concern over environmental degradation and the possible impact of stratospheric ozone depletion as well as climate change," all of which it proposes to consider from the perspective of "ecological security." In other words, these are all serious crises that must be combated with the same seriousness as any other threat to national security. Not the least of the problems with this approach is that the claims about the environment this course takes for granted rest on a set of debatable assumptions. For instance, while there is a scientific consensus that the earth is currently undergoing a period of increased temperatures, there is vigorous debate about the causes and implications of this warming. The instructor is not a climatologist or meteorologist and consequently in advancing such claims is merely expressing his personal prejudice, not any professional expertise. Had he considered the range of opinions about global warming, he could have given his students a rich educational experience. Instead, he gives them premasticated political correctness.

Rather than a cautious and scholarly examination of the political consequences of changing weather patterns, the course has an alarmist environmentalist agenda. One course section is revealingly titled "The Global Water Crisis." Students are directed to links to a number of one-sided environmental websites—the Environmental News Network, Friends of the Earth,[20] and other radical grassroots environmental organizations—but there are no links to sites that might present a more skeptical understanding of these issues. For instance, while left-wing environmentalist groups have long advocated expanded intervention by governments to provide access to water, conservative environmentalists have argued that private enterprises and market mechanisms would be more efficient in allocating global water resources. Students taking this course would not only be incapable of judging the merits of the disputing sides, they would be unaware that such a debate exists.

Introduction to Peace and Conflict Studies *IR 310*[21]

INSTRUCTOR: Douglas Becker, Visiting Lecturer in the School of International Relations

This course, offered as part of a minor in peace and conflict studies, is more accurately described as a training program in antiwar activism. On matters of war and peace, the course description poses the following question: "What can peace-minded individuals and groups do to lessen the outbreak of war and/or ameliorate its consequences?" Each of the assigned texts strengthens the antiwar and activist position. For example, *The Political Economy of Armed Conflict* is a project by the International Peace Academy, an antiwar research institute affiliated with the United Nations. In the introduction, the editors write that the "the promotion of a more concerted global regulatory effort is indispensable to effective conflict resolution." While many knowledgeable observers have pointed to the potential dangers of a global government, including its potential for abuse and hence for engendering conflict on an unprecedented scale, no text offering such criticisms is provided in this course. Nor has the instructor assigned texts critical of the UN, a scandal-ridden institution dominated by dictatorial regimes.

Another assigned reading, *Beyond Appeasement: Interpreting Interwar Peace Movements in the World,* supports "international peace movements" because of their capacity for "delegitimizing . . . preparations for war and legitimizing norms that underlay global international organization and hence the construction of the United Nations." The author rejects the notion that these movements are "ideologically monolithic."

According to her, they are derived from "the diverse intellectual, social and political currents of radical progressivism, romanticism, feminism, liberalism, and socialism," as though variations of left-wing politics were a fair representation of the political spectrum.

Still another book used in the course is *War Is a Force That Gives Us Meaning,* a collection of essays by the radical journalist Chris Hedges. Hedges disparages the U.S.-led war on terrorism as a "crusade." To Hedges's reductive antiwar beliefs and partisan analysis the course offers no contrary perspective.

Barbra Streisand Academics: The Gender Studies Program

In a self-description that appears on its homepage, the Gender Studies Program explains that among its primary goals is to examine the "functions and images of women and men from feminist perspectives." Consistent with that goal, the courses offered through the program are devoted to feminist ideology and political activism.

Introduction to Feminist Theory and the History of the Women's and Men's Movements *SWMS 301*[22]

INSTRUCTOR: Diana York Blaine, Adjunct Professor of Gender Studies and the Writing Program

Notwithstanding the word "history" in its title, this is not a history course but an instruction in feminist ideology. Of the three main texts, one is a collection of writings from a feminist perspective, titled *Feminist Theory: A Reader;* another is the novel *Woman on the Edge of Time,* by feminist activist Marge Piercy; the final text is *Feminism Is for Everybody,* by the all-purpose radical feminist bell hooks, which calls for "feminist political solidarity." There are many ways to describe such a work, but academic scholarship is not one of them. Not only is the course composed solely of feminist political texts, it also discusses subjects ("Capitalism and Its Discontents") that the professor, whose background is in "gender studies," has no competence to address.

Professor Blaine is not known for her professionalism. In May 2006, she caused a scandal at USC after linking to topless pictures of herself on her personal blog, which she had earlier said, in an unfortunate turn of phrase, was meant for USC students seeking "further exposure to my ideas once our class time together has ended." When criticized for exposing her students to more than her ideas, Professor Blaine was unapologetic, lashing out against the "outpouring of hatred against me and my un-mutilated middle-aged breasts, which I had the audacity to have photographed in several spontaneous life moments and the unmitigated gall to share with others." Considered against this background, the fact that Professor Blaine's course is the work of a politically engaged amateur ought not, perhaps, to come as a surprise.

Feminist Theory *SWMS 560*[23]

INSTRUCTOR: Sharon Hays, Barbra Streisand Professor in Contemporary Gender Studies

It is fitting that the professor of this course should occupy a chair endowed by one of Hollywood's more dogmatic left-wing activists. For although the course discusses a number of feminist schools—including liberal feminism, socialist/Marxist feminism, radical feminism, psychological feminism, spiritual feminism, and ecological feminism—there is nothing to indicate that students are anywhere given the chance to consider substantive criticism of feminist ideology, as opposed to superficial differences between its affiliated schools. The course makes the usual number of unsubstantiated assumptions from the feminist perspective, asserting, naturally, the "social construction of gender differences," a concept that has spread like a computer virus in American higher education. This ideological approach, while inappropriate for an academic course, is consistent with the agenda of the professor, Sharon Hayes, who views her scholarship as a means of carrying on the "the unfinished business of feminism."[24]

Overcoming Prejudice *SWMS 384*[25]

INSTRUCTOR: Joseph Hawkins, Lecturer in the Department of Anthropology

As its catalogue description makes abundantly clear, this is a course in political activism. It is described as an "analysis of the most effective strategies and techniques for reducing prejudice against racial/ethnic minorities, women, gays and lesbians, and others subjected to stigma." Few would dispute the principle that such prejudices should be opposed, but is the proper function of a university to create activists to achieve this end? Equally problematic is that the course expands the definition of "prejudice" to include categories such as "heterosexism" (discrimination against nonheterosexuals) and "homophobia." There are no similar expansions of the definition of prejudice to include homosexism or, for that matter, heterophobia.

Texts assigned for this course seem to have been selected to correspond to the political assumptions of the professor. For example, an assigned section from the book *Working for Social Justice: Visions and Strategies for Change* suggests an activist approach, offering "strategies for personal and collective action" that can be used for "working toward social justice." Another required text is *Readings for Diversity and Social Justice: An Anthology on Racism, Anti-Semitism, Sexism, Heterosexism, Ableism, and Classism*. Although that title reads like a parody of academic political correctness, this is an actual book—a collection of essays by left-wing ideologues such as the ubiquitous Joe Feagin,[26] Cornel West,[27] and bell hooks.[28] The editors of this book subscribe to a number of radical claims, including that political activism—in the form of "social change" and "social justice"—is not only an appropriate subject for the classroom but one demanded by professional ethics. "We believe that it is unethical to critically examine issues of social oppression in the classroom without offering hope, a vision for the future and practical tools for change," they write. By this way of thinking, it would be unethical to express pessimism even if such an outlook were warranted by the empirical evidence.

Drilling home the "hope" that your program of "social justice" offers, and whipping your students into activism—this is recruitment to a political cause masquerading as an undergraduate degree program.

If courses as extreme and politically oriented as these pass muster at USC, one wonders just what a professor or a department would need to do to actually arouse the concerns of the university and its administration. If professors can state their political agendas as frankly as many of them do in the course descriptions examined here, is there any limit to what they might do in the classroom?

As bad as the situation is at USC, matters are worse at a school located several hundred miles up the coast: the University of California at Santa Cruz, which yields to no institution in its assaults on academic decency and academic standards.

12

The Worst School in America

UNIVERSITY OF CALIFORNIA, SANTA CRUZ
TUITION: $7,539 IN-STATE
$27,123 OUT-OF-STATE

Nestled in a redwood glade on cliffs above the Pacific Ocean, the University of California at Santa Cruz would seem to be located in an environment ideally suited for the contemplative life. In the hard sciences, it can be said that Santa Cruz handsomely fulfills its academic expectations. Its physics program is ranked among the best in the country, while its Department of Astronomy and Astrophysics, which houses the Lick Observatory, is a world-class scientific institution. But inside the classrooms of its liberal arts division something besides the life of the mind is being nourished. In these environs, UC Santa Cruz is beyond any doubt the most radical university in the United States, its curricula anything but academic.

Emblematic of the politicized state of this public institution was the appointment in February 2005 of Denice Denton as university chancellor. A professor of engineering, Denton had made a name for herself as a radical feminist and antiwar activist. In her brief career as chancellor she made an additional mark as one of the academics whose angry protests led to the resignation of Harvard president Larry Summers. Denton's intemperate behavior led to a series of scandals (including a $600,000 renovation of her university residence and a $192,000-a-year university post for her lesbian lover) that brought her career to an abrupt end. The blowback from these and other episodes, along with her tormented private life, culminated in her suicide on June 24, 2006, barely eighteen months after her appointment.

The fiefdom that academic radicals have established at Santa Cruz continues without her. The school's most celebrated faculty member is Angela Davis, a lifelong Communist who ran as the party's vice presidential nominee, received a Lenin Prize from the East German police state, and retained her party membership card even after the fall of the Berlin Wall.[1] Davis is one of seven designated "University Professors," a title normally reserved "for scholars of international distinction," which provides her with a six-figure income. Admired by professorial radicals across the country, Davis has produced nothing in her academic career besides hackneyed Marxist political tracts. Her real distinction is to be a tireless agitator for radical causes, including her personal crusade to free criminals and abolish the "prison-industrial complex."

This former Black Panther militant once purchased an arsenal of weapons for a would-be hijacker whose ill-fated hostage-taking resulted in the killing of three people, including a California judge. She holds an academic chair in Santa Cruz's History of Consciousness Program, which awarded a Ph.D. to another Black Panther Party member—in fact, to its leader—Huey Newton. Newton's sole academic credentials were his radical rap sheet and a political tract exculpating the criminal organization he headed and presenting it as a victim of government persecution. Santa Cruz accepted this worthless document as his doctoral thesis.

The Department of Community Studies is one of a cornucopia of radical studies programs available to Santa Cruz students. One department offering is "The Theory and Practice of Resistance and Social Movements," whose contents are described in the Santa Cruz catalogue in these terms: "The goal of this seminar is to learn how to organize a revolution. We will learn what communities past and present have done and are doing to resist, challenge, and overcome systems of power including (but not limited to) global capitalism, state oppression, and racism."[2]

Similarly devoted to revolutionary agendas is Santa Cruz's Women's Studies program, one of the oldest and most influential in the country. Its creators have renamed it the Department of Feminist Studies to reflect their real agenda, which is to provide a training center for political radicals. The chief architect of these academic programs is Bettina Aptheker, a former Communist Party comrade of Professor Davis and a well-known Berkeley radical in her own right.[3] Like Huey Newton, Aptheker received her Ph.D. from the Santa Cruz History of Consciousness program, which allowed her to submit as a "scholarly" thesis a collection of political articles previously rejected by the Communist Party's publishing house because of her deviation on the "woman question" (Aptheker is a lesbian activist).

In her autobiography, *Intimate Politics: How I Grew Up Red, Fought for Free Speech, and Became a Feminist Rebel,* she describes her initial reluctance to take on an academic career,[4] and explains how she overcame her hesitation when Marge Frantz, a lecturer in American Studies at Santa Cruz and, like Aptheker, a Bay Area Communist, advised her, "It's your revolutionary duty!"[5] Aptheker was duly made the instructor for the "Introduction to Women's Studies" course in the fledgling program: "I redesigned the curriculum and re-titled it, 'Introduction to Feminism,' making it more overtly political, and taught the class in the context of the women's movement."

According to Aptheker, most of her students "were activists themselves"[6] and nothing remotely academic entered her lesson plan: "Teaching became a form of political activism for me, replacing the years of dogged meetings and intrepid organizing with the immediacy of a liberatory practice."[7] This abusive approach to education was made possible by the abdication of university authorities and the shirking of their legal obligations to students and the public.

In its formal regulations, California's public university system makes clear that its campuses must observe clearly defined academic standards and that political indoctrination is an abuse of its classrooms and students. This is a contract not only between the university's faculty and its administration but also between the university and the public, whose taxpayers support it. While professors are "free within the classroom to express the widest range of viewpoints," university regulations require that these viewpoints must "accord with the standards of scholarly inquiry and professional ethics." The Standing Orders of the Regents, passed in September 2005, make unmistakably clear that political indoctrination and partisan interest have no place in the university curriculum and that the regents are obligated to maintain its standards:

> [The Regents] are responsible to see that the University remain aloof from politics and never function as an instrument for the advance of partisan interest. Misuse of the classroom by, for example, allowing it to be used for political indoctrination, for purposes other than those for which the course was constituted, or for providing grades without commensurate and appropriate student achievement, constitutes misuse of the University as an institution.[8]

In the liberal arts programs of the University of Santa Cruz, however, the violation of this policy and the consequent abuse of the institution and its students is a routine fact of academic life.

Organizing the Revolution: The Department of Community Studies

In contravention of the Standing Orders of the Regents, the clear purpose of the Community Studies Program (as described on the departmental web page) is overtly political rather than academic: "The UCSC faculty offers courses related to social justice—including broad structural and social changes and community based organizing." The use of the term "social justice" signals, as we've seen, a left-wing perspective, and sure enough, the departmental website provides several telling examples of politicized curricula.[9] Department courses fall under several "social justice domains," such as "labor studies, including the history of the working class," "youth cultures, youth activism and empowerment," "race and racism," "cultural work in social change," "gay and lesbian issues," "social justice, sustenance and sustainability in agro-food systems," and "resistance and social movements." The department makes explicit its commitment to training political activists when it states that the Community Studies major "provides an opportunity for the student who is committed to social justice to work on a full-time basis beyond the university."

The way the department frames the subject matter automatically excludes students who do not subscribe to this left-wing party line. The entire process violates the students' academic freedom and every academic standard set by the Regents of the University, although no university official seems to care. By requiring students to adhere to a political orthodoxy, the Department of Community Studies also violates the fundamental contract between the Regents and the taxpayers of California, who are funding, unbeknownst to them, a training program in radical politics.

Theory and Practice of Economic Justice *CMMU 100E*[10]

INSTRUCTOR: Mary Beth Pudup, Associate Professor and Chair of the Department of Community Studies

"Economic justice" is an ideological term, not an analytical one. This course promulgates left-wing propaganda about what constitutes a "just" economic order, offering a one-sided critique of free-market capitalism. The course ascribes the unequal outcomes of competition to the inherent injustice of free-market systems, rather than to the unequal distribution of natural abilities. The link to radical activism is also explicit in the syllabus, which is fixated on the "economic justice movement in the U.S." and its "targeting of inequalities arising from contemporary capitalist structures such as the labor market, credit market, and housing market."

Students in the Community Studies program are required to do volunteer work in line with the program's mission to develop future political activists, and this course encourages students to sign up with organizations that are part of the "economic justice movement."

Among the organizations that Professor Pudup suggests is the Coalition of University Employees, a clerical union within the University of California system. This means that the taxpayers of California are funding a program that trains agitators whose goal is to raise the costs of a university education. Another recommended organization is the anti–free trade activist group Corpwatch.

Professor Pudup doesn't even seem qualified to teach this course. Her academic degree is in geography, not economics, and from her published academic résumé it appears that she has published a single scholarly article on subsistence agriculture in Appalachia and has coedited a book on Appalachian culture in the nineteenth century. It is not evident how this minimal record of publications would qualify her for tenure at any major university, let alone for a departmental chair.

Community Organizing *CMMU 181*[11]

INSTRUCTOR: Mike Rotkin, Lecturer and Field Study Coordinator in the Department of Community Studies

The title of this course states its political agenda bluntly: its goal is to turn students into political organizers for radical organizations. Students are required to understand the "theory and practice of community organizing," and to that end must do "a minimum of four hours a week of practical organizing with a community group." Assignments for the course are designed to encourage students to think like political activists and organizers. In the first such assignment, students are asked to "develop or explain your community group's organizing strategy," while in their final paper they are required to produce an "overall organizational, strategic, and tactical approach to the solution of some social or environmental problem."

Books assigned for the course uniformly reflect the political agendas of the radical Left. A core text is *Reveille for Radicals,* by Saul Alinsky, dean of radical community organizers. A second, *Activists' Handbook* by Randy Shaw, enumerates the strategies and tactics for effecting "progressive change." Yet another, *Making the News: A*

Guide for Activists and Nonprofits by environmentalist radical Jason Salzman, instructs activists in ways they can "creatively manipulate the media." Besides these required books, students are also encouraged to draw lessons in political organizing from radicals such as Howard Zinn, Abbie Hoffman, and the late labor organizer César Chávez.

The professor for this course, Mike Rotkin, is not an academic but a longtime member of the Santa Cruz City Council who describes himself as a "radical" and a "political activist for life."

Feminist Organizing and Global Realities *CMMU 100Q*[12]

INSTRUCTOR: Nancy E. Stoller, Professor of Community Studies

Professor Stoller signed a U.C. petition urging the university to divest from Israel, and was seen by students tearing down fliers announcing an upcoming talk by a visiting lecturer, Itamar Marcus of Palestinian Media Watch.[13] This gives a sense of her commitment to the traditional academic values of open inquiry and objectivity. Her research specialties are gender and health, the politics of nonnormative sexuality, and grassroots organizing. She is involved with several community-based action-research and organizing projects addressing the impact of incarceration on individuals and public health. Nothing in Professor Stoller's academic résumé, in short, indicates that she is qualified to teach this course dealing with the global economy.

In keeping with the department's mission to train political activists, the first half of the course is devoted to the required text *Women's Activism and Globalization: Linking Local Struggles and Transnational Politics,* a compendium of essays by feminist antiglobalization activists coedited by Stoller. The second half of the course, students are informed, is designed to "prepare you more specifically for your activist work in the fields of gender and sexuality." The aim of the course is not simply that students should study feminist theory, but that they should practice it as political operatives—at taxpayers' expense. The instructor explains in her syllabus that her course is not merely an introduction to feminism but "an introduction *to the theory and practice of feminist organizing* in a global context" (emphasis hers).

Women's Health Activism *CMMU 148*[14]

INSTRUCTOR: Nancy E. Stoller, Professor of Community Studies

This course's political agenda, already adumbrated in its title, is spelled out in Professor Stoller's course description. She explains, "In this course, the emphasis is on *activism—making change, especially from the grass roots*" (emphasis hers). Specifically, she means *feminist* activism, as she notes that the course "is designed for students interested in a feminist approach to women's health." In case students don't get the picture, Stoller adds that papers "must be focused on activism. They are not to be about an illness per se or a theoretical analysis of a problem. They must focus on organizing by women . . . concerning a threat to women's health." Examples of topics the professor finds appropriate include profiling a "currently active California feminist health organization," or conducting a "national comparison of feminist activism concerning a specific feminist health challenge." As these examples suggest, the course is designed to familiarize students with feminist dogmas and the organizations and campaigns that attempt to put those dogmas into practice.

Books assigned in the course are written exclusively from a radical perspective. In *Killing the Black Body,* author Dorothy Roberts claims that the federal government is waging a racial war against the "reproductive rights" of black women. An assigned collection of feminist writings includes an article titled "Not Feminist, but Not Bad: Cuba's Surprisingly Pro-Woman Health System." Another assignment is *The Vagina Monologues*, by feminist author Eve Ensler. Instead of examining the work critically, students are required to perform a section from the play in front of the class. This was no doubt the procedure in religious monasteries during the Middle Ages, when students were required to perform Morality Plays exemplifying church doctrine.

Environmental Justice *CMMU 110*[15]

INSTRUCTOR: Max Boykoff, Graduate Student

The term "environmental justice" is a left-wing catchphrase for political activism, encompassing such familiar radical formulas as economic redistribution. Among the questions students taking this course are asked to consider are the following:

> How do rights-based movements of distributive justice relate to various environmental problems? How have environmental justice movements worked to combat asymmetrical power relations as well as social, economic and political inequality? Have environmental justice movements actually dealt appropriately with issues of race, class, culture and gender inequalities?[16]

The syllabus continues, "Readings in this class will trace the early historical roots and conceptualizations of 'environmental justice' as a mechanism for change, but also its more current engagements with culture, equity, and power." Uncritical promotion of radical ideology is thus the principal, even sole, aim of this course.

The texts assigned take the students deeper into the professor's tunnel vision. The stated purpose of one required text, *Environmentalism Unbound,* to "plant the seeds for a new kind of environmentalism that can contribute to a new type of social agenda" and to challenge "the structures of power within the contemporary urban, industrial, and global order"—or, as the author identifies the enemy more pointedly, "expansive, resource-based capitalism."

Another required text, *Dead Heat: Globalization and Global Warming,* treats global warming not as a scientific question but as a subset of the social justice movement: "In this book, we argue that the battle against global warming is key to the larger battle for global justice." While meteorologists may argue about the severity of the problem and the extent of its consequences—indeed, while the problem itself is a contested issue—the authors assume that the threat is not only inarguable but lethal, and that it is directed at the poor:

"The science clearly shows, in mercilessly numeric terms, that . . . the consequences of global warming will soon be quite severe, and even murderous, particularly for the poor and vulnerable." The authors dismiss anyone who would dare question their alarmist claims: "But the skeptics can go to hell, and we're basically going to ignore them." There is nothing scholarly in this blithe dismissal of critics; it is a political stump speech that reflects the tenor of this course.

Theory and Practice of Resistance and Social Movements

CMMU 100P[17]

INSTRUCTOR: Paul Ortiz, Associate Professor in the Department of Community Studies

Illustrating how acceptable political extremism has become in the Department of Community Studies, this is a course whose stated goal is "to learn how to organize a revolution" (of course an anticapitalist revolution). Appropriately, the syllabus is introduced with a quote from the Communist writer C. L. R. James. The syllabus goes on to state, "We will learn what communities past and present have done and are doing to resist, challenge, and overcome systems of power including (but not limited to) global capitalism, state oppression, and racism."[18]

One section of the course, titled "Women in Struggle; Gender and Organizing," requires students to read about the Communist Worker's Party of Brazil. Another section, titled "Capitalism, Slavery, and Internationalism," centers on such traditional radical themes as "liberation theology" (i.e., religious Marxism), "radical Christianity," and "anti-capitalism." A third section of the course, titled "Workers' Culture, Religion, and State Terror," focuses on "organizing against multinational corporations; sustaining a movement in a one-party state; surviving state and corporate-sponsored terrorism," and it addresses "the question of armed insurrection."

Students are provided with a glossary of terms that preclude any skepticism or contrary perspectives: "Capitalist societies," the class glossary explains, "breed on hierarchy and inequality." The professor,

Paul Ortiz, describes himself "as a historian/activist of social change," but to judge from the outlines of his course, the historian aspect is very much under the thumb of the activist. His curriculum is a textbook example of the kind of academic abuse that the University of California's academic freedom policy proscribes.

Radical organizing courses such as this belong not at a public university but at the headquarters for MoveOn.org or a cadre training school for the Green Party.

"A Unified Field Theory of Liberation": The Department of Feminist Studies

Introduction to Feminisms *FMST 1A*[19]

INSTRUCTOR: **Bettina Aptheker, Professor, Feminist Studies and History**

This course is a case study in the politicized approach that Bettina Aptheker brought to Santa Cruz. The class fulfills the academic mission she outlined in her autobiography, which is to form the "juxtaposition of Marxism and feminism into a unified field theory of liberation." The course introduces students to a "gendered analysis of philosophical, scientific, historical, economic, political, and cultural issues from feminist perspectives." Professor Aptheker summarizes her course as an attempt to synthesize feminist theory and to make it more "accessible" to students—that is, to immerse students in a sectarian ideology. Aptheker provides a one-sided overview of this politically charged subject, with no critical apparatus and no texts skeptical of its agendas.

Feminist Methods of Teaching *FMST 196*[20]

INSTRUCTOR: **Bettina Aptheker, Professor, Feminist Studies and History**

Aptheker has described her teaching philosophy as a "revolutionary praxis," a Marxist term of art for political organizing. The crux of her approach, she says, is to break down the distinction between subjective and objective truth, what she refers to as "breaking down dualisms." This old-fashioned Marxism allows her to inject a "women-centered perspective" into the curriculum to correct what she claims is the "male-centered" bias of traditional university study.

While the University of California regulations require faculty to evaluate students solely on the basis of criteria related to their academic performance, this course adopts an opposite approach. "Feminist Methods of Teaching" is geared toward undergraduate students who assist in teaching Aptheker's introductory course on feminism, and the professor urges the would-be teaching assistants to focus on such supposedly critical criteria as "racial diversity" and "violence against women" when they "conduct sections and evaluate student papers." It is far from obvious what academic merit there is in such criteria, or how they can be neutrally applied.

Women and the Law *FMST/POLI 112*[21]

INSTRUCTOR: Gina Dent, Associate Professor, Feminist Studies, History of Consciousness, and Legal Studies

While Gina Dent is listed as a professor of "legal studies," her faculty biography makes no mention of any academic background that would qualify her to teach law. Her doctorate is in English and Comparative Literature. This course violates the university's policy that professors exhibit specific competence in the subjects they teach.

Obscured by its neutral title is the fact that this course is simply another exercise in radical feminist politics. To the extent that the law is discussed, it is only to explicate the guiding suppositions of feminist theory—for example, the notion that complex institutions such as the law should be viewed from the ideologically constrained prism of "gender." Unsurprisingly, the course is also informed by "critical race theory," which integrates Marxism with racial politics, and the class's underlying theme is that "the law" is inherently oppressive. To this end the course "examines how the law structures rights [unfairly], offers protections [to the privileged], produces hierarchies, and sexualizes power."

Assignments for the course are designed not to examine this theory critically but to ratify its political agendas. The course website encourages students to read "feminist jurisprudence" and assorted "feminist legal theories," as well as publications from left-wing political groups. Students are directed to an ACLU website assailing the PATRIOT Act as an assault on American freedoms, though its connection to a course called "Women and the Law" is not apparent.

Introduction to Feminist Science Studies *FMST 80L*[22]

INSTRUCTOR: Astrid Schrader, Graduate Student

In this course, feminist politics ventures into the realm of the natural sciences. The course description states, "We will examine a variety of feminist approaches to scientific methods and practices." Relying on objective evidence about the natural world, science does not easily lend itself to the yoke of ideology. To overcome this problem, the course includes a full-bore assault on the very idea of scientific objectivity, although its instructor, Astrid Schrader, is not a scientist or science major but a graduate student in the History of Consciousness Program.

Students are required to read essays like "The Science Question in Feminism and the Privilege of Partial Perspective" by the radical feminist Donna Haraway, who is a professor (and the former chair) of the History of Consciousness at Santa Cruz, and a faculty patron of Bettina Aptheker's academic career. In this essay, Haraway claims that science has never been truly objective—the history of science, according to Haraway, has been "tied to militarism, capitalism, colonialism, and male supremacy"—and calls for "a doctrine of embodied objectivity that accommodates paradoxical and critical feminist science projects," or what Haraway terms "feminist objectivity." In short, only a "science" that is consistent with feminist prejudices can be considered genuinely "objective." And what could be more Orwellian than that?

An Academic Home for Black Panthers and Communists: The History of Consciousness Department

The History of Consciousness Department at UCSC is among the most famous—or notorious—academic programs in the country. This is less the legacy of the department's academic achievements—which are nugatory—than of its association, throughout its nearly three-decade-long history, with radical politics and questionable standards. Asked about the degree awarded to Huey Newton in the 1970s, historian Page Smith, the founder of the program, explained that he had created the program "to demonstrate that the PhD is a fraud."[23] The program's political agendas are easily discerned in its mission statement, which focuses on "the intersection of race, sexuality, and gender," the standard trinity of radical academic theory.

Radical Critiques of Penalty *HISC 208 A/B*[24]

INSTRUCTOR: Angela Y. Davis, Professor, History of Consciousness and Feminist Studies

In keeping with her relentless campaign against the "prison-industrial complex," the Communist and former Black Panther Angela Davis teaches this radical course, whose "major goal," according to the catalogue description, is "to identify ways of disarticulating crime and punishment using race, class and gender as principal analytical categories." Davis provides a more comprehensible definition of what she means in her book *Are Prisons Obsolete?,* in which she urges readers to acquire a more "nuanced understanding" of the "punishment system." This understanding is as follows: "We would recognize that 'punishment' does not follow from 'crime' in the neat logical discourses offered by discourses [*sic*] that insist on the justice of imprisonment, but rather punishment—primarily through imprisonment (and sometimes death)—is linked to the agendas of politicians, the profit drive of corporations, and media representations of crime. Imprisonment is associated with the racialization of those most likely to be punished. It is associated with their class . . .

gender structures the punishment system as well."[25] To translate this linguistic mess, prisons do not exist to serve justice by punishing individuals who inflict injury on others but rather to carry out the sinister agendas of capitalist elites against minorities and the poor. Even Marx did not believe nonsense like this.

The main text for Davis's course is *Discipline and Punish: The Birth of the Prison,* by the Maoist sociologist Michel Foucault. A founding text of sorts for the radical antiprison movement, the book deplores the very "principle of penal detention" and also calls for the abolition of prisons. Another text, *Compelled to Crime: The Gender Entrapment of Battered Black Women,* relates the stories of thirty-seven women in Rikers Island prison and attempts to rehabilitate them as innocent victims who were "compelled" to commit crime in order to "confront the deadly conditions of institutionalized racism, persistent poverty, and violence" of American society. Not a single text assigned in the course subjects such extreme and absurd claims to academic scrutiny.

Feminist Theory *HISC 217*[26]

INSTRUCTOR: Donna Haraway, Professor in the Department of History of Consciousness and the Department of Feminist Studies

Professor Haraway refers to herself as a 1960s counterculture holdover, and ten years ago in her most famous tract—*A Cyborg Manifesto*—she actually described herself as a cyborg.[27] The thrust of this manifesto is that the line between human beings and machines has been erased. In her latest book *Primate Visions,* Haraway contends that the line between animals and humans is also nonexistent. This book received a negative review from a British biological anthropologist in the *New York Times,* on the grounds that her arguments were—no surprise here—incoherent. Her course in "Feminist Theory" is organized entirely—and narcissistically—around the views expressed in her new book. These views she equates *ex cathedra* with "feminism."

"What does feminist theory have to say about species, human-animal co-shapings, and the problem of categories for humans and animals?" Professor Haraway asks in the course syllabus. She then supplies the answer, explaining that feminist theory says there is no meaningful distinction to be made between the two, that humans are merely another form of animal, and that any view of humans as fundamentally different from the rest of the animal kingdom is a form of wrongheaded "human exceptionalism." So much for Greeks, Christianity, the Enlightenment, and in fact the entire Western intellectual tradition before 1960. So much for feminists who don't share her bizarre views. The entire course, Professor Haraway explains, is based on the proposition that "we [humans] have never been human."

What would be the fate of a student who argued in behalf of "human exceptionalism"? Would the judgment on the student be that he or she "did not understand the course"?

As presented, Professor Haraway's curriculum excludes any perspectives that might challenge her eccentric opinions, which are offered not only as the scientific word on such matters but as *the* feminist view as well. This is indoctrination, but not very cleverly presented. The course sounds like something created by the fertile comic imagination of the novelist of academe David Lodge.

Foundations in Science Studies *HISC 250*[28]

INSTRUCTOR: Donna Haraway

This seminar, also taught by Professor Haraway, has the same underlying purpose: to promote her idiosyncratic view that there is no significant distinction to be drawn between humans and other animal species. As Haraway explains in the course syllabus:

> My sole and inflexible expectation is that everyone make an heroic effort to bring together—in a serious and sustained way—more than one way of knowing, for example, philosophy and biology; fiction and behavioral ecology; anthropology and cognitive sciences; science studies and animal stories; sociology,

> physiology, and visual studies; or many other combinations. The premise of this requirement is that taking seriously animal-human encounters necessitates inhabiting theories, methods, histories, and experiences that the animal/human divide—whether that usually found in the human sciences or the natural sciences—presumes and enforces to be separate.

In comprehensible English, students taking this course must accept her claim—Professor Haraway is "inflexible" on this point—that humans and animals cannot and should not be understood separately. Such blatant ideological compulsion stands in stark contrast to the standards of professionalism required by University of California regulations.

Racism and Imperialism *HISC 230*[29]

INSTRUCTOR: Neferti Tadiar, Assistant Professor in the Department of History of Consciousness

This course is predicated on the claim that the "practices of modern imperialism" are motivated by racism. Not content with this charge, the course claims that emergent global capitalism is also racist. Both these views are staples of Marxist theory, and, not coincidently, reading assignments for the course consist mainly of writings by Marxist writers like Lenin, C. L. R. James, Frantz Fanon, and Aimé Cesaire, among others.

Professor Tadiar has no obvious academic qualification to teach these subjects. She is not a historian of imperialism, nor a political scientist, nor even an economist. Her academic credential is in Comparative Literature. According to her academic website, "Her work concerns the role of cultural production and social imagination in the creation of wealth, power, marginality and liberatory movements in the context of global relations." So she can teach this course because she is familiar with airy theories of "cultural production" and "social imagination," and the discredited prejudices of the Marxist Left.

Conspiracy Theory: The Department of Politics

Like the Department of Feminist Studies, the Department of Politics provides a self-description that reflects its commitment to agitation rather than cogitation. Its mission statement frankly asserts its goal of creating an "activist citizenry."

The Politics of the War on Terrorism *Politics 72*[30]

INSTRUCTOR: Bruce D. Larkin, Professor Emeritus of Politics

Ostensibly an overview of the War on Terrorism, this course is in fact a left-wing case against U.S. policy. Students are informed that the Bush administration lied to make the case for the war in Iraq. In support of this allegation, the syllabus denies that the terrorist attacks of September 11 were carried out by al Qaeda: "How did Bush and Cheney build the fiction that al-Qaeda was a participant in the 9/11 attacks?" This question is particularly bizarre, since Osama bin Laden has publicly claimed responsibility for the attacks, providing details that only a planner could know. Students are also told that in undertaking the war, the Bush administration "silenced Democratic critics in Congress," although exactly how an opposition party can be silenced in a democracy is not explained, especially since Democrats have savagely attacked Republican White Houses for ages.

Another section of the syllabus focuses on the Middle East conflict, with the implication that Israeli interests are driving the war on terror. The conspiratorial belief that Israel controls American foreign policy is a longtime theme of the instructor, Bruce Larkin. On his personal blog, Professor Larkin lodges the following complaint about the Bush administration: "They have not explained a connection many suspect: the intimate parallels between their choices and the objectives of Israel's Likud." But there are no such parallels, since the Likud intelligence establishment was focused on the threat from Iran and was not in favor of invading Iraq. This is not a scholarly or analytic course on the war on terrorism. It is an introduction to the antiwar, anti-Israel, anti-Semitic, and anti-Bush views of the professor. It is a parody of academic inquiry.

America and the World *Politics 177*[31]

INSTRUCTOR: Ronnie Lipschutz, Professor of Politics

According to its catalogue description, this course not only examines the "political, economic, and cultural relationship between the United States and the rest of the world," it also includes a "special focus on U.S. involvement in the Middle East and Persian Gulf, and the politics and economics of that region as well as the extent to which domestic politics influenced foreign policy and vice versa." Such a broad focus would prove an ambitious undertaking for a scholar with training in military history, economics, and foreign policy, yet Professor Lipschutz has expertise in none of these areas. His doctorate from UC Berkeley was awarded by the "Energy and Resources Group," whose mission is to "transmit and apply critical knowledge to enable a future in which human material needs and a healthy environment are mutually and sustainably satisfied." That is to say, his academic credential was awarded by a program in environmental activism.

"America and the World" is a course in Professor Lipschutz's political prejudices, which are radical and left. Typical of the required readings for the course is *The Sorrows of Empire: Militarism, Secrecy, and the End of the Republic,* by Chalmers Johnson. Johnson claims that "the United States dominates the world through military power," that it is "a military juggernaut intent on world domination," and that American military bases constitute a "new form of empire." In keeping with this theme Johnson describes his text as a "guide to the American empire as it begins to spread its imperial wings."

A similar theme is taken up by a second required text, *The Tragedy of American Diplomacy,* by the late William Appleman Williams. Williams was an academic godfather of the New Left. His well-known arguments about America's foreign policy are grounded in a Marxist view that the pursuit of foreign markets dictates its directions. Although Williams's work has been subjected to severe review for its faulty logic and insecure factual basis, students taking this course are kept in the dark about such critical perspectives. No books are assigned that deviate from the ideological premises of the instructor.

Thinking Green: Politics, Ethics, Political Economy

Politics 214[32]

INSTRUCTOR: Ronnie Lipschutz, Professor of Politics

Described as a survey of the "political thought and practice" of the environmentalist movement, this is a course in how to think like an environmental leftist. Students are required to read works by radical authors such as Edward Abbey, whose book *The Monkey Wrench Gang* is often credited with popularizing "ecotage"—vandalism and violence in the service of environmentalist extremism. Another book, *Eco-socialism,* by the author David Pepper, states its purpose in these terms: "This book tries to help the cause of eco-socialist politics by describing and explaining the forms of socialism—particularly Marxist socialism—and anarchism on which they must be based."

In addition to radical texts, radical environmentalist organizations feature prominently in the curriculum. One section of the syllabus, titled " 'Radical' Ecologies," includes an uncritical discussion of groups such as Earth First!, an environmentalist organization notorious for its practice of ecoterrorism. Sections on "ecofeminism," "ecosocialism," and "environmental justice" also reflect the political agendas of the course.

Social Forces and Political Change *Politics 200B*[33]

INSTRUCTOR: Michael Urban, Professor of Politics.

Though couched in academic language, Politics 200 is simply one more training course in political activism:

> This seminar concerns the transformation of social forces into political ones. Accordingly, it focuses on the formation,

> articulation, mobilization and organization of political interests and identities, their mutual interaction and their effects on the structures and practices of states and societies, as well as on the effects of those same structures and practices on them. The major themes under consideration, here, are (1) the social bases of political action—class, gender, race and other determinants of social division and political identity—and (2) the relevant forms of political agency and action, including the development of political consciousness and the representation of interests and identities in the public sphere.

The course seeks to impress on students the virtues of political activism and to shape their political outlook—a mission appropriate for an activist organization or political party. In accordance with the political nature of its mission, all the texts used in the course provide positive descriptions of left-wing activism. For example, *Power in Movement: Social Movements and Contentious Politics*, by Sidney Tarrow, draws heavily on Marxism and directs its attention primarily to "peace," environmental, and feminist movements. *Challenging Codes: Collective Action in the Information Age* encourages "collective action" and "resistance" in all spheres of life and claims that motherhood is a form of oppression against which women should rebel. ("The social practice of childbirth, entirely medicalized and managed by the male-dominated health system, still effectively prevents a woman from living the experience of life-giving as hers alone," author Albert Melucci writes.)

Sections of the course focus on the problems of organizing the political movements the instructor favors. Thus one section examines "resource mobilization and rational action," while another concentrates on "political opportunity and framing."

"The United States Recreated Rather than Abolished Slavery": The American Studies Program

A program of American Studies might be expected to encompass a wide range of academic courses on American history, culture, and politics. UC Santa Cruz takes a different approach. The stated intent of the program is to have students see the United States through a theoretical framework of "racial, ethnic, gender, sexual, class, and regional dynamics"—that is, through an ideological prism constructed by the political Left. Courses offered are rooted largely in instructions in identity politics and political activism, expose students to polemical indictments of American society, and introduce them to radical organizations they might join to advance the agendas of the Left.

Asian Americans in Film and Video *AMST 172*[34]

INSTRUCTOR: Rebecca Hurdis, Graduate Student in American Studies

Billed as a course on the "history of, and relevance of film and video production within Asian America," this is in fact an attack on American society, which is presented as racist in its treatment of Asian-Americans. American racism is the common theme of virtually all the texts and films featured in the course. Students are assigned, for instance, a chapter from the book *Asian American Women and Men: Labor, Laws and Love,* in which author Yen Le Espiritu claims that "racist and gendered immigration policies and labor conditions have worked in tandem to keep Asian Americans in an assigned, subordinate place." In addition, the author alleges that the American film industry is based on "white cultural and institutional racism against Asian males" due to its alleged "preoccupation with the death of Asians—a filmic solution to the threats of the Yellow Peril."

Students are also required to read *The Joy Fuck Club: Prolegomenon to an Asian American Porno Practice,* in which author Richard Fung describes the United States as a "racist society" and claims that Asians have experienced "rejection" in America "according to the established racial hierarchies."

A similar theme is central to *Asian America Through the Lens: History, Representations, and Identities,* from which students are required to read a chapter titled "Marginal Cinema and White Criticism." In this chapter, author Jun Xing alleges that "practices of cultural marginalization and appropriation" are routinely directed toward Asian-Americans. According to the author, the recognition that Asian-American filmmakers such as Academy Award–winning director Ang Lee have received "signifies not a true assimilation of Asians into the American mainstream, but rather a mere repositioning of their marginality in the motion picture industry." This sort of "can't win for losing" logic would relegate *any* recognition of Asian achievement into the category of marginalization. The author blithely proceeds, however, to his preordained conclusion: "The lack of critical attention [to Asian filmmaking] can be attributed to ideological and instructional racism."

American Prison Literature: 1960 to Present *AMST 180*[35]

INSTRUCTOR: Rashad Shabazz, Doctoral Student in the History of Consciousness Department

From the syllabus it is clear that this course has a goal more far-reaching than surveying prison "literature" since 1960. Thus, the "course also serves in part as a history of radical political movements and economic changes to America's economy." On closer inspection, it is to these radical movements—and their condemnation of the United States and, especially, its criminal justice system—that the course is devoted. Indeed, the primary qualification of the course's professor, self-described "prison abolitionist" Rashad Shabazz, to teach this subject is his loudly trumpeted status as a "prison rights activist."

Three of the four assigned texts are by onetime members of the Black Panther Party. Among them is *Live from Death Row,* a series of commentaries about prison and politics by death row inmate Mumia Abu-Jamal. The book's running theme is the convicted cop killer's belief that the American justice system is "racist." In a representative passage from the book, Mumia claims that his conviction and subsequent life behind bars stem from the fact that "American courts are reservoirs of racist sentiment and have historically been hostile to black defendants." What students would not learn from reading his apologetics is that ballistics tests, eyewitnesses, and extensive legal reviews all confirmed his guilt.

Another required text is *Soledad Brother,* a collection of prison letters by George Jackson, a maximum-security inmate who murdered several prison guards and was himself killed trying to escape. Founder of a notorious prison gang, the Black Guerrilla Family, Jackson uses these letters to vent about "racist America." "The whole of Western Europeans' existence here in the U.S. has been the same one long war with different peoples," he writes in a typical comment.

The course also assigns the autobiography of Jackson's onetime lover and political comrade, none other than Angela Davis. Here is an indication of the academic incest at Santa Cruz: the instructor in this American Studies course is a doctoral student in the History of Consciousness program and has assigned the autobiography of the program's most famous professor—a lifelong Communist and political extremist—without a single critical commentary.

The fourth required text is *The New Abolitionists: (Neo) Slave Narrative and Contemporary Prison,* an anthology of writings by convicted criminals who describe themselves as political prisoners. In the introduction to the book, editor Joy James calls prisoners "slaves" of the " 'master' state." According to James, "Prison is the modern day manifestation of the plantation," a favorite theme of Angela Davis herself. By maintaining prisons, "the United States recreated rather than abolished slavery."

Socialist Studies: The Department of Sociology

Although sociology is a traditionally defined academic discipline, the Sociology Department at UC Santa Cruz seems determined to undermine its connection to scholarly endeavors. Central to the mission of the department is not any scholarly inquiry, but "social justice"—that generally recognized code for a left-wing political agenda associated with the redistribution of resources and wealth. According to the department's mission statement, these predetermined political goals are built into the study of sociology:

> Sociology combines the elements of a search for social order with a vision of a just, free, and egalitarian society, a vision that may require fundamental social change. Developing an understanding of this double aspect of the sociological tradition, the interrelationship between social order and social change, is one of the teaching goals of sociologists at Santa Cruz.[36]

Since a socialist future is the goal of study in the Department of Sociology at Santa Cruz, it is hardly surprising that the courses offered bear no relation whatsoever to scholarship or academic inquiry.

Issues and Problems in American Society *Sociology 10*

INSTRUCTOR: Anthony J. Villarreal, Graduate Student in the Department of Sociology

On its face, this would appear to be a standard course in sociology, concerned as it is with exploring "sociological approaches to the study of social problems in the U.S." But the syllabus for the course makes clear that only one "sociological" approach is to be considered: radical political activism. "Our goal [is] not only to critically analyze the world, but ultimately, to change it," a paraphrase of Marx's famous thesis on Feuerbach. Sections of the course are presented under such titles as "Imagining Local/Global Social Change," reflecting the instructor's hubris that, as a graduate student, he knows—where others have failed to know—exactly how this should be done.

Of the three texts assigned, not one can properly be described as a sociological text. One, of course, is *Are Prisons Obsolete?* by Angela Davis. Another required text is *The Exception to the Rulers: Exposing Oily Politicians, War Profiteers, and the Media That Love Them*. The author is the radical radio journalist Amy Goodman, and the book is a polemical attack on the Bush administration (which Goodman refers to as an "OILYgarchy" that seeks "perpetual control of global oil"). It is also a defense of convicted terrorist accomplice Lynne Stewart and convicted cop killer Mumia Abu-Jamal, whom Goodman calls an "outspoken voice for the thousands of people on death rows around this country." The remaining assigned text is *Tangled Memories: The Vietnam War, the AIDS Epidemic, and the Politics of Remembering*. In a typical section, author Marita Sturken writes, "The way a nation remembers war and constructs its history is directly related to how that nation further propagates war. Hence, the rewriting of the Vietnam War in contemporary films directly affected the manufactured 'need' for the United State's involvement in the Persian Gulf."

In the course syllabus, instructor Villareal claims that "Differences of viewpoints, orientation, and experience are expected and welcomed in class discussions." Given the relentlessly one-sided reading material he provides, this merely shows Villareal's contempt for students who might take him seriously in this.

Society and Nature *Sociology 125*[37]

INSTRUCTOR: Brian J. Gareau, Graduate Student in the Department of Sociology

In the syllabus for this course, students are told that "many sociologists link the severity of environmental degradation to a particular way in which modern society is organized today, capitalism." Accordingly, the course itself is yet another rehearsal of radical dogmas—yet one more attack on free-market capitalism, this time in the name of environmentalism. The well-established fact that the socialist Soviet Union created by far the most degraded natural environment of any modern society (see, e.g., *Ecocide in the USSR: Health and Nature Under Siege,* by Murray Feshbach et al., 1993) is kept out of the sight of Gareau's captive student audience. Students will not learn that the Communist regime in Russia drained the world's largest inland sea or caused the radioactive contamination of an area larger than Europe.

The course syllabus is refreshingly candid about its commitment to a one-sided exposition of radical prejudices, specifically its anti-capitalist agendas: "the course will review theories that are critical of capitalism as a social formation, explain how it functions, and describe its environmental implications." No texts will be assigned that examine the benefits that free-market practices bring to the environment. Instead, each of the three assigned books is distinguished by its anticapitalist theme. In *Imperial Nature: The World Bank and Struggles for Social Justice in the Age of Globalization*, for instance, author Michael Goldman uses the World Bank to launch a broader fusillade against free markets, or what he calls alternatively the "rapacious accumulation strategies of global capital," "neoliberal capitalism," and the "onslaught of neoliberal capitalist development." Marxist writer John Bellamy Foster mounts a similar attack in his book *Ecology Against Capitalism*, arguing that Marxism is the best guiding theory for environmentalist politics.

Marxism, in fact, provides the recurring ideological orientation for this course, whose sections focus on "Marxist critiques" of capitalism, the "Greenness of Marxism," "Marxist Political Ecology," and "Labor movements as environmental movements."

All the above-mentioned courses have the complete support of the departments in which they are offered and the approval of the central university administration at UC Santa Cruz. This is the case despite the fact that every single one of these courses is in flagrant violation of the University of California rules on the presentation of course material in an objective and scholarly manner. The departments they appear in are not traditional academic departments at all, but taxpayer-funded centers of radical activism, supported by the Santa Cruz administration.

In fact, when we completed our investigation into the situation at UCSC, we sent a copy to all twenty-six members of the Board of Regents of the University of California. Only one regent, John Moores, responded and expressed concern. He is now retired.

But it is not just the Santa Cruz administration at the state university system of California that allows these offenses to continue. The courses we have reviewed here are also supported by the national professional associations and by the accrediting agencies that pass on university curricula.

In that sense, while it is safe to say that Santa Cruz is the most radical university in America, we cannot chalk up its assaults on academic freedom to the eccentricities of a few faculty members. The problems at Santa Cruz, just like those at all the other colleges and universities documented in this book, reveal a profound and widespread corruption of the academic system. Public or private, big or small, our institutions of higher learning have allowed large parts of their curriculum to be hijacked by radicals, and have abandoned their fundamental mission in the process.

Most disturbing of all is the unwillingness of administrators and trustees to defend their institutions and enforce the professional standards of a modern research university.

Conclusion
The End of the University as We Know It*

The abuses described in these pages document the dramatic changes that have occurred in the liberal arts curriculum of American universities over the past forty years. These changes include the subvention of academic goals by political agendas, the abandonment of scientific methods of inquiry, the devaluing of academic expertise, and the replacement of intellectual discourse with programs designed to instill sectarian doctrines.

Alarms about these developments were first sounded two decades ago in books such as Allan Bloom's *The Closing of the American Mind* and Dinesh D'Souza's *Illiberal Education*. Equally critical texts followed, including Roger Kimball's *Tenured Radicals,* Neil Hamilton's *Zealotry and Academic Freedom,* Richard Bernstein's *Dictatorship of Virtue,* and Daphne Patai's and Noretta Koertge's *Professing Feminism: Education and Indoctrination in Women's Studies.* Organizations such as the National Association of Scholars, the American Council of Trustees and Alumni, and Students for Academic Freedom, and the website Noindoctrination.org document the abuses. All these commentators drew attention to the way in which academic practices had departed from the standards set by the American Association of University Professors

*This chapter was written by David Horowitz.

(AAUP) nearly a hundred years ago, which became the foundation of the modern research university.

In October 2007, the AAUP—now a staunch defender of ideological trends in the academic curriculum—issued a report to answer critics and their rapidly accumulating data.[1] The report, called "Freedom in the Classroom," is a striking departure from the academic principles that the AAUP had once done so much to foster. It is a ratification of the destructive trends that are taking university practices back to an era when institutions of higher learning were controlled by religious denominations and their curricula were governed by the authority of the church rather than the principles of scientific inquiry.

An exercise in denial, the AAUP report examines none of the principal critiques of universities and their curricula. Instead, it devotes its entire discussion of indoctrination to a four-year-old complaint raised by a group calling itself the Committee for a Better North Carolina. The complaint concerned a single text the University of North Carolina had assigned as part of a summer reading program to all incoming freshmen: Barbara Ehrenreich's *Nickel and Dimed*—the left-wing tract that has appeared several times in these pages. The committee described the assignment of one extremely partisan text as a case of "indoctrination," a characterization the AAUP seizes on to dismiss not only the committee's complaint but the unexamined complaints of other critics as well.

The assignment of any one book, the AAUP argues, is not a *prima facie* case for indoctrination. This is certainly correct but hardly related to the problem at hand. The Committee for a Better North Carolina was not constructing a formal argument about the nature of indoctrination in university courses. It was addressing a specific case that it found problematic. By focusing on this narrow complaint, the AAUP report is able to avoid the serious issues that critics have raised while disparaging them as philistines who fail to understand the nature of academic discourse or the freedoms that make it possible.

But even as an answer to the Committee for a Better North Carolina, the AAUP's response is an act of bad faith. The committee never argued that the university should not have assigned the Ehrenreich text. Instead it maintained that if college freshmen were required to read a partisan text on a contested issue, they ought to be provided with a divergent point of view for comparison. That position is in accord with the AAUP's own past statements on academic freedom, which instruct professors to provide students with "divergent opinions" on "controversial matters," and to be fair-minded in doing so:

> The university teacher, in giving instructions upon controversial matters, while he is under no obligation to hide his own opinion under a mountain of equivocal verbiage, should, if he is fit in dealing with such subjects, set forth justly, without suppression or innuendo, the divergent opinions of other investigators . . . and he should, above all, remember that his business is not to provide his students with ready-made conclusions, but to train them to think for themselves, and to provide them access to those materials which they need if they are to think intelligently.[2]

The AAUP's long-standing position is quite clear. If a professor is "fit to deal with such matters" (e.g., Ehrenreich's book on the nature and causes of poverty), that professor should present students with the divergent positions of others and "provide them access to those materials which they need if they are to think intelligently." It is not a stretch to think that this would mean providing an alternative text.

The report also fails to consider the ideologically one-sided nature of the North Carolina faculty who would be charged with teaching Ehrenreich's book. As professors Neil Gross and Solon Simmons show in their 2007 Harvard study, 95 percent of the professors on liberal arts faculties are likely to share liberal or left-wing approaches to social issues, including those discussed in Ehrenreich's text.[3] In these circumstances, the concern about the assignment of a single polemical text by a socialist author acquires added urgency. But the AAUP report never gets to the level of such specifics; it does not even mention the fact that the required text assigned was written by an ideological radical. Instead it lectures the plaintiffs: "The Committee for a Better North Carolina could not possibly have known whether the assignment of Ehrenreich's *Nickel and Dimed,* which explores the economic difficulties facing low-wage workers in America, was an example of indoctrination or education. It is a fundamental error to assume that the assignment of teaching materials constitutes their endorsement. An instructor who assigns a book no more endorses what it has to say than does the university library that acquires it."

But is this really the case? The text was assigned not by an individual teacher but by the university—and to *all* incoming freshmen. This is quite different from a faceless librarian's decision to stock a book on a library shelf.

In addition, Ehrenreich's text was hardly the only controversial selection in North Carolina's summer reading program. The previous year's assignment—a book on the Koran—had also provoked a public reaction because of what many perceived as its one-sided and uncritical views on the nature of Islam. They suspected that a Christian apologetic required of all incoming freshmen would have been regarded in a wholly different light by those defending the UNC decision. These suspicions were heightened by the fact that the assignment came on the heels of the 9/11 attacks by radical Islamists. Yet the university faculty ignored the critics' complaints and the following year assigned another one-sided text—again without providing critical materials. The next year, 2003, UNC officials assigned an anti–capital punishment polemic, *The Death of Innocents: An Eyewitness Account of Wrongful Executions,* by Sister Helen Prejean, which the university improbably described as a narrative "told calmly and with tolerance for differing sides of the contentious issue of the death penalty in the United States."[4] Prejean is a prominent anti–capital punishment activist, famous for her memoir *Dead Man Walking,* and her title itself—with the phrases "death of innocents" and "wrongful executions"—telegraphs that it is anything but "tolerant." Reviewers not connected with the university readily recognized the book as a "searing indictment of capital punishment" (*Booklist*) and "a passionate indictment of the American criminal justice system" *(Publishers Weekly),* observing that in *The Death of Innocents* she "continues her crusade against capital punishment" *(Washington Post).* None of this is addressed in the AAUP report.

Moreover, the AAUP's dismissive claim that the Committee for a Better North Carolina made "a fundamental error" in assuming that "the assignment of teaching materials constitutes their endorsement" does not prove that indoctrination was *not* taking place in the freshmen reading program. To provide such proof would have required the AAUP to produce the class lessons of the North Carolina faculty and demonstrate that they provided students with critical materials for evaluating Ehrenreich's contentions. The AAUP made no effort to do so.

Dogma as "Truth"

The AAUP report reiterates several principles over which there is no disagreement—"Indoctrination occurs whenever an instructor insists that students accept as truth propositions that are in fact professionally contestable"; "Instructors indoctrinate when they teach particular propositions as dogmatically true"; and "It is not indoctrination when, as a result of their research and study, instructors assert to their students that in their view particular propositions are true, even if these propositions are controversial within a discipline." But solving the current and widespread problem of indoctrination requires more than lip service to basic principles.

Our own formulation of a principle that would distinguish education from indoctrination is as follows: Indoctrination takes place when professors teach a point of view that is contested within the spectrum of scholarly or intellectually responsible opinion as though it were scientific fact. Professors should make their students aware that such opinions are contested, and must not teach their point of view as though it were fact. Students should be provided with materials that would allow them to draw their own conclusions about contested positions.

This definition is not without problems. Outside the hard sciences, where contested issues can be resolved by experiment and authorities are certified by objective measures, the question of what constitutes scholarly or intellectually responsible opinion is obviously problematic, and cannot be resolved at the margins of discourse. It is probably better to err on the side of acknowledging challenges to an orthodoxy in the humanities and social sciences, even if those challenges are marginal, than to make absolute claims to truth that these disciplines cannot sustain. The process of making such acknowledgments is a way of teaching students about democratic ways of thinking, and encouraging them to respect the pluralism of ideas.

Respect for the contested nature of nonscientific opinions is the foundation of both an educational discourse and a democratic culture, which brings us to the truly disturbing aspect of the AAUP report—its defense of the very practices that threaten academic freedom and academic values.

The report states that it is not necessary for liberal arts professors to observe the principle of acknowledging that a discourse is contested *if they can enforce a consensus among their departmental peers:* "It is not indoctrination for professors to expect students to comprehend ideas and apply knowledge that is accepted as true within a relevant discipline." The AAUP statement does not say that ideas can be taught as truth if they are regarded as true "within the spectrum of scholarly and intellectual opinion" or even "within the spectrum of scientific opinion." Instead, the AAUP report says a dogma can be taught as truth if it is accepted as true "within a relevant discipline."

This is an alarming departure from all past doctrines of academic freedom and academic standards. In the humanities and the liberal arts, no sectarian doctrine, no ideology should be taught as "truth." Teaching a doctrine as truth—teaching an orthodoxy—is the mission of religious and authoritarian institutions. It is the antithesis of a liberal education.

The AAUP's new interpretation of truth is designed to legitimize the state of affairs that has been dissected at length in this book.

Many of the courses we have analyzed are offered by the newly minted academic disciplines created since the 1960s, which are the result not of new scholarship or scientific developments but of sectarian political movements within the university. Most prominent among these new disciplines is Women's Studies, which freely acknowledges its origins in a political movement and defines its educational mission in political terms. Recall the preamble to the Constitution of the National Women's Studies Association which proclaims that "Women's Studies owes its existence to the movement for the liberation of women; the feminist movement exists because women are oppressed." Women's Studies is then "equipping women not only to enter the society as whole, as productive human beings, but to transform the world to one that will be free of all oppression."[5]

When the AAUP report says that professors are not indoctrinating students when they "expect [them] to comprehend ideas and apply knowledge that is accepted as true within a relevant discipline," it is really saying that the training of students in sectarian ideologies, such as radical feminism, is an acceptable function of modern research universities. This is an abrogation of students' academic freedom. It severs the link between scientific method and academic professionalism. It undermines the very concept of a university education as it has been understood for the past hundred years, or ever since American institutions of higher learning declared their independence from religious denominations.

The AAUP has issued its new defense of indoctrination fully cognizant of the fact that numerous academic disciplines have incorporated sectarian ideologies as "scholarly truths" and view their academic mission as instilling these doctrines in their students. These ideological programs include Women's Studies, African-American Studies, Peace Studies, Cultural Studies, Chicano Studies, Gay Lesbian Studies, Post-Colonial Studies, Whiteness Studies, Community Studies, and recently politicized disciplines such as Cultural Anthropology and Sociology. At the University of California Santa Cruz, the Women's Studies Department has dropped all pretense of being a scholarly discipline and has renamed itself the Department of Feminist Studies to signify that it is a political training facility. It has done so without a word of complaint or caution from university administrators, the Women's Studies Association, or the AAUP.

The AAUP's new doctrine is a transparent attempt to justify the transformation of the university into a home for sectarian creeds by shielding them from the scrutiny of scientific method. In the new dispensation, political control of a discipline is the sole basis for establishing "truth," which closes off critical debate. The idea that political power can establish "truth" is a conception so at odds with the intellectual foundations of the modern research university that the AAUP committee could not state it so baldly. Hence the disingenuous compromise of "truth within a relevant discipline."

One of the architects of this compromise is Professor Robert Post, a leading expert on academic freedom and an author of the AAUP report. In an article that appeared in a collection of essays by liberal scholars titled *Academic Freedom After September 11,* Post wrote an excellent summary of the principles that have informed university governance since 1915, when the AAUP's "Declaration of Principles on Academic Freedom and Academic Tenure" was published. In the essay, entitled "The Structure of Academic Freedom," Post wrote: "[A] key premise of the '1915 Declaration' is that faculty should be regarded as professional experts in the production of knowledge. . . . The mission of the university defended by the 'Declaration' depends on a particular theory of knowledge. The 'Declaration' presupposes not only that knowledge exists and can be articulated by scholars, but also that it is advanced through the free application of highly disciplined forms of inquiry, which correspond roughly to what [philosopher] Charles Peirce once called 'the method of science' as opposed to the 'method of authority.' "[6]

The method of authority, of course, is precisely the method now recommended by Post and the AAUP committee—the authority of the discipline. The method of authority violates not only the AAUP's stated principles but also Robert Gordon Sproul's famous 1934 statement affirming that the university must not become a platform for sectarian creeds ("Where it becomes necessary in performing this function of a university, to consider political, social, or sectarian movements, they are dissected and examined, not taught, and the conclusion left, with no tipping of the scales, to the logic of the facts.").[7] Not coincidentally, it was Post who recommended that the University of California remove the long-standing Sproul statement from its academic freedom policy.

The sectarian curriculum is exemplified by Women's Studies, which, as this book has demonstrated, treats the controversial claim that gender is "socially constructed" as though it were an established fact. This idea is the basis for Women's Studies programs throughout the American university system. To force students to accept as true a doctrine that is contested by the findings of modern biology, neuroscience, and evolutionary psychology is precisely what is meant by indoctrination. Yet the AAUP has found a way to redefine indoctrination so that it can be included in the academic curriculum. According to the AAUP's principle of "truth within a relevant discipline," it is not indoctrination for Women's Studies professors to assert a dogma as truth.

This is the point to which we have come: a discipline can define what is true even if that "truth" is refuted by a massive body of scientific data.

A Slippery Slope

At the time the AAUP report was finalized, the association's official journal, *Academe,* featured two articles defending the feminist indoctrination of university students. The first was "Impassioned Teaching," the article in which AAUP regional president Pamela Caughie proudly announces her aim of indoctrinating students in feminist dogma, writing, "I feel I am doing my job well when students become practitioners of feminist analysis and committed to feminist politics."[8] In the second article, feminist professor Julie Kilmer describes how it is necessary to publicly expose and intimidate students who "resist" such indoctrination, while providing suggestions as to how to do it.[9]

The publication of two such articles can hardly be regarded as coincidental. They identify the slope on which the AAUP and the academy now find themselves.

It is a slope slippery in more ways than one. The doctrine of "truth within a relevant discipline" may work in one direction when the discipline is controlled by ideological leftists, but in quite another should a discipline come under the aegis of different political factions. Suppose, for example, antagonists of Darwin's theory of evolution were to establish a new academic field of Intelligent Design Studies. What academic principle would prevent them from teaching their contested theories as truth? The same would apply to conservatives or Republicans, Holocaust deniers or 9/11 conspiracy theorists, animal rights activists or racists—in fact, to any political movement that was able to take control of a university department and structure its curriculum as a new academic "discipline."

Far from setting off alarm bells for the current AAUP leadership, this prospect is apparently perfectly acceptable—probably because there is a smug confidence that leftist dominance of the university culture will endure. Thus, Professor Michael Berube, a member of the AAUP's National Council, has already endorsed the idea: "I don't see that there's anything wrong with a situation in which students learn to practice feminist analysis and become committed to feminism. . . . I don't see that there's anything wrong with a situation in which students learn to practice conservative analysis and become committed to conservatism."[10] It would be hard to imagine a more anti-intellectual, antischolarly statement from a reputable academic.

Like many of his colleagues, Berube argues that indoctrination is not really indoctrination if students are "free not to do those things without penalty"[11]—that is, if they can object to a professor's classroom advocacy without fear of reprisal. But how would students know in advance that there would be no penalty for refusing to embrace a professor's political assumptions? How would they deal with Professor Kilmer's threats to "expose" them and break down their "resistance"? How would Women's Studies majors be able to resist the feminist assumptions of the Women's Studies curriculum and still be judged good students by its ideologically committed and monolithic faculty—especially if its professors are advocating only one point of view in their classrooms, using the mode of discourse that Pamela Caughie has described as "impassioned teaching"?

In her article for *Academe,* Caughie explains: "I can hardly teach feminism as if it were simply an object of analysis and not a vital force in my life."[12] But what student, realizing that feminist dogmas are a vital force in the life of his or her professor, would take the risk of challenging the instructor in class, particularly when his or her grade is dependent on the professor's approval? If Caughie cannot teach without proselytizing, she should seek employment with a feminist advocacy organization, not on the faculty of a modern research university, which claims to operate under guidelines instituted to separate it from the religious institutions of the past.

Even the term "impassioned teaching" runs counter to previous AAUP statements on academic freedom. For example, the AAUP's 1940 statement, which is part of the template of most modern research universities, asserts that scholars and educators should be "restrained" rather than impassioned: "As scholars and educational officers . . . [professors] should at all times be accurate, should exercise appropriate restraint [and] should show respect for the opinions of others."

Under these guidelines, professors are obligated to hold back their ardor, to teach students to be skeptical, to assess the evidence, to respect the divergent views of others, and to support the pluralism of ideas on which democratic culture is based. It is their obligation to provide students with materials that would allow them to weigh more than one side of controversial issues, and thus to learn to think intelligently and to think for themselves.

That is why the AAUP's new position is such a shocking departure from academic tradition, and such a disturbing betrayal of academic freedom. The current AAUP leadership has laid down a challenge that everyone concerned about the future of the academy must answer.

Of course, the challenge does not come simply from the AAUP. The fact that this national organization has forsaken its longstanding principles of academic freedom reflects how firmly established radicalism and the practice of indoctrination have become in institutions of higher learning across the country. As the case studies in this book show, literally thousands of university courses have become forums for professors to advance their own extremist political agendas.

The AAUP is just the latest organization of many to have abandoned its responsibility to protect the principle of academic freedom. The culprits are not simply the professors who use their classrooms to recruit and train political activists. Just as guilty are the department chairs, school administrators, university presidents, and regents and trustees who allow the indoctrination to continue even though it is at odds with the educational mission.

Here, the case studies examined in this book are instructive. When we completed our investigations, we sent a copy of our findings to the trustees and top administrators of each of the twelve colleges chronicled in these pages. Aside from the decision of Temple University to restructure its summer freshman reading program, the response was nil. This reflects the lack of oversight or public intervention. As long as faculties and administrators continue to turn a blind eye to these abuses—and as long as students, alumni, parents, and trustees fail to stand up to the abuses—these trends will continue unabated and unaddressed. And should that happen, it will most certainly spell the end of the modern research university as we know it.

Notes

INTRODUCTION: AN ACADEMIC TRAGEDY

1. Policy on Course Content, approved June 19, 1970. Amended September 22, 2005 www.universityofcalifornia.edu/regents/policies/6065.html. This is the September 2005 statement.
2. Official catalog description of the course. Community Studies 100P, Instructor, Paul Ortiz. Ortiz is an associate professor. http://reg.ucsc.edu/soc/aci/winter2002/cmmu.html#100p.
3. www.discoverthenetworks.org/individualProfile.asp?indid=1524.
4. Bettina Aptheker, *Intimate Politics: How I Grew Up Red, Fought for Free Speech, and Became a Feminist Rebel* (Emeryville, CA: Seal Press, 2006), p. 13.
5. Ibid., p. 473.
6. Ibid., p. 405.
7. Ibid., p. 406.
8. www.accessmylibrary.com/coms2/summary_0286-25351356_ITM.
9. For a recent review of this disturbing phenomenon by a liberal academic, see Stanley Fish, *Save the World on Your Own Time* (New York: Oxford University Press, 2008).
10. www.wjh.harvard.edu/~ngross/lounsbery_9-25.pdf. I have discussed the reasons for this exclusion and the methods by which it is accomplished in the introduction to my book, *The Professors*, and will not repeat them here. Horowitz, op cit., pp. xxxi–xli. See also, Mark Bauerlein, "Liberal Group-think Is Anti-Intellectual," *The Chronicle of Higher Education*.
11. The studies have been conducted by Daniel Klein, Charlotta Stern, Stanley Rothman, Robert Lichter, Neil Nevitte, Neil Gross and Solon Simmons; http://cms.studentsforacademicfreedom.org//index.php?option=com_content&task=view&id=1898&Itemid=40.
12. 1915 *Declaration of Principles on Academic Freedom and Tenure*.
13. Rule APM 0–10, University of California, Berkeley, Academic Personnel Manual.
14. Interviews with Martin Trow and Robert Post.
15. Pamela Caughie, "Impassioned Teaching," *Academe*, July–August, 2007.
16. Steven Pinker, *The Blank Slate* (New York: Viking, 2002), pp. 341–343.
17. www.insidehighered.com/views/2007/06/19/neal.

CHAPTER 1. WHITE DEVILS: DUKE UNIVERSITY

1. http://www.npr.org/templates/story/story.php?storyId=9533535.
2. http://www.goduke.com/ViewArticle.dbml?DB_OEM_ID=4200&ATCLID=264739.
3. http://www.dukenews.duke.edu/mmedia/pdf/socialdisasterad.pdf.
4. Ibid.
5. http://www.diverseeducation.com/artman/publish/printer_7059.shtml.
6. http://www.amconmag.com/article/2007/feb/26/00013.
7. Stuart Taylor and K. C. Johnson, *Until Proven Innocent* (New York: Macmillan, 2007), pp. 108–109.
8. http://dukenews.duke.edu/mmedia/features/lacrosse_incident/lange_baker.html.
9. Ibid.
10. http://www.barnard.edu/sfonline/sport/holloway_01.htm.
11. Ibid.
12. http://www.blackcommentator.com/180/180_white_male_privilege.html.
13. http://www.foxnews.com/printer_friendly_story/0,3566,191232,00.html.
14. http://www.diverseeducation.com/artman/publish/printer_7059.shtml.
15. http://www.concernedukefaculty.org.
16. Karla Holloway, *Codes of Conduct: Race, Ethics, and the Color of Our Character* (New Brunswick, NJ: Rutgers University Press, 1995), pp. 7–42.
17. B. Denise Hawkins, "Karla Holloway to Lead African and African-American Studies at Duke University," *Black Issues in Higher Education,* May 2, 1996.
18. Christina Asquith, "Duke Fallout Continues as Top Black Professor Resigns from Race Committee," *Diverse,* Jan. 10, 2007.
19. Emily Eakin, "Black Captive in a White Culture," *New York Times,* May 5, 2001.
20. Houston Baker, *The Journey Back* (Chicago: University of Chicago Press, 1984), p. 82.
21. James Atlas, "Battle of the Books," *New York Times Magazine,* 1988.
22. Roger Kimball, *Tenured Radicals: How Politics Has Corrupted Our Higher Education* (New York: Harper & Row, 1990), p. xiii.
23. Houston Baker, *Black Studies, Rap, and the Academy* (Chicago: University of Chicago Press, 1995), p. 102.
24. Ibid.
25. Eakin, "Black Captive in a White Culture."
26. Houston Baker, *South Again: Re-thinking Modernism/Re-reading Booker T* (Durham, NC: Duke University Press, 2001), p. 91.
27. http://durhamwonderland.blogspot.com/2007/10/flexible-forthcoming.html.
29. Wahneema Lubiano, "Wahneema Lubiano on Race, Class and Katrina," Sept. 6, 2005, posted at www.newblackman.blogspot.com/2005/09/wahneema-lubiano-on-race-class-and.html.
30. K. C. Johnson, "Wahneema's World," DurhaminWonderland.blogspot.com, Dec. 11, 2006, http://durhamwonderland.blogspot.com/2006/12/wahneemas-world.html.
31. Wahneema Lubiano, "Perfect Offenders, Perfect Victim: The Limitations of Spectacularity in the Aftermath of the Lacrosse Team Incident," posted at http://newblackman.blogspot.com/2006/04/social-disaster-voices-from-durham.html.
32. Ibid.
33. Ibid.
34. For example, the American Association of University Professors' 1915 "Declaration of the Principles on Academic Freedom and Academic Tenure" states that teachers

should avoid "taking unfair advantage of the student's immaturity by indoctrinating him with the teacher's own opinions before the student has had an opportunity fairly to examine other opinions upon the matters in question, and before he has sufficient knowledge and ripeness of judgment to be entitled to form any definitive opinion of his own." Full text available at www.campus-watch.org/article/id/566.

35. K. C. Johnson, "Duke Lacrosse and the Professions of Diversity," MindingtheCampus .com, May 22, 2007.
36. http://durhamwonderland.blogspot.com/2006/12/wahneemas-world.html ?widgetType=BlogArchive&widgetId=BlogArchive1&action=toggle&dir=open& toggle=MONTHLY-1164949200000&toggleopen=MONTHLY-1188619200000.
37. Jessica Dudek, "Mark Anthony Neal, PhD '96—Black Male Feminist," May 2006, posted at http://alumni.buffalo.edu/drpl/node/1887. Mark Anthony Neal, "Confessions of a ThugNiggaIntellectual," SeeingBlack.com, Sept. 12, 2003.
38. Greg Garber, "Turbulent times for Duke and Durham," ESPN.com, Apr. 3, 2006.
39. Mark Anthony Neal, "(White) Male Privilege, Black Respectability, and Black Women's Bodies," SeeingBlack.com, May 23, 2006.
40. K. C. Johnson, "Duke's Poisoned Campus Culture," InsideHigherEd.com, May 1, 2006.
41. Mark Anthony Neal, *Songs in the Key of Black Life: A Rhythm and Blues Nation* (New York: Routledge, 2003), p. 13.
42. Mark Anthony Neal, *Soul Babies: Black Popular Culture and the Post-Soul Aesthetic* (New York: Routledge, 2002), p. 3.
43. Dudek, "Mark Anthony Neal, PhD '96—Black Male Feminist."
44 http://www.aas.duke.edu/aaas/undergrad.
45. www.aas.duke.edu/reg/synopsis/view.cgi?term=1220&s=01&action=display&subj= AAAS&course=49S.
46. www.rethinkingmarxism.org/cms/node/884.
47. www.soc.duke.edu/courses/synopses.html.
48. www.aas.duke.edu/reg/synopsis/view.cgi?term=1220&s=01&action=display&subj= English&course=26S.
49. Cf. Paul Beatty, *The White Boy Shuffle* (Boston: Houghton Mifflin, 1996), From the Prologue.
50. www.aas.duke.edu/reg/synopsis/view.cgi?s=01&action=display&subj=SOCIOL& course=116&sem=1220.
51. Sara Rimer and Karen Arenson, "Top Colleges Take More Blacks, but Which Ones?" *New York Times,* June 24, 2004.
52. www.aas.duke.edu/reg/synopsis/view.cgi?s=68&action=display&subj=PUBPOL& course=264S&sem=1060.
53. http://ije.oxfordjournals.org/cgi/content/full/33/5/1159.
54. Ibid.
55. Cf. Noam Chomsky and Robert W. McChesney, *Profit over People: Neoliberalism and Global Order* (New York: Seven Stories Press 1998), p. 107.
56. www.aas.duke.edu/reg/synopsis/view.cgi?s=01&action=display&subj=CULANTH& course=113&sem=1000.

CHAPTER 2. WARD CHURCHILL U: UNIVERSITY OF COLORADO

1. www.colorado.edu/news/reports/churchill/download/WardChurchillReport.pdf.
2. www.9news.com/rss/article.aspx?storyid=74224.

3. www.colorado.edu/Sociology/gimenez/soc.5055/marx99.html.
4. Professor Gimenez has recently retired.
5. www.colorado.edu/Sociology/gimenez/soc.5055/marx99.html.
6. www.discoverthenetworks.org/Articles/University%20of%20%20at%20Boulder.htm#_Syllabus_for_the_14.
7. www.cddc.vt.edu/feminism/Gimenez.html.
8. Ibid.
9. Butler writes, "We have, I think, witnessed the conceptual and material violence of this practice in the United States's war against Iraq, in which the Arab 'other' is understood to be radically 'outside' the universal structures of reason and democracy and, hence, calls to be brought forcibly within." Darlene M. Juschka, *Feminism in the Study of Religion: A Reader* (New York: Continuum International Publishing Group, 2001), p. 633.
10. www.discoverthenetworks.org/Articles/Feminist%20Theory.doc.
11. Ibid. Emphasis added.
12. Ibid.
13. This department is discussed in Chapter 12 below.
14. www.discoverthenetworks.org/Articles/Graduate%20Feminist%20Methods.doc.
15. Ibid.
16. http://socsci.colorado.edu/SOC/Undergrad/Syllabi/1016_Morrow_Spr06.htm.
17. http://socsci.colorado.edu/SOC/Undergrad/Syllabi/1016_Hatch_Spr06.htm.
18. http://socsci.colorado.edu/SOC/Undergrad/Syllabi/1016-001%20Enarson%20Fall%2004.htm.
19. http://socsci.colorado.edu/SOC/Undergrad/Syllabi/1016_Morenberg_Sum06.pdf.
20. http://socsci.colorado.edu/SOC/Undergrad/Syllabi/1005_BJ.htm.
21. http://socsci.colorado.edu/SOC/Undergrad/Syllabi/1005_BJ.htm.
22. Ibid.
23. http://socsci.colorado.edu/SOC/Undergrad/Syllabi/3171_Hubbard_Fall05.htm.
24. http://sobek.colorado.edu/~steen/2031SyllabusFall04.doc.
25. www.discoverthenetworks.org/individualProfile.asp?indid=1058.
26. http://sobek.colorado.edu/~steen/2031SyllabusFall04.doc.
27. www.discoverthenetworks.org/Articles/University%20of%20Colorado%20at%20Boulder.htm#_Syllabus_for_the_20.
28. Joe Feagin and Melvin Sikes, *Living with Racism: The Black Middle-Class Experience* (Boston: Beacon Press, 1994), p. 2.
29. www.carolynnewberger.com/pdf/kozol-review.pdf.
30. www.commentarymagazine.com/cm/main/article.pdf?handle=com.commentarymagazine.content.Article::8545.
31. http://findarticles.com/p/articles/mi_m1282/is_n19_v45/ai_14667441/print.
32. Ibid.
33. http://socsci.colorado.edu/SOC/Undergrad/Syllabi/SOCY%203015%20Boardman%20Spr05.pdf.
34. Joe Feagin, *Racist America: Roots, Current Realities and Future Reparations* (New York: Routledge, 2001), p. 2.
35. Ibid., p. 107.
36. www.roxbury.net/race.html.
37. Ibid.
38. www.colorado.edu/WomenStudies/womensstudiesprogram.html.

39. www.discoverthenetworks.org/Articles/Introduction%20to%20Feminist%20Studies.doc.
40. Ibid.
41. www.colorado.edu/peacestudies/PACS%202500%20Syllabus.doc.
42. Ibid.
43. Jacqueline Bobo, Cynthia Hudley, and Claudine Michel, eds., *The Black Studies Reader* (New York: Routledge, 2004), p. 2.
44. William L. Van Deburg, *Modern Black Nationalism: From Marcus Garvey to Louis Farrakhan* (New York: NYU Press, 1997), pp. 160–63.
45. Bobo, Hudley, and Michel, eds., *The Black Studies Reader*, p. 2.
46. Donald Alexander Downs, *Cornell '69: Liberalism and the Crisis of the American University* (Ithaca, NY: Cornell University Press, 1999), pp. 190–240.
47. Ibid.
48. Noliwe M. Rooks, *White Money Black Power: The Surprising History of African American Studies and the Crisis of Race in Higher Education* (Boston: Beacon Press, 2007), p. 58.
49. Ibid.
50. Lewis Ricardo Gordon and Jane Anna Gordon, *A Companion to African-American Studies* (Oxford: Blackwell Publishing, 2006), p. 330.
51. http://spot.colorado.edu/~kingwm/SyllBlackAmerica.html.
52. Eugene Halton, *Bereft of Reason: On the Decline of Social Thought and Prospects for Its Renewal* (Chicago: University of Chicago Press, 1997), p. 11.
53. Arthur Schlesinger Jr., *The Disuniting of America: Reflections on a Multicultural Society* (New York: Norton, 1998), p. 160.
54. http://spot.colorado.edu/~kingwm/SyllCivilRights.html.
55. Ibid.
56. Cedric Robinson, *Black Movements in America* (New York: Routledge, 1997), p. 134.
57. www.discoverthenetworks.org/Articles/Queer%20Rhetorics.doc.
58. Ibid.
59. http://www.discoverthenetworks.org/Articles/Introduction%20to%20Lesbian.doc.
60. Ibid.
61. Emphasis added.

CHAPTER 3. UPTOWN MADRASSA: COLUMBIA UNIVERSITY

1. Both Roosevelts attended the law school, though each dropped out before graduating.
2. http://www.columbiaunbecoming.com.
3. http://www.columbia.edu/cu/news/07/09/lcbopeningremarks.html.
4. http://www.sipa.columbia.edu/resources_services/student_affairs/academic_policies/grievance_procedures.pdf.
5. Ibid.
6. Greg Lukianoff, "Social Justice and Political Orthodoxy," *The Chronicle of Higher Education,* Mar. 30, 2007. www.tc.columbia.edu/admissions/catalogdetail.htm?id=Teacher+Education.
7. www.tc.columbia.edu/news/article.htm?id=5392.
8. Lukianoff, "Social Justice and Political Orthodoxy."
9. Mona Charen, "Letting the PC slip Show," Townhall.com, Oct. 13, 2006.
10. www.tc.columbia.edu/news/article.htm?id=5392.
11. Sol Stern, "The Ed Schools' Latest—and Worst—Humbug," *City Journal,* Summer

2006. Ayers was quoted in a *New York Times* interview that appeared on September 11, 2001, saying, "I don't regret setting bombs. I feel we didn't do enough."

12. Angela Calabrese Barton, *Teaching Science for Social Justice* (New York: Teachers College Press, 2003), pp. 17–18.
13. Ibid.
14. Cynthia Stokes Brown, *Refusing Racism: White Allies and the Struggle for Civil Rights* (New York: Teachers College Press, 2002), p. 1.
15. Ibid.
16. Mahmood Mamdani, *When Victims Become Killers: Colonialism, Nativism, and the Genocide in Rwanda* (Princeton, NJ: Princeton University Press, 2001), pp. 8–9.
17. Ibid.
18. Adam Hochschild, *King Leopold's Ghost: A Story of Greed, Terror, and Heroism in Colonial Africa* (Boston: Houghton Mifflin, 1998), p. 2.
19. www.discoverthenetworks.org/Articles/Columbia%20University.htm#_Syllabus_for_the_6.
20. Ibid.
21. Ibid.
22. www.discoverthenetworks.org/Articles/Columbia%20University.htm#_Syllabus_for_the_3.
23. www.columbia.edu/cu/bulletin/uwb/subj/ANTH/G6129-20081-001/.
24. www.discoverthenetworks.org/Articles/Columbia%20University.htm#_Syllabus_for_the.
25. Ibid.
26. www.discoverthenetworks.org/individualProfile.asp?indid=1330.
27. www.discoverthenetworks.org/Articles/Columbia%20University.htm#_Syllabus_for_the.
28. www.discoverthenetworks.org/Articles/Columbia%20University.htm#_Syllabus_for_the_1.
29. Ibid.
30. Manning Marable, *Dispatches from the Ebony Tower: Intellectuals Confront the African American Experience* (New York: Columbia University Press, 2000). From front matter.
31. Ibid.
32. www.columbia.edu/cu/iraas/courses.html.
33. http://ellabakercenter.org/page.php?pageid=19&contentid=151.
34. http://mxgm.org/web/about-mxgm/putting-in-work.html.
35. Ibid.
36. www.themichiganjournal.com/home/index.cfm?event=displayArticlePrinterFriendly&uStory_id=bd33290f-ec07-42be-999e-9781f9ab792f.
37. Ibid.
38. www.discoverthenetworks.org/individualProfile.asp?indid=977.
39. www.discoverthenetworks.org/Articles/Columbia%20University.htm#_Syllabus_for_the_13.
40. Ibid.
41. www.discoverthenetworks.org/individualProfile.asp?indid=2230.
42. www.columbiaunbecoming.com/script.htm.
43. Douglas Feiden, *New York Daily News,* "Hate 101: Climate of Hate Rocks Columbia University," November 21, 2004.

44. www.discoverthenetworks.org/individualProfile.asp?indid=1347.
45. www.discoverthenetworks.org/individualProfile.asp?indid=1244.
46. Ahmadinejad's full comments were: "We don't have homosexuals like in your country. We don't have that in our country. We don't have this phenomenon; I don't know who's told you we have it."
47. Joseph Massad, *Desiring Arabs* (Chicago: University of Chicago Press, 2007), pp. 160–190.
48. Ibid.
49. Ibid.

CHAPTER 4. BREAKING THE RULES: PENN STATE UNIVERSITY

1. www.guru.psu.edu/POLICIES/OHR/hr64.html#A. "It is not the function of a faculty member in a democracy to indoctrinate his/her students with ready-made conclusions on controversial subjects. The faculty member is expected to train students to think for themselves, and to provide them access to those materials which they need if they are to think intelligently."
2. www.discoverthenetworks.org/Articles/Penn%20State.htm#_Syllabus_for_the.
3. www.discoverthenetworks.org/Articles/Penn%20State.htm#_Syllabus_for_the_24.
4. www.discoverthenetworks.org/individualProfile.asp?indid=1058.
5. www.discoverthenetworks.org/groupProfile.asp?grpid=6779.
6. www.womenstudies.psu.edu/.
7. www.personal.psu.edu/mpj/SYL001.html.
8. Ibid. Emphasis in original.
9. www.discoverthenetworks.org/Articles/Penn%20State.htm#_Another_Syllabus_for_1.
10. Ibid.
11. www.libraries.psu.edu/news/releases/spring2002/YoungFirstFriday102.html; www.discoverthenetworks.org/individualProfile.asp?indid=1544.
12. www.discoverthenetworks.org/Articles/Penn%20State.htm#_Syllabus_for_the_22.
13. www.discoverthenetworks.org/individualProfile.asp?indid=2217.
14. www.discoverthenetworks.org/Articles/Penn%20State.htm#_Syllabus_for_the_20.
15. www.geog.psu.edu/people/wright/.
16. Cf. Chris Weedon, *Feminism, Theory and the Politics of Difference* (Hoboken, NJ: Wiley-Blackwell, 1999), p. 154.
17. Chandra Mohanty, *Feminism Without Borders: Decolonizing Theory, Practicing Solidarity* (Durham, NC: Duke University Press, 2003), pp.10–13.
18. J. K. Gibson-Graham, *The End of Capitalism (As We Knew It)* (Oxford: Blackwell, 1996), p. 15.
19. www.discoverthenetworks.org/groupProfile.asp?grpid=6972.
20. www.discoverthenetworks.org/Articles/Penn%20State.htm#_Syllabus_for_the_21.
21. Ibid.
22. It should be noted that one section of Introduction to Women's Studies (WMST 001) taught by Mary Faulkner does meet the test of providing an actual debate on these issues, at least for one lesson that includes the essay "What's Wrong with Women's Studies," by Daphne Patai. Yet this assignment stands out as an exception and merely highlights the failure of others to do the same. https://cms.psu.edu/section/default.asp?format=course&id=200607FAUP+++RWMNST001+009&title=WMNST+001+%2C+Section+009%3A+INTRO+WMN+STUDIES.

23. Cf. Mohanty, *Feminism Without Borders.*
24. https://cms.psu.edu/section/default.asp?format=course&id=200607FAUP+++RWMNST003+004&title=WMNST+003+%2C+Section+004%3A+WMN%2C+HMNTS+%26+ARTS+.
25. Ibid.
26. www.miracosta.edu/home/gfloren/nochlin.htm.
27. http://academic.evergreen.edu/curricular/fopa/fopatext/fusco/fusco.html.
28. www.ecampus.com/book/1580050549.
29. www.discoverthenetworks.org/Articles/Penn%20State.htm#_Another_Syllabus_for_3.
30. Cf. Joe Feagin, *White Racism* (New York: Routledge, 1995). From front matter.
31. www.discoverthenetworks.org/Articles/Penn%20State.htm#_Syllabus_for_the_26.
32. Ibid.
33. See the discussion on p. 175–176.
34. www.discoverthenetworks.org/Articles/Penn%20State.htm#_Syllabus_for_the_28.
35. www.discoverthenetworks.org/individualProfile.asp?indid=1531.
36. www.psu.edu/bulletins/bluebook/courses/s_t_s/490.htm.
37. www.discoverthenetworks.org/individualProfile.asp?indid=2172.
38. www.frontpagemag.com/Articles/ReadArticle.asp?ID=15852.
39. A section of my letter referring to a student complaint about a specific course, which Dean Welch ignored, has been removed from the text.

CHAPTER 5. RADICAL DEGREES: UNIVERSITY OF TEXAS

1. "Teachers are entitled to freedom in the classroom in discussing their subject, but they should be careful not to introduce into their teaching controversial matter which has no relation to their subject." www.aaup.org/AAUP/pubsres/policydocs/1940statement.htm. For a discussion of the AAUP statements on academic freedom, see Horowitz, *Indoctrination U: The Left's War Against Academic Freedom* (New York: Encounter, 2007), chap. 1.
2. http://uts.cc.utexas.edu/~dcloud/undergrad.html. See also: www.discoverthenetworks.org/individualProfile.asp?indid=2183.
3. Professor Cloud has testified to the accuracy of the representation of her courses and syllabi in reference to *The Professors,* a text written by one of the authors: "There are the organizations and professors who have devoted themselves to refuting Horowitz's 'facts' about their publications and activism. I believe this also is a wrong approach, because his 'facts' about faculty syllabi and political affiliations are not in question." www.counterpunch.org/cloud03082007.html.
4. www.discoverthenetworks.org/individualProfile.asp?indid=939; www.discoverthenetworks.org/individualProfile.asp?indid=2221.
5. www.discoverthenetworks.org/Articles/UT-Austin.htm#_Freshman_Seminars_http://wwwhost.utexas.
6. Professor Richardson's academic resume can be found here: www.biosci.utexas.edu/ib/faculty/RICHARDS.HTM#edu.
7. www.utexas.edu/cola/centers/cwgs/about/.
8. www.utexas.edu/courses/arens/wgs1/wgs1syll.html.
9. http://rtf.utexas.edu/pdf/syllabi/spring01/386C.pdf.
10. Ibid.

11. www.cwrl.utexas.edu/~hogan/fall03/links.html.
12. Hogan has since taken an appointment at Louisiana State University.
13. http://www.discoverthenetworks.org/Articles/UT-Austin.htm#_Syllabus_for_the_7.
14. Chris Weedon, *Feminist Practice and Poststructuralist Theory* (Oxford: Blackwell, 1997), pp. 1–10.
15. Steven Cohan and Ina Rae Clark, *Screening the Male: Exploring Masculinities in Hollywood Cinema* (New York: Routledge, 1993), p. 176.
16. www.discoverthenetworks.org/Articles/UT-Austin.htm#_Syllabus_for_the_7.
17. http://rtf.utexas.edu/pdf/syllabi/fall04/359S.pdf.
18. Ibid.
19. http://web.austin.utexas.edu/cola/students/courses/coursedetail.cfm?courseID=11527.
20. Ibid.
21. Ibid. Emphasis added.
22. http://web.austin.utexas.edu/cola/students/courses/coursedetail.cfm?courseID=10520.
23. Jonathan Schell, *The Unconquerable World: Power, Nonviolence, and the Will of the People* (New York: Metropolitan Books, 2003), p. 144.
24. Michael Nagler, *Is There No Other Way?* (Albany, CA: Berkeley Hills Books, 2003).
25. www.cwrl.utexas.edu/~boade/309kspring06/unit1.shtml.
26. www.cwrl.utexas.edu/~watts/309NA/syllabus2.html.
27. www.discoverthenetworks.org/individualProfile.asp?indid=1740.
28. www.utexas.edu/courses/arens/marx/marxdesc.html.
29. http://web.austin.utexas.edu/cola/students/courses/coursedetail.cfm?courseID=9661.
30. http://uts.cc.utexas.edu/~dcloud/movements.pdf.
31. Howard Zinn, *A People's History of the United States: 1492–Present* (New York: HarperCollins, 2003), p. 125.
32. Mary Eleanor Triece, *Protest and Popular Culture: Women in the U.S. Labor Movement, 1894–1917* (Boulder, CO: Westview Press, 2001).
33. Jeff Goodwin, *The Social Movements Reader: Cases and Concepts* (Oxford: Blackwell, 2003).
34. www.discoverthenetworks.org/Articles/UT-Austin.htm#_Syllabus_for_Cloud's_1.
35. Julia Wood, *Gendered Lives: Communication, Gender & and Culture* (Florence, KY: Thomson Wadsworth, 2005), p. 1.
36. Kate Bornstein, *My Gender Workbook: How to Become a Real Man, a Real Woman, the Real You, or Something Else Entirely* (New York: Routledge, 1998), p. 26.
37. Ibid.
38. Ibid.
39. www.discoverthenetworks.org/Articles/UT-Austin.htm#_Syllabus_for_Cloud's_1.
40. www.discoverthenetworks.org/Articles/UT-Austin.htm#_Syllabus_for_Cloud's_2.
41. Ibid.
42. http://uts.cc.utexas.edu/~dcloud/ideology.pdf.
43. http://uts.cc.utexas.edu/~rjensen/tc357/tc357syllabus.htm.
44. Richard W. Leeman, *African-American Orators: A Bio-Critical Sourcebook* (Westport, CT: Greenwood Press, 1996), p. 65.
45. Paul, Wong, *Race, Ethnicity, and Nationality in the United States: Toward the Twenty-First Century* (Boulder, CO: Westview Press, 1999), pp. 14–24.
46. www.thirdworldtraveler.com/Herman%20/Manufac_Consent_Prop_Model.html.

CHAPTER 6. IDEOLOGY UNDER THE SUN: UNIVERSITY OF ARIZONA

1. www.u.arizona.edu/~spikep/433F96.htm.
2. Ibid.
3. Ibid.
4. www.u.arizona.edu/~spikep/335s03syl.htm.
5. Ibid.
6. Ibid.
7. www.u.arizona.edu/~spikep/461f98.htm.
8. Ibid.
9. www.discoverthenetworks.org/Articles/University%20of%20Arizona.htm#_Syllabus_for_the.
10. Ibid.
11. www.gened.arizona.edu/nparezo/cultural%20pres%20syllabus%202006.htm.
12. Patricia Pierce Erikson, Helma Ward, and Kirk Wachendorf, *Voices of a Thousand People: The Makah Cultural and Research Centers* (Lincoln: University of Nebraska Press, 2002), p. 31.
13. Michael Brown, *Who Owns Native Culture?* (Cambridge, MA: Harvard University Press, 2003), pp. 101–117.
14. Ibid.
15. Ibid.
16. www.ic.arizona.edu/ic/mcbride/theory/ws305.htm.
17. www.marxists.org/archive/marx/works/1847/wage-labour/ch02.htm; www.marxists.org/archive/marx/works/1847/wage-labour/ch05.htm.
18. www.ic.arizona.edu/ic/mcbride/theory/305marx.htm.
19. www.koni.ch/cyborg/.
20. www.egs.edu/faculty/haraway/haraway-the-ironic-dream-of-a-common-language.html.
21. www.u.arizona.edu/~lbriggs/Courses/WS%20539.html.
22. Laura Briggs, *Reproducing Empire: Race, Sex, Science, and U.S. Imperialism in Puerto Rico* (Berkeley, CA: University of California Press, 2002).
23. http://en.wikipedia.org/wiki/Puerto_Rico_status_referenda.
24. www.u.arizona.edu/~lbriggs/Courses/WS%20539.html.
25. Ibid.
26. www.u.arizona.edu/~lbriggs/Courses/WS%20586.html.
27. Ibid.
28. Anna Lowenhaupt Tsing, *In the Realm of the Diamond Queen* (Princeton, NJ: Princeton University Press, 1993), p. 33.
29. Dorothy Roberts, *Shattered Bonds: The Color of Child Welfare* (New York: Basic Civitas Books, 2002), p. 98.
30. Roberts, p. 6.
31. www.thirdworldtraveler.com/Haiti/Haiti_Under_Seige.html.
32. Donald Pease and Amy Kaplan, *Cultures of United States Imperialism* (Durham, NC: Duke University Press, 1993), p. 4.
33. www.u.arizona.edu/~jlarson/Soc313/.
34. Ibid.
35. Ibid.
36. www.u.arizona.edu/~jlarson/background.html.

37. http://driedsage.blogspot.com/.
38. www.u.arizona.edu/~spikep/101s03syl.htm.
39. http://gened.arizona.edu/gened/.
40. www.u.arizona.edu/~spikep/101s03syl.htm.
41. Ibid.
42. Ibid.
43. Ibid.
44. www.u.arizona.edu/~sung/english101/#Syllabus.
45. www.thirdworldtraveler.com/Zinn/Occupied_Country.html.
46. www.discoverthenetworks.org/individualProfile.asp?indid=2221.
47. www.discoverthenetworks.org/individualProfile.asp?indid=1232.
48. www.u.arizona.edu/~sung/english101/#Syllabus.
49. Jeffrey Javier, "Faculty Responds to Horowitz," *Arizona Daily Wildcat*, Feb. 2, 2007, http://media.wildcat.arizona.edu/media/storage/paper997/news/2007/02/02/News/Faculty.Responds.To.Horowitz-2693740.shtml.
50. Saxon Burns, "McCarthyism 101," *Tucson Weekly,* Jan. 25. 2007, http://www.tucsonweekly.com/gbase/Currents/Content?oid=oid%3A91732.
51. http://media.wildcat.arizona.edu/media/storage/paper997/news/2007/02/05/Opinions/Fighting.Fire.With.Nothing.Horowitz.Off.The.Mark.But.So.Is.Gpsc-2696427.shtml.

CHAPTER 7. SCHOOL OF INVERTED VALUES: ARIZONA STATE UNIVERSITY

1. www.asu.edu/clas/justice/.
2. Ibid.
3. www.asu.edu/clas/justice/courses/fall2005/jus-321-quan.pdf.
4. Ibid.
5. Cf. Sheldon H. Danziger and Peter Gottschalk, *America Unequal* (Cambridge, MA: Harvard University Press, 1995),
6. www.city-journal.org/html/6_1_a2.html.
7. www.asu.edu/clas/justice/courses/fall2005/jus-430-quan.pdf.
8. Ibid.
9. www.asu.edu/clas/justice/courses/fall2005/jus-105-garrett.pdf.
10. Ibid.
11. Ibid.
12. www.discoverthenetworks.org/Articles/Arizona%20State%20University.htm#_Syllabus_for_the_5.
13. Ibid.
14. Cf. David L. Altheide, *Terrorism and the Politics of Fear* (Lantham, MD: Alta Mira Press, 2006).
15. www.iranian.com/YahyaKamalipour/2003/January/US/.
16. www.discoverthenetworks.org/Articles/Arizona%20State%20University.htm#_Syllabus_for_the_24.
17. www.jillfisher.net/papers/WST300.pdf.
18. Ibid.
19. Published in 1982 (Brooklyn, NY: Verso), *I, Rigoberta Menchu* catapulted Menchu, a Quiche Mayan from Guatemala, to international fame, won her the Nobel Peace Prize, and made her an international emblem of the dispossessed indigenous peoples of the Western Hemisphere and their attempt to rebel against the oppression of European

conquerors. But it has been exposed as a fabrication, and one of the greatest intellectual and academic hoaxes of the twentieth century. It was actually written by a French leftist, Elisabeth Burgos-Debray, wife of the Marxist Regis Debray, who provided the "foco strategy" for Che Guevara's failed effort to foment a guerrilla war in Bolivia in the 1960s. Moreover, many of the book's most important claims about Menchu's suffering and oppression are little more than Marxist fantasy. See http://www.discoverthe networks.org/individualProfile.asp?indid=1124.

20. www.discoverthenetworks.org/Articles/Arizona%20State%20University.htm#_Syllabus_for_the_17.
21. Ibid.
22. www.asu.edu/clas/americanindian/Mission.htm.
23. www.discoverthenetworks.org/Articles/Arizona%20State%20University.htm#_Syllabus_for_the_1.
24. www.discoverthenetworks.org/individualProfile.asp?indid=1740.
25. The websites referenced include http://www.freeleonard.org/case/index.html; www.dickshovel.com/lsa23.html; http://www.aimovement.org/ggc/trailofbrokentreaties.html; and www.freepeltier.org/churchill_agents9a.htm.
26. www.asu.edu/clas/chicana/faculty_john.htm.
27. www.discoverthenetworks.org/Articles/Arizona%20State%20University.htm#_Syllabus_for_the_2.
28. Ibid.
29. Ibid.
30. www.discoverthenetworks.org/Articles/Arizona%20State%20University.htm#_Syllabus_for_the_26.
31. Ibid.
32. Ibid.
33. www.asu.edu/clas/aframstu/Documents/AFH/AFH%20294-Intro%20to%20Ethnic%20Studies%20-%20Fall%202005.pdf.
34. Ibid.
35. www.asu.edu/clas/aframstu/Documents/AFR/AFR%20494A-Minority%20Group%20Politics-Fall%202005.pdf
36. www.discoverthenetworks.org/individualProfile.asp?indid=1524.
37. www.discoverthenetworks.org/individualProfile.asp?indid=1516.
38. www.discoverthenetworks.org/individualProfile.asp?indid=1303.
39. www.asu.edu/clas/aframstu/Documents/AFH/AFH%20394%20UnRuly%20Voices%20AfAmWomen%20-%20Fall%202005.pdf.
40. Ibid.
41. www.asu.edu/clas/aframstu/Documents/AFS/AFS%20494L-Women,%20Ethnicity&%20Equality%20-%20Fall%202005.pdf.
42. Ibid.
43. www.asu.edu/clas/apas/courses.html.
44. Ibid.
45. Ibid.
46. Thomas Sowell, *Ethnic America* (New York: Basic Books, 1981).

CHAPTER 8. TEMPLE OF CONFORMITY: TEMPLE UNIVERSITY

1. http://books.guardian.co.uk/print/0,3858,4233337-99819,00.html.
2. Cf. James W. Loewen, *Lies My Teacher Told Me* (New York: The New Press, 1996), p. 274.
3. Cf. Danzy Senna, *Caucasia* (New York: Riverhead, 1999), p. 15.
4. Ibid., p. 21.
5. Ibid., p. 50.
6. Ibid., p. 86.
7. Ibid., p. 138.
8. Meri Nana-Ama Danquah *Shaking the Tree: A Collection of New Fiction and Memoir by Black Women* (New York: Norton, 2003), p. 15.
9. www.frontpagemag.com/Articles/Read.aspx?GUID={8773CC90-E19A-43FA-864C-3C80178C2B43}.
10. www.discoverthenetworks.org/Articles/Temple%20File.htm#_Temple_Course:_W051-701.
11. Mary Lefkowitz, *Not Out of Africa* (New York: Basic Books, 1996).
12. www.asante.net/articles/PHDTEMP.htm.
13. Cf. Lefkowitz, *Not Out of Africa,* p. 158.
14. http://astro.temple.edu/~karanja/Melanin%20Factors.htm.
15. http://astro.temple.edu/~karanja/Mental%20Health%20Issues.htm.
16. http://query.nytimes.com/gst/fullpage.html?res=9B07E6D8163DF937A25757C0A9649C8B63&sec=&spon=&pagewanted=3.
17. Ibid.
18. Ibid.
19. www.discoverthenetworks.org/individualProfile.asp?indid=2222.
20. www.discoverthenetworks.org/Articles/Temple%20File.htm#_African_American_Studies_1.
21. www.africawithin.com/wilson/wilson_books.htm.
22. www.discoverthenetworks.org/Articles/Temple%20File.htm#_African_American_Studies_3.
23. Ibid.
24. Ibid.
25. Cf. Robert Morkot, *The Egyptians* (New York: Routledge, 2005).
26. www.temple.edu/religion/faculty/gordon.html.
27. www.discoverthenetworks.org/individualProfile.asp?indid=813.
28. www.discoverthenetworks.org/Articles/Temple%20File.htm#_GUS_R055.
29. Beverly Daniel Tatum, "Defining Racism: 'Can We Talk?,' " in Maurianne Adams et al., eds., *Readings for Diversity and Social Justice: An Anthology on Racism, Antisemitism, Sexism, Heterosexism, Ableism, and Classism* (New York: Routledge, 2000), p. 79.
30. Cf. Peggy McIntosh, "White Privilege: Unpacking the Invisible Knapsack," *Independent School,* Winter 1990.
31. www.terry.uga.edu/~dawndba/4500Oppression.html.
32. Cf. N. Rodriguez, "The Real 'New World Order': The Globalization of Racial and Ethnic Relations in the Late Twentieth Century," in M. P. Smith and J. R. Feagin, eds., *The Bubbling Cauldron: Race, Ethnicity, and the Urban Crisis* (Minneapolis: University of Minnesota Press, 1995), pp. 211–25.
33. www.discoverthenetworks.org/individualProfile.asp?indid=899.

34. www.discoverthenetworks.org/individualProfile.asp?indid=2229.
35. http://frontpagemag.com/Articles/Read.aspx?GUID=F468BE35-2C3E-4091-8950-A6CB0B30C857.
36. Harold Meyerson, "A Clean Sweep: The SEIU's Organizing Drive for Janitors Shows How Unionization Can Raise Wages." See www.discoverthenetworks.org/individualProfile.asp?indid=1038.
37. www.praxis-epress.org/rtcp/mgmm.pdf.
38. www.discoverthenetworks.org/Articles/Temple%20File.htm#_Sociology_R059.
39. www.discoverthenetworks.org/individualProfile.asp?indid=2184.
40. www.discoverthenetworks.org/individualProfile.asp?indid=1874.
41. www.loc.gov/catdir/toc/ecip0616/2006021005.html.
42. www.discoverthenetworks.org/Articles/Temple%20File.htm#_History_184.
43. http://flagpole.com/News/Features/HowWouldJesusVoteGandhiKingArthur/2004-04-14.
44. www.discoverthenetworks.org/Articles/Temple%20File.htm#_History:_CO68.
45. Ibid.
46. www.discoverthenetworks.org/Articles/Temple%20File.htm#_History_271_.
47. Ibid.
48. Ibid.

CHAPTER 9. MOBILIZE U: MIAMI UNIVERSITY (OHIO)

1. www.units.muohio.edu/srp/aboutsrp.html.
2. www.insideout.org/documentaries/pax/radioprogram.asp.
3. http://casnov1.cas.muohio.edu/womensstudies/INDEX.HTM.
4. www.units.muohio.edu/womenscenter/.
5. www.units.muohio.edu/womenscenter/gender_issues/.
6. http://casnov1.cas.muohio.edu/womensstudies/.
7. http://casnov1.cas.muohio.edu/womensstudies/PROGRAMS/Seniorthesis.HTM.
8. www.discoverthenetworks.org/Articles/Miami%20University.htm#_Other_Courses_of_2.
9. Ibid.
10. www.discoverthenetworks.org/Articles/Miami%20University.htm#_Other_Courses_of_2.
11. Ibid.
12. www.discoverthenetworks.org/Articles/Miami%20University.htm#_Other_Courses_of_2.
13. www.discoverthenetworks.org/Articles/Miami%20University.htm#_Other_Courses_of.
14. www.ham.muohio.edu/news/2005/blackstudies.htm.
15. For an excellent report on these matters, see Heather Mac Donald, "What Really Happened in Cincinnati, *City Journal,* Summer 2001, www.city-journal.org/html/11_3_what_really_happened.html.
16. www.cas.muohio.edu/compass/2005/BWS.htm.
17. http://fna.muohio.edu/cce/index.html.
18. Rev. Damon Lynch III and Thomas A. Dutton, "Cincinnati's 'Beacon,'" *The Nation,* Jan. 10, 2005, www.thenation.com/docprem.mhtml?i=20050110&s=lynch.
19. www.politicalaffairs.net/article/articleview/52/1/27.

20. www.fna.muohio.edu/cce/_pdf/a_year_later.pdf.
21. Mac Donald, "What Really Happened in Cincinnati."

CHAPTER 10. POLITICALLY CORRECT U: UNIVERSITY OF MISSOURI

1. http://wgst.missouri.edu/index.html.
2. Ibid.
3. http://wgst.missouri.edu/fmemo_070119.html#two; http://diversity.missouri.edu/workshops/white-privilege/.
4. www.discoverthenetworks.org/Articles/University%20of%20Missouri.htm#_Other_Courses_of.
5. Ibid.
6. www.discoverthenetworks.org/Articles/University%20of%20Missouri.htm#_Other_Courses_of.
7. Ibid.
8. www.discoverthenetworks.org/Articles/University%20of%20Missouri.htm#_Other_Courses_of.
9. Ibid.
10. www.discoverthenetworks.org/Articles/University%20of%20Missouri.htm#_Syllabus_for_the_10.
11. Dr. Rogers appears to be an adjunct, but her status is not made clear on the university website.
12. www.discoverthenetworks.org/Articles/University%20of%20Missouri.htm#_Syllabus_for_the_10.
13. www.discoverthenetworks.org/Articles/University%20of%20Missouri.htm#_Other_Courses_of.
14. Ibid.
15. www.discoverthenetworks.org/Articles/University%20of%20Missouri.htm#_Other_Courses_of.
16. Ibid.
17. www.discoverthenetworks.org/Articles/University%20of%20Missouri.htm#_Syllabus_for_the.
18. http://web.missouri.edu/~women/courses_ws2006.html#1332.
19. http://web.missouri.edu/~women/courses_fs2007.html#4600.
20. Ibid.
21. http://web.missouri.edu/~women/courses_fs2007.html#4830.
22. http://web.missouri.edu/~women/courses_ws2007.html#4990.
23. Ibid.
24. http://web.missouri.edu/~women/courses_ws2007.html#4940.
25. No faculty position is listed for Jessica Jennrich.
26. http://web.missouri.edu/~women/courses_ws2007.html#4940.
27. http://peacestudies.missouri.edu/index.html.
28. http://peacestudies.missouri.edu/degree.html.
29. www.discoverthenetworks.org/Articles/University%20of%20Missouri.htm#_Syllabus_for_the_2.
30. www.abolitionist-online.com/interview-issue05_animal.rights.human.rights-david.nibert.shtml.

31. www.discoverthenetworks.org/Articles/University%20of%20Missouri.htm#_Another_Syllabus_for.
32. Ibid.
33. Howard Zinn, *The Power of Nonviolence: Writings of Advocates for Peace* (Boston: Beacon Press, 2002), p. ix.
34. www.discoverthenetworks.org/Articles/University%20of%20Missouri.htm#_Expanded_Course_Description_1.
35. Ibid.
36. http://www.discoverthenetworks.org/Articles/University%20of%20Missouri.htm.
37. http://english.missouri.edu/courses/fall.html.
38. http://en.wikipedia.org/wiki/Antonio_Negri See also www.discoverthenetworks.org/individualProfile.asp?indid=1436 and www.discoverthenetworks.org/individualProfile.asp?indid=1898.
39. www.discoverthenetworks.org/individualProfile.asp?indid=634.
40. www.discoverthenetworks.org/individualProfile.asp?indid=1942.
41. www.discoverthenetworks.org/Articles/University%20of%20Missouri.htm#_Expanded_Course_Description_3.
42. www.discoverthenetworks.org/Articles/University%20of%20Missouri.htm#_Expanded_Course_Description_4.
43. www.discoverthenetworks.org/Articles/University%20of%20Missouri.htm#_Expanded_Course_Description_5.
44. Ibid.
45. www.discoverthenetworks.org/Articles/University%20of%20Missouri.htm#_Syllabus_for_the_14.
46. Ibid.
47. www.discoverthenetworks.org/Articles/University%20of%20Missouri.htm#_Syllabus_for_the_12.
48. http://sociology.missouri.edu/New%20Website%20WWW/Faculty%20and%20Staff/David_Brunsma.htm.
49. Keith Boykin, *Beyond the Down Low: Sex, Lies, and Denial in Black America* (New York: Carroll & Graf, 2006), p. 179.
50. www.discoverthenetworks.org/individualProfile.asp?indid=1330.
51. www.discoverthenetworks.org/Articles/University%20of%20Missouri.htm#_Syllabus_for_the_13.
52. Eduardo Bonilla-Silva, *White Supremacy and Racism in the Post-Civil Rights Era* (Boulder, CO: Lynne Rienner Publishers, 2001), p. 90.
53. Ibid., p. 2.
54. Patricia Hill Collins, *Black Feminist Thought: Knowledge, Consciousness, and the Politics of Empowerment* (New York: Routledge, 2000), pp. 5–52.
55. David R. Roediger, *The Wages of Whiteness: Race and the Making of the American Working Class* (Brooklyn, NY: Verso, 1999), p. 5.

CHAPTER 11. TROJAN RADICALISM: UNIVERSITY OF SOUTHERN CALIFORNIA

1. Emma Hildreth Adams, *To and Fro in Southern California* (Manchester, NH: Ayer Company Publishing, 1976), p. 142.
2. www.discoverthenetworks.org/Articles/University%20of%20Southern%20California.htm#_Syllabus_for_the.

3. www.discoverthenetworks.org/Articles/University%20of%20Southern%20California.htm#_Abbreviated_Syllabus_for.
4. www.discoverthenetworks.org/Articles/University%20of%20Southern%20California.htm#_Abbreviated_Syllabus_for_1.
5. www.discoverthenetworks.org/Articles/University%20of%20Southern%20California.htm#_Abbreviated_Syllabus_for_3.
6. www.discoverthenetworks.org/Articles/University%20of%20Southern%20California.htm#_Syllabus_for_the_15.
7. Ibid.
8. www.discoverthenetworks.org/Articles/University%20of%20Southern%20California.htm#_Syllabus_for_the_16.
9. www.census.gov/Press-Release/www/releases/archives/income_wealth/005647.html.
10. www.discoverthenetworks.org/Articles/University%20of%20Southern%20California.htm#_Syllabus_for_the_13.
11. www.discoverthenetworks.org/Articles/University%20of%20Southern%20California.htm#_Syllabus_for_the_14.
12. http://sowkweb.usc.edu/news/item.php?id=107.
13. www.choike.org/nuevo_eng/informes/2279.html.
14. www.usc.edu/dept/LAS/ir/programs/581.pdf.
15. www.discoverthenetworks.org/individualProfile.asp?indid=1244.
16. www.usc.edu/schools/college/news/october_2006/laurie_brand.html.
17. www.usc.edu/dept/LAS/ir/programs/316.pdf.
18. www.usc.edu/dept/LAS/ir/programs/509.pdf.
19. www.discoverthenetworks.org/Articles/University%20of%20Southern%20California.htm#_Syllabus_for_the_32.
20. www.discoverthenetworks.org/groupProfile.asp?grpid=6934.
21. www.discoverthenetworks.org/Articles/University%20of%20Southern%20California.htm#_Syllabus_for_the_38.
22. www.discoverthenetworks.org/Articles/University%20of%20Southern%20California.htm#_Syllabus_for_the_20.
23. www.discoverthenetworks.org/Articles/University%20of%20Southern%20California.htm#_Syllabus_for_the_18.
24. www.usc.edu/schools/college/news/december_2005/hays.html.
25. www.discoverthenetworks.org/Articles/University%20of%20Southern%20California.htm#_Syllabus_for_the_19.
26. www.discoverthenetworks.org/individualProfile.asp?indid=2202.
27. www.discoverthenetworks.org/individualProfile.asp?indid=813.
28. www.discoverthenetworks.org/individualProfile.asp?indid=2217.

CHAPTER 12. THE WORST SCHOOL IN AMERICA: UNIVERSITY OF CALIFORNIA, SANTA CRUZ

1. www.discoverthenetworks.org/individualProfile.asp?indid=1303.
2. http://reg.ucsc.edu/soc/aci/winter2002/cmmu.html#100p.
3. www.discoverthenetworks.org/individualProfile.asp?indid=2165.
4. Bettina Aptheker, *Intimate Politics* (New York: Seal Press, 2006), p. 473: "I was not sure I wanted a tenure track position at the university with all that that implied about serving on faculty committees, publishing under pressure and attending scholarly conferences."

5. Ibid.
6. Ibid., p. 405.
7. Ibid., p. 406.
8. Policy on Course Content, approved June 19, 1970. Amended September 22, 2005. www.universityofcalifornia.edu/regents/policies/6065.html.
9. http://communitystudies.ucsc.edu/about_us/.
10. www.discoverthenetworks.org/Articles/University%20of%20California%20-%20Santa%20Cruz.html#_Other_Courses_of_1.
11. www.discoverthenetworks.org/Articles/University%20of%20California%20-%20Santa%20Cruz.html#_Syllabus_for_the_87.
12. www.discoverthenetworks.org/Articles/University%20of%20California%20-%20Santa%20Cruz.html#_Syllabus_for_the_95.
13. www.spme.net/cgi-bin/facultyforum.cgi?ID=1999.
14. www.discoverthenetworks.org/Articles/University%20of%20California%20-%20Santa%20Cruz.html#_Syllabus_for_the_97.
15. www.discoverthenetworks.org/Articles/University%20of%20California%20-%20Santa%20Cruz.html#_Syllabus_for_the_13.
16. Ibid.
17. www.discoverthenetworks.org/Articles/University%20of%20California%20-%20Santa%20Cruz.html#_Syllabus_for_the_76.
18. http://reg.ucsc.edu/soc/aci/winter2002/cmmu.html#100p.
19. http://feministstudies.ucsc.edu/PDFs/CourseOfferingsFall2006.pdf.
20. www.discoverthenetworks.org/Articles/University%20of%20California%20-%20Santa%20Cruz.html#_Aptheker's_Courses.
21. http://reg.ucsc.edu/soc/aci/fall2003/wmst.html#112.
22. www.discoverthenetworks.org/Articles/University%20of%20California%20-%20Santa%20Cruz.html#_Syllabus_for_the_2.
23. Interview with one of the authors.
24. http://humwww.ucsc.edu/FMST/PDFs/HISC208ASyllabus.pdf.
25. Angela Davis, *Are Prisons Obsolete?* (New York: Seven Stories Press, 2003), p. 112.
26. www.discoverthenetworks.org/Articles/University%20of%20California%20-%20Santa%20Cruz.html#_Syllabus_for_the_80.
27. Hari Kunzru, "You Are Cyborg," interview with Donna Haraway, *Wired*, February 1997.
28. www.discoverthenetworks.org/Articles/University%20of%20California%20-%20Santa%20Cruz.html#_Syllabus_for_the_43.
29. www.discoverthenetworks.org/Articles/University%20of%20California%20-%20Santa%20Cruz.html#_Syllabus_for_the_44.
30. www.discoverthenetworks.org/Articles/University%20of%20California%20-%20Santa%20Cruz.html#_Syllabus_for_the_35.
31. http://ic.ucsc.edu/~rlipsch/Pol177/syllabus.html.
32. www.discoverthenetworks.org/Articles/University%20of%20California%20-%20Santa%20Cruz.html#_Syllabus_for_the_38.
33. http://reg.ucsc.edu/soc/aci/fall2006/poli.html#200B.
34. http://summer.ucsc.edu/classes/syllabus/reader.php?f=7ee555391ecdcbf2a3d29c5b70964c85.

35. http://summer.ucsc.edu/classes/syllabus/reader.php?f=2e51b031138d2c12eef3ca95f920d334.
36. www.sociology.ucsc.edu.
37. http://summer.ucsc.edu/classes/syllabus/reader.php?f=0091ec2384d1c3e733674905ce9c2fd1.

CONCLUSION: THE END OF THE UNIVERSITY AS WE KNOW IT

1. www.aaup.org.
2. 1915 Declaration of Principles on Academic Freedom and Tenure.
3. Neil Gross and Solon Simmons, "The Social and Political Views of American Professors," www.wjh.harvard.edu/~ngross/lounsbery_9-25.pdf.
4. www.unc.edu/srp/srp2007/.
5. www.accessmylibrary.com/coms2/summary_0286-25351356_ITM.
6. Beshara Doumani, ed., *Academic Freedom After September 11* (Brooklyn, NY: Zone Books, 2006), p. 69
7. Rule APM 0-10, University of California, Berkeley, Academic Personnel Manual.
8. Pamela Caughie, "Impassioned Teaching," *Academe,* July–August 2007.
9. Julie Kilmer, "Retain Your Rights as a Liberal Educator," *Academe,* July–August 2007.
10. Michael Berube, "Freedom to Teach." InsideHigherEd.com. See comment by Berube, response to Professor Ethan, September 13. www.insidehighered.com/views/2007/09/11/berube.
11. Ibid.
12. Caughie, "Impassioned Teaching."

Acknowledgments

The authors wish to thank Tom Ryan for research assistance in the writing of this book.

Index

Page numbers beginning with 289 refer to notes.

About the Author

David Horowitz is the author of three previous books on universities: *Uncivil Wars* (2001), *The Professors* (2005), and *Indoctrination U* (2007).

Jacob Laksin is a senior editor at *Frontpagemag.com*